SPOTLIGHT

W9-CCD-481

OLYMPIC PENINSULA CAMPING & HIKING

TOM STIENSTRA & SCOTT LEONARD

How to Use This Book

ABOUT THE CAMPGROUND PROFILES

The campgrounds are listed in a consistent, easy-to-read format to help you choose the ideal camping spot. If you already know the name of the specific campground you want to visit, or the name of the surrounding geological area or nearby feature (town, national or state park, forest, mountain, lake, river, etc.), look it up in the index and turn to the corresponding page. Here is a sample profile:

Campground name and number →

❶ SOMEWHERE USA CAMPGROUND

Icons noting activities and facilities at or nearby the campground

General location of the campground in relation to the nearest major town or landmark →

Scenic rating: 10

south of Somewhere USA Lake

Rating of scenic beauty on a scale of 1-10 with 10 the highest rating

BEST (

Each campground in this book begins with a brief overview of its setting. The description typically covers ambience, information about the attractions, and activities popular at the campground.

Symbol indicating that the campground is listed among the author's top picks

Campsites, facilities: This section notes the number of campsites for tents and RVs and indicates whether hookups are available. Facilities such as restrooms, picnic areas, recreation areas, laundry, and dump stations will be addressed, as well as the availability of piped water, showers, playgrounds, stores, and other amenities. The campground's pet policy and wheelchair accessibility is also mentioned here.

Reservations, fees: This section notes whether reservations are accepted, and provides rates for tent sites and RV sites. If there are additional fees for parking or pets, or discounted weekly or seasonal rates, they will also be noted here.

Directions: This section provides mile-by-mile driving directions to the campground from the nearest major town or highway.

Contact: This section provides an address, phone number, and website, if available, for the campground.

ABOUT THE ICONS

The icons in this book are designed to provide at-a-glance information on activities, facilities, and services available on-site or within walking distance of each campground.

- 🥾 Hiking trails
- 🚲 Biking trails
- 🏊 Swimming
- 🎣 Fishing
- 🚤 Boating
- 🛶 Canoeing and/or kayaking
- ❄️ Winter sports

- ♨️ Hot springs
- 🐕 Pets permitted
- 🛝 Playground
- ♿ Wheelchair accessible
- 🚐 RV sites
- ⛺ Tent sites

ABOUT THE SCENIC RATING

Each campground profile employs a scenic rating on a scale of 1 to 10, with 1 being the least scenic and 10 being the most scenic. A scenic rating measures only the overall beauty of the campground and environs; it does not take into account noise level, facilities, maintenance, recreation options, or campground management. The setting of a campground with a lower scenic rating may simply not be as picturesque that of as a higher rated campground, however other factors that can influence a trip, such as noise or recreation access, can still affect or enhance your camping trip. Consider both the scenic rating and the profile description before deciding which campground is perfect for you.

ABOUT THE TRAIL PROFILES

Each hike in this book is listed in a consistent, easy-to-read format to help you choose the ideal hike. From a general overview of the setting to detailed driving directions, the profile will provide all the information you need. Here is a sample profile:

Map number and hike number →

1 SOMEWHERE USA HIKE
9.0 mi/5.0 hrs   👫3 ⛰8 ← Difficulty and quality ratings

Round-trip mileage → (unless otherwise noted) and the approximate amount of time needed to complete the hike (actual times can vary widely, especially on longer hikes)

at the mouth of the Somewhere River ← General location of the trail, named by its proximity to the nearest major town or landmark

BEST ← Symbol indicating that the hike is listed among the author's top picks

Each hike in this book begins with a brief overview of its setting. The description typically covers what kind of terrain to expect, what might be seen, and any conditions that may make the hike difficult to navigate. Side trips, such as to waterfalls or panoramic vistas, in addition to ways to combine the trail with others nearby for a longer outing, are also noted here. In many cases, mile-by-mile trail directions are included.

User Groups: This section notes the types of users that are permitted on the trail, including hikers, mountain bikers, horseback riders, and dogs. Wheelchair access is also noted here.

Permits: This section notes whether a permit is required for hiking, or, if the hike spans more than one day, whether one is required for camping. Any fees, such as for parking, day use, or entrance, are also noted here.

Maps: This section provides information on how to obtain detailed trail maps of the hike and its environs. Whenever applicable, names of U.S. Geologic Survey (USGS) topographic maps and national forest maps are also included; contact information for these and other map sources are noted in the Resources section at the back of this book.

Directions: This section provides mile-by-mile driving directions to the trailhead from the nearest major town.

Contact: This section provides an address and phone number for each hike. The contact is usually the agency maintaining the trail but may also be a trail club or other organization.

ABOUT THE ICONS

The icons in this book are designed to provide at-a-glance information on the difficulty and quality of each hike.

 The **DIFFICULTY** rating (rated **1-5** with **1** being the lowest and **5** the highest) is based on the steepness of the trail and how difficult it is to traverse

 The **QUALITY** rating (rated **1-10** with **1** being the lowest and **10** the highest) is based largely on scenic beauty, but also takes into account how crowded the trail is and whether noise of nearby civilization is audible

ABOUT THE DIFFICULTY RATINGS

Trails rated 1 are very easy and suitable for hikers of all abilities, including young children.

Trails rated 2 are easy-to-moderate and suitable for most hikers, including families with active children 6 and older.

Trails rated 3 are moderately challenging and suitable for reasonably fit adults and older children who are very active.

Trails rated 4 are very challenging and suitable for physically fit hikers who are seeking a workout.

Trails rated 5 are extremely challenging and suitable only for experienced hikers who are in top physical condition.

MAP SYMBOLS

┄┄┄	Expressway	(80)	Interstate Freeway	✗	Airfield
━━━	Primary Road	(101)	U.S. Highway	✗	Airport
━━━	Secondary Road	(21)	State Highway	○	City/Town
▪▪▪▪	Unpaved Road	(66)	County Highway	▲	Mountain
··········	Ferry		Lake	▲	Park
━▪━▪━	National Border		Dry Lake	)(	Pass
━▪▪━	State Border		Seasonal Lake	◉	State Capital

ABOUT THE MAPS

This book is divided into chapters based on major regions in the state. Each chapter begins with a map of the region, which is further broken down into detail maps. Sites are noted on the detail maps by number.

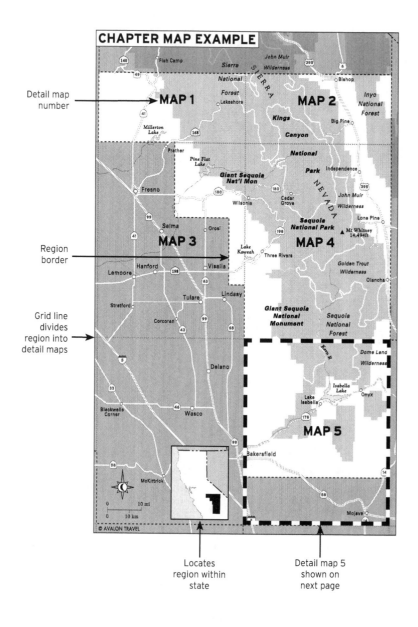

Detail map number

Region border

Grid line divides region into detail maps

Locates region within state

Detail map 5 shown on next page

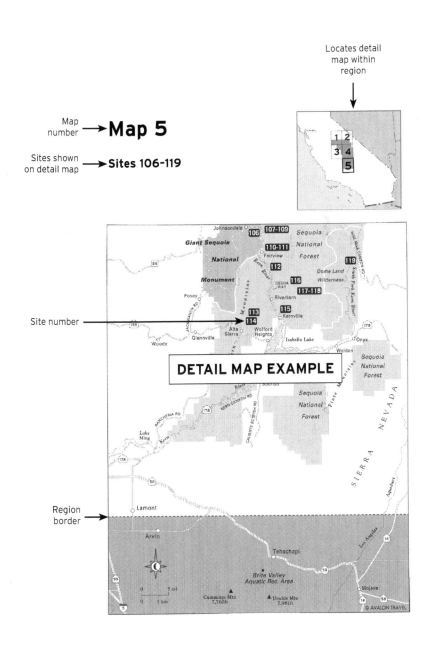

Locates detail
map within
region

Map
number ➔ **Map 5**

Sites shown ➔ **Sites 106-119**
on detail map

Site number ⟶

DETAIL MAP EXAMPLE

Region
border ➔

Camping and Hiking Tips

THE 10 ESSENTIALS

The 10 Essentials are just that—indispensable items that you should carry every time you hit the trail. No matter where you're headed, you never know what you're going to come across (or what's going to come across you); being prepared can help to prevent problems before they start.

Clothing

Here in Washington, the weather can turn at the drop of a hat. In every season, rain is an inevitability. We didn't get a reputation for wet weather for nothing. During the summer, sudden thundershowers or snowstorms can give even experienced hikers a surprise. So it's best to bring extra clothing for those unexpected weather fronts.

Clothing that can ward off the cold is extremely important. Most accidents in the wilderness are the result of, or complicated by, hypothermia, which can set in quickly and with little warning. Once a person starts getting cold, the ability to think and troubleshoot heads downhill. Symptoms of hypothermia include fatigue, drowsiness, unwillingness to go on, a feeling of deep cold or numbness, poor coordination, and mumbling. To avoid this, bring clothes that are easily layered. During the summer, that can be as simple as a warm fleece. During the winter, wool or synthetic fleeces are effective against the cold. A stocking cap is extremely helpful since a big chunk of body heat is lost through the head. Extra socks are helpful for keeping feet warm and comfortable. Remember that you can be vulnerable even in the summer—bitter July snowstorms are not unprecedented.

Rain gear, such as a waterproof jacket, pants, and a hat or hood, is equally important during all seasons, but especially during the fall and spring when it's practically impossible to head outdoors without rain. Even if there is no rain in the forecast, be prepared for it. (Local weather reporters are forecasting for the cities, not the mountains.) And short but serious rainstorms are the year-round norm, not the exception, in Washington.

When dressing for a hike, it's important to avoid cotton clothing, especially if rain is a possibility. Once cotton gets wet, it can draw off body heat, causing hypothermia to set in quickly. Wool and polypropylene are good alternatives. If you get wet wearing cotton, take it off if you have another layer that is not cotton.

Water

Be sure to drink lots of water, even if it's not that hot out. Staying properly hydrated can prevent heat exhaustion. Symptoms of heat exhaustion include excessive sweating, gradual weakness, nausea, anxiety, and eventually loss of consciousness. Usually, the skin becomes pale and clammy or cold, the pulse slows, and blood pressure may drop. Heat exhaustion is often unexpected but very serious; someone experiencing heat exhaustion will have difficulty getting out of a wilderness setting and will need assistance—not always an easy task.

When day hiking, you can probably carry from the trailhead all the water you'll need for the hike. Two liters per person is a good rule of thumb. Carrying water with you or having a method of filtering water is important—never drink untreated water in the

HIKING WITH KIDS

1. **Prepare, prepare, prepare.** Heading out on the trail with kids calls for extra preparation. The 10 Essentials are more important than ever. And be ready for the unexpected: Bring something extra to drink and eat, and bring proper rain/sun protection. And don't hesitate to involve them – kids often love to help pack.
2. **Pick the right hike.** Kids are much more likely to enjoy hiking if the trail is appropriate for their age and ability. And don't assume the trail will need to include peaks and summits for kids to enjoy the journey: From bugs and animals to streams and forests, kids will find something in nature to interest them (if they aren't wiped from the hike).
3. **Gear up.** Hiking with children doesn't mean you have to drop a week's pay at REI. But making sure you and your little hiker have the proper gear is important for safety and enjoyment. Comfortable footwear and weather-appropriate clothing are musts. A backpack for your child helps them feel involved in the "work" of hiking; just make sure it's not too heavy. And parents should be carrying extra water and food for all.
4. **Be flexible.** Hiking is not mandatory. Our parents may have insisted that discomfort builds character, but kids often know when enough is enough for their bodies. Accommodating a request to turn around before the intended destination can be rewarded by a request for another trip soon. Remember, the point is for each hiker to enjoy the journey.
5. **Be attentive.** When hiking with children, there are more factors to keep in mind. Kids may be getting wet or cold, sunburned or overheated. Many hikes have inherent danger, such as cliffs, snakes, poison oak, or slippery ground. Keep an eye on your little hikers and they will be around for many hikes to come.

wild. A stream may look crystal clear and be ice cold, but it can also be full of nasty parasites and viruses. If you catch a case of *giardia* or *cryptosporidia*, you could be incapacitated for a full week. Carrying a stove or a filter can be impractical on day hikes. The best back-up method is to carry iodine and chlorine tablets that quickly and easily purify water. They're lightweight and come in handy in a pinch. If you don't mind a strange taste in your water, these will do the trick.

Food

The lore of the backcountry is filled with tales of folks who head out for a quick day hike and end up spending a night (or more) in the wilderness. Planning on just an afternoon away from the kitchen, they don't bring enough food to last into the night or morning. Not only is an empty stomach a restless stomach, it can be dangerous, as well. A full stomach provides energy to help ward off hypothermia and keeps the mind clear for the task at hand: Not getting even more lost.

When packing food for an outing, include a little extra gorp or an extra energy bar. This will come in extremely handy if you find yourself wandering back to the trailhead later than planned. A grizzled old veteran of the backcountry once passed on a helpful tip for packing extra food. Extra food is meant for an emergency; the last thing you want to do is eat it in a nonemergency and then need it later. So, he packed something nutritious that he'd consider eating only in an emergency: canned dog food.

Fire Starter

Some people prefer matches while others choose to bring along a lighter. Either way, it's important to have something with which to start a fire. Don't think that you can start your fire by rubbing two sticks together. Even when it's dry, sticks don't like to start up easily. So be certain to purchase some quality waterproof matches (you can make your own with paraffin wax and wooden matches), or carry a couple of lighters. Regardless of your choice, keep them packed away in a safe and dry place (like a sandwich baggie). Besides a starter, bring along something to keep the fire going for a bit. Fire pellets are available at any outdoor store. Do-it-yourselfers will be glad to know that toilet paper is highly flammable, as are cotton balls dipped in Vaseline. Starting a fire when it's cold, dark, and wet can save your life.

Map and Compass

You need to carry a map and compass on your person *every* time you hit the trail, whether you're going up Mount Si with the rest of Seattle or venturing into the vacant backcountry of North Cascades National Park. No matter how familiar you think you are with a trail, you can get lost. Not only should you carry a map and compass, but you also need to know how to use them.

A map is not always a map. You can't rely on the map that AAA gave you out on the trail. Instead, it's best to purchase a quality topographic map for use on the trail. A quality topographic map allows hikers to follow their steps more accurately and is infinitely more helpful for figuring out where you are when you're lost. Green Trails of Seattle makes high-quality topo maps for 90 percent of Washington trails. The USGS and National Geographic also make good topo maps.

Now that it's the 21st century, GPS devices are becoming more popular. These are great toys to play with while out on the trail. Some folks even swear by them. But a GPS device often won't work in a thick forest canopy. A good old-fashioned

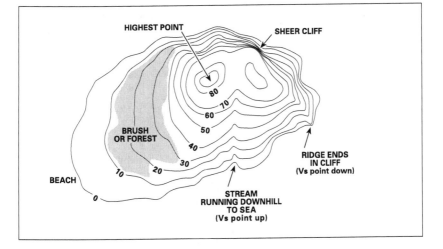

compass, on the other hand, is significantly cheaper and won't ever die on you when the batteries run out.

First-Aid Kit

A first-aid kit is an important essential to carry while out on the trail. With twigs, rocks, and bears lurking around every corner, hiking can be dangerous business. Injuries can range from small abrasions to serious breaks, and a simple but well-stocked first-aid kit can be a lifesaver. It's best to purchase a first-aid kit at an outdoors store. Kits come in different sizes, depending on intended use, and include the fundamentals. Also, a number of organizations provide medical training for backcountry situations. Courses run from one-day seminars in simple first aid all the way to month-long classes for wilderness EMT certification. Outdoors enthusiasts who venture out on a regular basis should consider a course in Wilderness First Aid (WOOFA) or Wilderness First Response (WOOFER).

Band-aids come in every kit but are only helpful for small, nonserious cuts or abrasions. Here are a few things that are especially important and can come in handy in an emergency:

• Ibuprofen: It works very well to combat swelling. Twist an ankle or suffer a nasty bruise and reducing the swelling quickly becomes an important consideration.

• Athletic tape and gauze: These are helpful in treating twisted or strained joints. A firm wrap with athletic tape will make the three-mile hobble to the car less of an ordeal.

• Travel-size supplies of general medicines: Items like Alka-Seltzer or NyQuil are multipurpose and practical.

Finally: The only thing better than having a first-aid kit on the trail is not needing one.

Sun Protection

Most hikers don't think that fierce sunburns are a serious concern in notoriously gray Washington. But during the summer, the sun can be extremely brutal, especially at higher altitudes where a few thousand feet of atmosphere can be sorely missed. A full day in the blazing sun is hard on the eyes as well.

Don't let the sun spoil an otherwise great day in the outdoors. Sunscreen is worth its weight in gold out on the trail. Be sure to apply it regularly, and keep kids lathered up as well. It helps to bring a hat and lightweight clothing with long sleeves, both of which can make sunscreen almost unnecessary. Finally, many hikers swear by a good pair of sunglasses. Perhaps obvious during the summer, sunglasses are also a snowshoer's best friend. Snow blindness is a serious threat on beautiful sunny days during the winter.

All of these measures will make a trip not only safer but more enjoyable as well. Avoiding sunburn is also extremely helpful in warding off heat stroke, a serious condition in the backcountry.

Light Source

Even veteran hikers who intend to go out only for a "quick" day hike can end up finishing in the dark. There were just too many things to see, too many lakes to swim in, and too many peaks to bag on that "short" hike. Often, getting back to the car or camp before it's dark requires the difficult task of leaving a beautiful place while it's still light out. Or perhaps while out on an easy forest hike, you're on schedule to get back before dark, but the thick forest canopy brings on night an hour or two early. There are lots of ways to get stuck in the outdoors in the dark. And what good are a map and compass if you can't see them? Plan ahead and bring an adequate light source. The market is flooded these days with cheap (and not so cheap) headlamps. Headlamps are basically small flashlights that fit around your head. They're great because they're bright and they keep your hands free, so you're better able to beat back brush on the trail or fend off hungry fellow campers around the dinner stove.

Multipurpose Knife

For outdoors enthusiasts, the multipurpose Swiss Army knife is one of the greatest things since sliced bread. Handy utility knives come in all shapes and sizes and are made by about a hundred different companies. A high-quality utility knife will come in handy in a multitude of situations. The features available include big knives and little knives, saws and scissors, corkscrews and screwdrivers, and about 30 other fun little tools. They are useful almost everywhere, except at the airport.

Emergency Kit

You'll probably have a hard time finding a pre-prepared emergency kit for sale at any store. Instead, this is something that you can quickly and inexpensively assemble yourself.
• Space blanket: Find these at any outdoor store or army surplus store. They're small, shiny blankets that insulate extremely well, are highly visible, and will make do in place of a tent when needed.
• Signal mirror: A signal mirror is handy when you're lost. Catch the glare of the sun, and you can signal your position to search-and-rescue hikers or planes. The small mirror that comes attached to some compasses works perfectly.
• Whistle: Again, if you get really lost, don't waste your breath screaming and hollering. You'll lose your voice quickly, and it doesn't carry far anyhow. Blow your whistle all day or night long, and you'll still be able to talk to the trees (or yourself).

ON THE TRAIL

It's Friday afternoon, work has been a trial all week, and there's only one thing on your mind: getting outdoors and hitting the trail for the weekend. For many of us, nature is a getaway from the confines of urban living. The irony of it all, however, is that the more people head to the backcountry, the less wild it truly is. That means that it takes a collective effort from all trail users to keep the outdoors as pristine as it was 100 years ago. This effort is so important, in fact, that the organization Leave No Trace has created an ideology for low-impact use of our wilderness. (For more information on the Leave No Trace Center for Outdoor Ethics and their values, check out their website at www.lnt.org.) Here are a few principles that we all can follow to ensure that the great outdoors continues to be great.

Planning Your Trip

A little careful planning and preparation not only makes your trip safer, but it also makes it easy to minimize resource damage. Make sure you know the regulations, such as group size limits or campfire regulations, before hitting the trail. Prepare for any special circumstances an area may have, such as the need for ice axes or water filters. Many

HIKING ETIQUETTE

1. **Leave no trace.** We love hiking for the opportunity to leave civilization behind and enjoy nature. Thus, we all need to leave the trail as nice – or nicer – than we found it. Pack all litter out (even litter that others may have left behind, if you're so inclined). Do not leave graffiti or other marks on trees or rocks. Let wildlife stay wild by not feeding or harassing animals. If you find something interesting, it's likely that someone else will also find it interesting: Be sure to leave rocks, flowers, and other natural objects where you find them.

2. **Stay on the trail.** Washington trails are heavily used. While just one person cutting a switchback or zipping off trail through a meadow has little consequence, the cumulative damage from many hikers wandering off trail is all too easy to spot. Avoid erosion and unsightly way-trails by hiking only on established trails.

3. **Yield to uphill hikers.** Hikers who are headed up an incline have the right-of-way. After all, uphill hikers have built up momentum and are working hard to put trail beneath their feet. Downhill hikers should find a safe place to step off the trail and allow others to pass.

4. **Keep dogs under control.** Yes, we all love to take our best friends out on the trail. But they need to stay on the trail. Out-of-control dogs can easily end up lost in the woods. While a leash is not always necessary, one should be carried at all times and used when on a busy trail. Where dogs are not permitted, it is bad form and even dangerous to take them along.

5. **Be respectful of others.** Be aware of your noise level, and make way for others. Common courtesy creates community on the trail and enhances everyone's experience. Remember, our public lands belong to no one and everyone at the same time.

places are used heavily during summer weekends. Schedule your trip for a weekday or off-season, and you'll encounter far fewer fellow bipeds.

Hiking and Camping

One of the most important principles for hikers and campers here in Washington is to minimize our impact on the land. Many of our greatest and most heavily used trails visit fragile environments, such as alpine meadows and lakeshores. These ecosystems are easily injured by hikers and campers. Take care to travel only on the main trail, never cut a switchback, and avoid the social trails—small, unofficial trails that are made over years by hikers cutting trails—that spiderweb through many a high meadow. When camping, pitch camp in already established sites, never on a meadow. Take care in selecting a site for a camp kitchen and when heading off for the bathroom. Being aware of your impact not only improves the experience for yourself but also for those who follow you.

Packing Out Your Trash

It goes without saying that trash does not belong in the great outdoors. That goes for all trash, regardless of whether it's biodegradable or not. From food packaging to the food itself, it has to go out the way it came in: on your back. Ditto for toilet paper. As far as human waste goes, dig a cat hole for your waste, and pack all toilet paper and hygiene products in bags. It may be nasty, but it's only fair for others.

Leaving What You Find

The old saying goes, "Take only photographs and leave only footprints." Well, if you're walking on durable surfaces such as established trails, you won't even leave footprints. And it's best to leave the artifacts of nature where they belong: in nature. By doing so, you ensure that others can enjoy them as well. If you see something interesting, remember that it is only there because the hiker in front of you left it for you to find. The same goes for attractive rocks, deer and elk antlers, and wildflowers. Avoid altering sites by digging trenches, building lean-tos, or harming trees.

Lighting Campfires

Thanks to Smokey the Bear, we all know the seriousness of forest fires. If you're going to have a fire, make sure it's out before going to sleep or leaving camp. But there are other important considerations for campfires. Here in Washington, many national forests and wildernesses have fire bans above 3,500 feet. At these higher altitudes, trees grow slowly and depend greatly on decomposition of downed trees. Burning downed limbs and trees robs the ecosystems of much-needed nutrients, an impact that lasts centuries. Carry a camp stove any time you plan on cooking while backpacking.

Encountering Wildlife

Hiking is all about being outdoors. Fresh air, colorful wildflowers, expansive mountain views, and a little peace and quiet are what folks are after as they embark on the trail. The great outdoors is also home to creatures big and small. Remember, you are in their home: No chasing the deer. No throwing rocks at the chipmunks. No bareback riding the elk. And no wrestling the bears. In all seriousness, the most important way we can respect wildlife is by not feeding them. Chipmunks may be cute, but feeding them only makes them fat and dependent on people for food. Keep a clean camp without food on the ground, and be sure to hang food anytime you're separated from it. A good bear hang is as much about keeping the bears out of the food as it is about keeping the mice and squirrels from eating it.

Nearly all wildlife around Seattle is completely harmless to hikers; bears and cougars are the only wildlife that pose a danger to us humans. Fortunately, the vast majority of encounters with these big predators result in nothing more than a memorable story. Coming across bears and cougars may be frightening, but these encounters don't need to be dangerous as long as you follow a few simple precautions.

BEARS

Running into a bear is the most common worry of novice hikers when they hit the trail. Bears are big, furry, and naturally a bit scary at first sight. But in reality, bears want little to do with people and much prefer to avoid us altogether. The chance of getting into a fistfight with a bear is rare in Washington. In our state's history, there have only been three attacks and one fatality recorded. As long as you stay away from bear cubs and food, bears will almost certainly leave you alone.

What kind of bear will you see out on the trail? Most likely, you won't see one at all, but if you do, it will probably be a black bear, although Washington is home to grizzly bears as well. Black bears, whose thick coats range from light tan to cinnamon to black, are by far the most numerous, with approximately 25,000 spread throughout our state. Grizzly bears are much more rare, numbering less than 50, and are primarily located along the Canadian border in the Pasayten Wilderness and Selkirk Mountains. Grizzlies have a distinctive hump between their shoulders.

The old image of Yogi the Bear stealing picnic baskets is not that far off. Bears love to get a hold of human food, so proper food storage is an effective way to avoid an unwanted bear encounter. When camping, be sure to use a bear hang. Collect all food, toiletries, and anything else with scent; place it all in a stuff sack and hang the sack in a tree. The sack should be at least 12 feet off the ground and eight feet from the tree trunk.

Should you come across a bear on the trail, stay calm. It's okay to be scared, but with a few precautions, you will be completely safe. First, know that your objective is not to intimidate the bear but simply to let it know you are not easy prey. Make yourself look big by standing tall, waving your arms, or even holding open your jacket. Second, don't look it in the eye. Bears consider eye contact to be aggressive and an invitation to a confrontation. Third, speak loudly and firmly to the bear. Bears are nearsighted and can't make out objects from afar. But a human voice means humans, and a bear is likely to retreat from your presence. If a bear advances, it is very likely only trying to get a better look. Finally, if the bear doesn't budge, go around it in a wide circle. In case the unlikely should occur and the bear attacks, curl up in a ball, stay as still as possible, and wait for the attack to end. If the bear bites, take a cheap shot at the nose. Bears hate being hit on their sensitive noses. Trying to hit a bear from this position is difficult. It can work if you can cover your neck with one hand and swing with the other. Protecting yourself is first priority. If the bear is especially aggressive, it's necessary to fight back. Most important, don't let fear of bears prevent you from getting out there; it's rare to see a bear and even rarer to have a problem with one.

COUGARS

With millions of acres of wilderness, Washington is home to cougars, bobcats, and lynx. Bobcats and lynx are small and highly withdrawn. If you encounter one of these recluses, you're in a small minority. Cougars are also very shy, and encounters with these big cats are rare; only 2,500 cougars live in our state. Cougar attacks are extremely uncommon; there have been few in recent years and only one fatality ever in Washington. You're more likely to be struck by lightning than attacked by a cougar. In most circumstances, sighting a cougar will just result in having a great story to tell.

If you should encounter a cougar in the wild, make every effort to intimidate it. First, don't run! A cougar views something running from it as dinner. Second, make yourself bigger by waving your arms, jumping around, and spreading open a jacket. Cougars have very little interest in a tough fight. Third, don't bend down to pick up a rock; you'll only look smaller to the cougar. Fourth, stare the cougar down—a menacing stare-down is intimidating for a cougar. Finally, should a cougar attack, fight back with everything you have and as dirtily as possible.

Respecting Other Hikers

If you are considerate of others on the trail, they are likely to return the favor. This includes such simple things as yielding right-of-way to those who are trudging uphill, keeping noise to a minimum, and observing any use regulations, such as no mountain bikes and no fires. If possible, try to set up camp off trail and out of sight. Together, everyone can equally enjoy the beauties of hiking in Washington.

Hiking with Dogs

Though not everyone may have a dog, nearly everyone has an opinion about dogs on the trail. Hiking with canine friends can be a great experience, not only for us but for them, as well. What dog doesn't love being out on the trail, roaming the wild and in touch with his ancestral roots? That's great, but there are a few matters that must be considered before taking a dog on a hike.

First, be aware that national parks do not allow dogs on any trail at any time. However, dogs are allowed throughout national forests and any wildernesses contained within them. Second, dogs should remain on the trail at all times. Dogs can create an enormous amount of erosion when roaming off trail, and they're frequent switchback cutters. Third, dogs must be under control at all times. Leashes are not always mandatory because many dogs are obedient and do very well while unleashed. But if you're not going to use a leash, your dog should respond to commands well and not bother other hikers. Finally, be aware that dogs and wildlife don't mix well. Dogs love to chase chipmunks, rabbits, deer, and anything else that moves. But from the chipmunk's point of view, a big, slobbering beast chasing you is stressful and unequivocally bad. Not only that, but dogs can incite aggression in bears or cougars. An unleashed dog can quickly transform a peaceful bear into a raging assault of claws and teeth. Plus, bears and cougars find dogs to be especially tasty. Don't hesitate to bring your dog out on the trail as long as you take the dog's interests, as well as other hikers' interests, into consideration.

PERMITS

You've got your pack ready, done your food shopping, purchased the right maps, and even wrestled the kids into the car. But do you have the right permits? Here in Washington, there are several permits that you may need before you can hit the trail. Headed for a national forest? Read up on the Northwest Forest Pass. Driving down to Mount Rainier or the Olympics? You probably need a National Parks Pass. Backpacking in a national park? Don't forget your backcountry camping permit.

Northwest Forest Pass

The Northwest Forest Pass (NWFP) is the most widely used permit in our state. The pass is accepted at 680 day-use recreation sites in Washington and Oregon. Almost every trailhead in every national forest in Washington requires a NWFP for parking. Remarkably, a Northwest Forest Pass is all that is required in the North Cascades National Park. The Colville National Forest is the one agency that does not participate in the NWFP program; access to trailheads in the Colville is free. Senior citizens take note: In lieu of a NWFP, the federal Golden Eagle, Golden Access, and Golden Age passes are accepted.

The Northwest Forest Pass costs $30 and is valid for one year from date of purchase. It's interchangeable between vehicles in the same household. Day passes may also be purchased at a cost of $5 per day. More than 240 vendors across the northwest offer the pass, including all ranger stations, most outdoor stores, and many service stations in recreational areas. Passes can also be ordered online through Nature of the Northwest at www.naturenw.org. Proceeds from Northwest Forest Passes go toward improvements at recreational sites, including refurbishing trailheads, trail maintenance and construction, and environmental education. There is a lot of controversy over the pass, as critics contend that national forests are public lands and already paid for by federal taxes. They have a point, but the revenue serves to supplement ever-dwindling forest service budgets.

National Parks Passes and Permits

No question, the United States has the world's premier national park system. From Acadia National Park in Maine to Denali National Park in Alaska, the United States has taken care to preserve our most important ecosystems for future generations to enjoy. Here in Washington, we have the North Cascades, Olympic, and Mount Rainier National Parks to savor. This book includes coverage only of Mount Rainier National Park. The four hikes inside the park require fees for car access to the trailheads. Access to Carbon River Road and Mowich Lake Road require one of three passes: a Single Visit Vehicle Permit ($10 and good for seven days), a Mount Rainier National Park Annual Pass ($30 and good for one year), or any of the national parks passes, which are good for one year at all national parks in the United States. National parks passes include: the National Parks Pass ($50 and good at any national park in the United States for one year), the Golden Access Pass (available for people who are blind or permanently disabled and allows lifetime admittance to any national park for free), and the Golden Age Pass (available to people 62 years or older and allows lifetime admittance to any national park for a one-time fee of $10).

OLYMPIC PENINSULA CAMPING

© NATALIA BRATSLAVSKY/123rf.com

BEST CAMPGROUNDS

CAMPING

Vast, diverse, and beautiful, the Olympic Peninsula

is like no other landscape in the world. Water borders the region on three sides: the Pacific Ocean to the west, the Strait of Juan de Fuca to the north, and the inlets of Hood Canal to the east. At its center are Olympic National Park and Mount Olympus, with rainforests on its slopes feeding rivers and lakes that make up the most dynamic river complex in America.

Only heavy rainfall for months on end from fall through spring and coastal fog in the summer have saved this area from a massive residential boom. At the same time, those conditions make it outstanding for getaways and virtually all forms of recreation. A series of stellar camp-grounds ring the perimeter foothills of Mount Olympus, both in Olympic National Park and at the state parks and areas managed by the Department of Natural Resources. Your campsite can be your launch pad for adventure – just be sure to bring your rain gear.

In winter, campers can explore the largest array of steelhead rivers anywhere – there is no better place in America to fish for steelhead. Almost every one of these rivers provides campsites, often within walking distance of prime fishing spots.

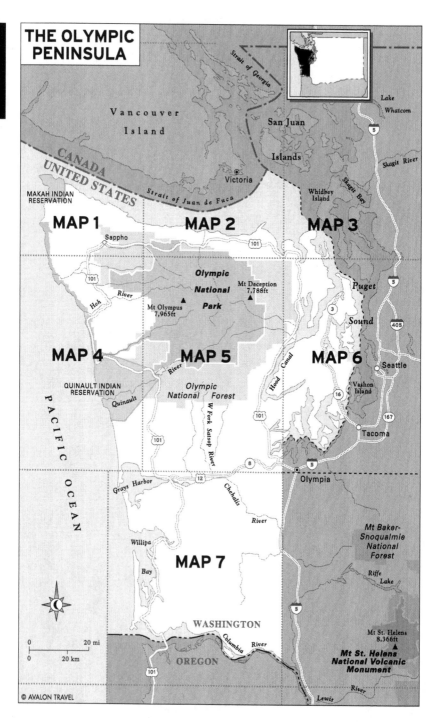

CAMPING

THE OLYMPIC PENINSULA

Strait of Georgia

Lake Whatcom

Vancouver Island

San Juan

Islands

Skagit River

CANADA
UNITED STATES

Strait of Juan de Fuca

Victoria

Whidbey Island

Skagit Bay

MAKAH INDIAN RESERVATION

MAP 1

Sappho

101

101

Hoh River

MAP 2

101

Olympic National Park

Mt Deception 7,788ft

Mt Olympus 7,965ft

MAP 3

Puget

3

Sound

5

405

MAP 4

QUINAULT INDIAN RESERVATION

Quinault

River

MAP 5

Olympic National Forest

W Fork Satsop River

Hood Canal

101

MAP 6

16

Vashon Island

Seattle

Tacoma

167

PACIFIC

101

8

5

Olympia

OCEAN

Grays Harbor

12

Chehalis River

Mt Baker-Snoqualmie National Forest

Riffe Lake

Willipa

Bay

MAP 7

5

WASHINGTON

Columbia River

Mt St. Helens 8,366ft

Mt St. Helens National Volcanic Monument

OREGON

101

River

Lewis

0   20 mi
0   20 km

© AVALON TRAVEL

Map 1

Campgrounds 1-7

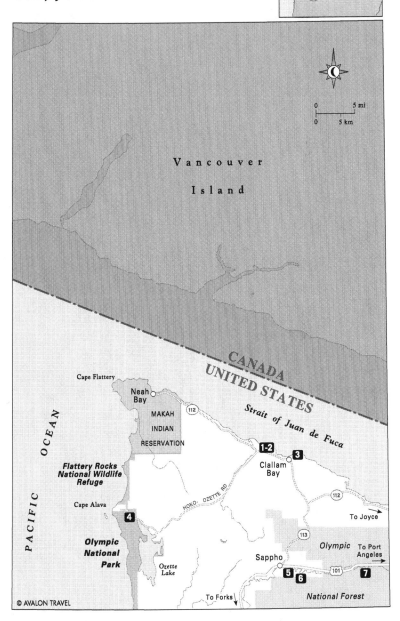

CAMPING

Map 2

Campgrounds 8-23

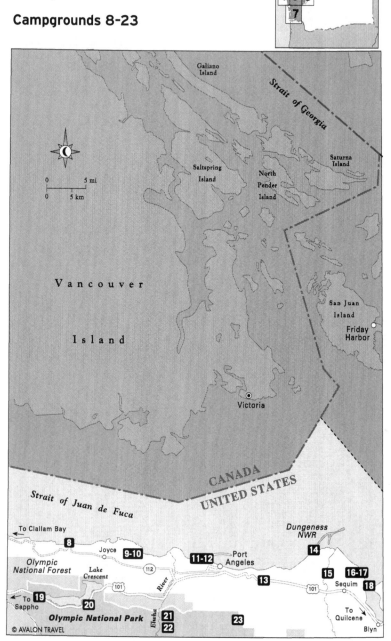

Map 3

Campgrounds 24-28

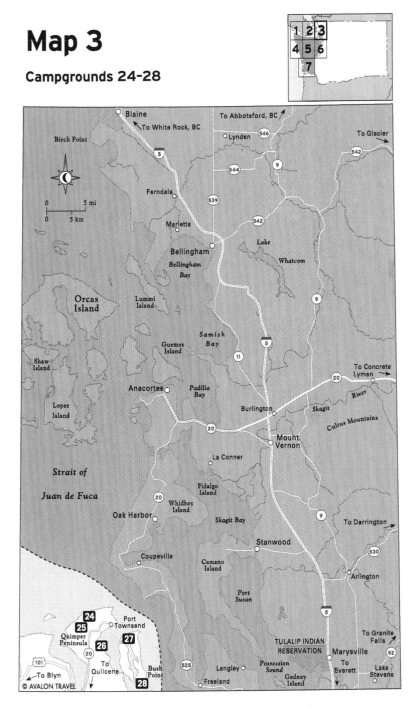

CAMPING

Map 4

Campgrounds 29-50

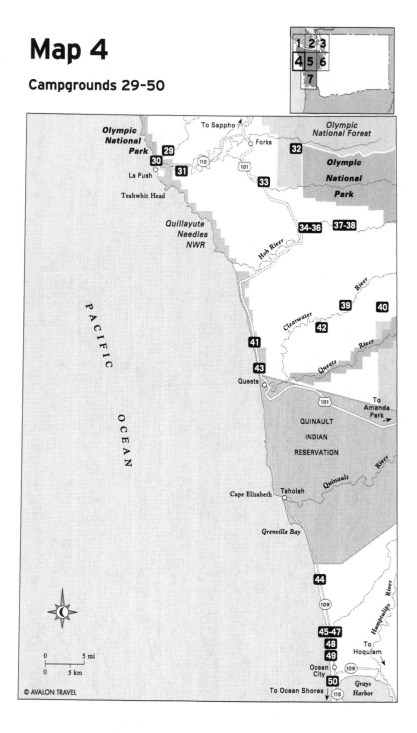

Map 5

Campgrounds 51-79

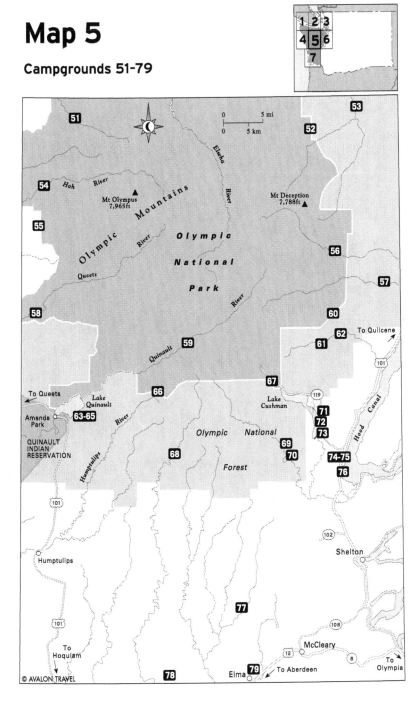

CAMPING

Map 6

Campgrounds 80-99

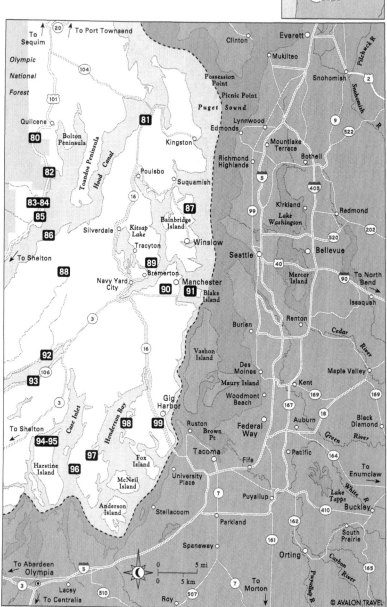

Map 7

Campgrounds 100-130

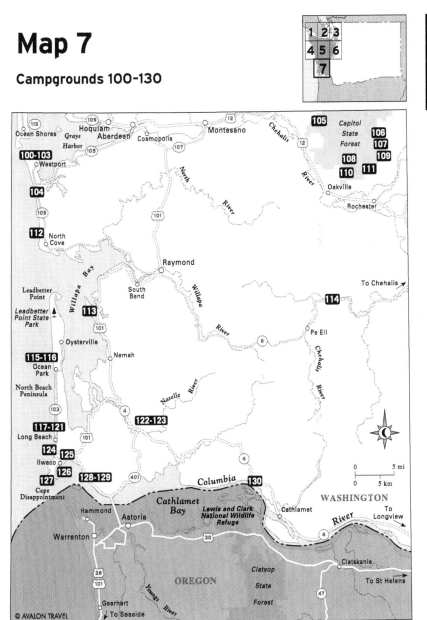

■ VAN RIPER'S RESORT

Scenic rating: 7

on Clallam Bay in Sekiu

Part of this campground hugs the waterfront and the other part sits on a hill overlooking the Strait of Juan de Fuca. Most sites are graveled, many with views of the strait. Other sites are grassy, without views. Note that some of the campsites are rented for the entire summer season. Hiking, fishing, and boating are among the options here, with salmon fishing being the principal draw. The beaches in the area, a mixture of sand and gravel, provide diligent rock hounds with agates and fossils.

Campsites, facilities: There are 100 sites with full or partial hookups (30 amps) for tents or RVs of any length. Some sites are pull-through. Other lodging includes two cabins, a mobile home, a house, and 12 motel rooms. Picnic tables are provided, and fire rings and cable TV are available at some sites. Restrooms with flush toilets and showers, drinking water, a dump station, firewood, and ice are available. A store, café, and coin laundry are located within one mile. Boat docks, launching facilities, and rentals are available. Leashed pets are permitted; no pets are allowed in cabins or other buildings.

Reservations, fees: Reservations are not accepted for campsites. Sites are $14–28 per night. Open April–September. Some credit cards are accepted.

Directions: Directions: From Port Angeles, take U.S. 101 west and drive 41 miles to Sappho Junction and Highway 113. Continue north on Highway 113 for nine miles to a fork with Highway 112. Take Highway 112 for two miles to Sekiu and Front Street. Turn right and drive 0.25 mile to the resort on the right.

Contact: Van Riper's Resort, 360/963-2334, www.vanripersresort.com.

■ OLSON'S RESORT

Scenic rating: 5

in Sekiu

Olson's Resort is large with full services, and the nearby marina is salmon-fishing headquarters. In fact, the resort caters to anglers, offering all-day salmon fishing trips and boat moorage. Chartered trips can be arranged by reservation. A tackle shop, cabins, houses, and a motel are also available. Other recreation options include hiking, boating, and beachcombing for agates and fossils.

Campsites, facilities: There are 100 sites for tents or RVs of any length (no hookups), 45 sites with for tents or RVs of any length (full hookups), seven cabins, 14 motel rooms, and four houses available. Picnic tables are provided, and fire rings are available at some sites. Restrooms with flush toilets and showers, drinking water, a dump station, coin laundry, convenience store, bait and tackle, and ice are available. Boat docks, launching facilities, boat rentals, bait, tackle, fish-cleaning station, gear storage, gas, and diesel fuel are also available on-site. A restaurant is located one mile away. Leashed pets are allowed, with certain restrictions.

Reservations, fees: Reservations are not accepted. Sites are $18–28 per night, plus $2 per person per night for more than two people. Some credit cards are accepted. Open year-round.

Directions: From Port Angeles, drive 41 miles west on U.S. 101 to Sappho Junction and Highway 113. Continue north on Highway 113 for nine miles to a fork with Highway 112. Take Highway 112 for two miles to Sekiu and Front Street. Turn right and drive one block to the resort on the right.

Contact: Olson's Resort, 360/963-2311, www.olsonsresort.com.

3 SAM'S MOBILE HOME AND RV PARK

Scenic rating: 5

on Clallam Bay

Sam's is an alternative to other resorts on Clallam Bay. It's a family-oriented park with grassy sites and many recreation options nearby. A mobile home park is adjacent to the RV park. Beaches are within walking distance. Those wanting to visit Cape Flattery, Hoh Rain Forest, or Port Angeles will find this a good central location.

Campsites, facilities: There are 21 sites, including some pull-through sites, with full hookups for RVs of any length and one tent site. Picnic tables are provided. Restrooms with flush toilets and showers, a dump station, cable TV, and coin laundry are available. Propane gas, gasoline, a store, café, and ice are located within one mile. Boat docks, launching facilities, and boat rentals are located within two miles. Leashed pets are permitted.

Reservations, fees: Reservations are accepted. RV sites are $24 per night, tent sites are $15 per night, $2 per person per night for more than two people. Credit cards are not accepted. Open year-round.

Directions: From Aberdeen, drive north on U.S. 101 for 119 miles to Sappho and Highway 113. Turn north on Highway 113 and drive nine miles to Clallam Bay and Highway 112. Continue straight on Highway 112 and drive into Clallam Bay. Just as you come into town, the park is on the right at 17053 Highway 112.

Contact: Sam's Mobile Home and RV Park, 360/963-2402.

4 OZETTE

Scenic rating: 6

on Lake Ozette in Olympic National Park

Many people visit this site located on the shore of Lake Ozette just a few miles from the Pacific Ocean. Set close to a trailhead road and ranger station, with multiple trailheads nearby, this camp is a favorite for both hikers and boaters and is one of the first to fill in the park.

Campsites, facilities: There are 15 sites for tents or RVs up to 21 feet long. Picnic tables and fire grills are provided. Vault toilets, drinking water (summer season only), and garbage bins are available; pit toilets are available in winter. Some facilities are wheelchair accessible. Leashed pets are permitted.

Reservations, fees: Reservations are not accepted. Sites are $12 per night, plus a $15 national park entrance fee per vehicle. Open year-round, weather permitting.

Directions: From Port Angeles, drive west on U.S. 101 to the junction with Highway 112. Bear right on Highway 112 and drive to Hoko-Ozette Road. Turn left and drive 21 miles to the ranger station. The camp parking lot is across from the ranger station on the northwest corner of Lake Ozette.

Contact: Olympic National Park, 360/565-3130, fax 360/565-3147, www.nps.gov/olym.

5 BEAR CREEK MOTEL AND RV PARK

Scenic rating: 7

on Bear Creek

This quiet little spot is set where Bear Creek empties into the Sol Duc River. It's private and developed, with a choice of sunny or shaded sites in a wooded setting. There are many recreation options in the area, including fishing, hunting, and nature and hiking trails leading to the ocean. Sol Duc Hot Springs is 25 miles north and well worth the trip. A restaurant next to the camp serves family-style meals.

Campsites, facilities: There are 10 pull-through sites for tents or RVs of any length (full hookups). Picnic tables and fire rings are provided. Restrooms with flush toilets and showers, drinking water, a dump station, a café, coin laundry, and firewood are available. A motel is also available on the premises. Boat-launching facilities are located within 0.5 mile. Leashed pets are permitted.

Reservations, fees: Reservations are not accepted. Sites are $25 per night. Some credit cards are accepted. Open year-round.

Directions: From Aberdeen, drive north on U.S. 101 to Forks. Continue past Forks for 15 miles to Milepost 205 (just past Sappho) to the park on the right at 205860 Highway 101 West.

Contact: Bear Creek Motel and RV Park, 360/327-3660, www.hungrybearcafémotel.com.

6 BEAR CREEK

Scenic rating: 8

on the Sol Duc River

BEST (

Fishing for salmon and hiking along the Sol Duc River make this a good launch point for recreation. There are also good opportunities for wildlife-viewing and photography, including a wheelchair-accessible viewing platform overlooking the Sol Duc River. This camp is also popular in the fall with hunters.

Campsites, facilities: There are 14 tent sites. Vault toilets and fire pits are available. There is no drinking water, and garbage must be packed out. Some facilities are wheelchair accessible. Leashed pets are permitted.

Reservations, fees: Reservations are not accepted. There is no fee for camping. Open year-round.

Directions: From Olympia on I-5, take Exit 104 and drive north on U.S. 101 to the Aberdeen/Highway 8 exit. Turn west on Highway 8 and drive 36 miles to Aberdeen. Continue through Aberdeen four miles to U.S. 101 and turn north and drive to Forks. Continue past Forks for 15 miles to Milepost 206 (two miles past Sappho) to the campground on the right.

Contact: Department of Natural Resources, Olympic Region, 360/374-6131, fax 360/374-5446, www.dnr.wa.gov.

7 KLAHOWYA

Scenic rating: 9

on the Sol Duc River in
Olympic National Forest

Klahowya features great views of Lake Crescent and Mount Olympus. It's a good choice if you don't want to venture far from U.S. 101 yet want to retain the feel of being in Olympic National Forest. Set along the Sol Duc River, this 32-acre camp is pretty and wooded, with hiking trails in the area. A favorite, Kloshe Nanitch Trail, is across the river and leads up to a lookout on Snider Ridge overlooking Sol Duc Valley. Pioneer's Path Trail, an easy, wheelchair-accessible, 0.3-mile loop with interpretive signs, starts in the camp. Fishing for salmon and steelhead, in season, can be good about 0.25 mile downstream from camp; always check regulations. This camp gets medium use.

Campsites, facilities: There are 53 sites for tents or RVs up to 30 feet long and two walk-in sites requiring a 700-foot walk. Picnic tables and fire grills are provided. Drinking water, garbage bins, and vault and flush toilets are available. An amphitheater with summer interpretive programs is also available. A boat ramp is nearby. Some facilities are wheelchair accessible. Leashed pets are permitted.

Reservations, fees: Reservations are not

accepted. Sites are $10 per night, $5 per night per additional vehicle. Open May–late September, weather permitting.

Directions: From U.S. 101 in Port Angeles, drive west for about 33 miles (10 miles west of Lake Crescent) to the campground on the right side of the road, close to Milepost 212. (Coming from the other direction on U.S. 101, drive eight miles east of Sappho to the campground.)

Contact: Olympic National Forest, Pacific Ranger District, 360/374-6522, fax 360/374-1250, www.fs.fed.us.

8 LYRE RIVER

Scenic rating: 7

on the Lyre River

This prime spot is one of the rare free campgrounds on the Olympic Peninsula. Although quite primitive, it does offer drinking water and an even more precious commodity in these parts: privacy. The camp is set along the Lyre River, about 0.5 mile from where it enters the Strait of Juan de Fuca. A popular camp for anglers, Lyre River offers good salmon fishing during fish migrations; always check fishing regulations. A wheelchair-accessible fishing pier is available.

Campsites, facilities: There are 10 primitive tent sites. Picnic tables, fire grills, and tent pads are provided. Vault toilets and drinking water are available. Garbage must be packed out. A roofed group shelter is available. Some facilities are wheelchair accessible. Leashed pets are permitted.

Reservations, fees: Reservations are not accepted. There is no fee for camping. Open year-round.

Directions: From U.S. 101 in Port Angeles, drive north five miles to a fork with Highway 112. Turn right (west) on Highway 112 and drive about 15 miles to Milepost 46. Look to the right for a paved road between Mileposts

46 and 47; then turn right (north) and drive 0.4 mile to the camp entrance road on the left.

Contact: Department of Natural Resources, Olympic Region, 360/374-6131, fax 360/374-5446, www.dnr.wa.gov.

9 CRESCENT BEACH RV PARK

Scenic rating: 6

on the Strait of Juan de Fuca

Set on a half-mile stretch of sandy beach, this campground makes a perfect weekend spot. Popular activities include swimming, fishing, surfing, sea kayaking, and beachcombing. It borders Salt Creek Recreation Area, with direct access available. Numerous attractions and recreation options are available in Port Angeles.

Campsites, facilities: There are 41 sites with full or partial hookups (30 and 50 amps) for tents or RVs of any length, and a grassy area for tent camping. Picnic tables and fire rings are provided. Restrooms with flush toilets and coin showers, coin laundry, pay phone, recreation field, and horseshoe pits are available. A dump station is nearby. Leashed pets are permitted.

Reservations, fees: Reservations are accepted. Sites are $35–40 per night, $5 per person per night for more than two people, $5 per extra vehicle (one-time fee per stay) unless towed, and $5 per night per pet. Weekly and monthly rates are available. Credit cards are accepted. Open year-round.

Directions: From U.S. 101 in Port Angeles, drive north five miles to a fork with Highway 112. Turn right (west) on Highway 112 and drive 10 miles to Camp Hayden Road (between Mileposts 53 and 54). Turn right on Camp Hayden Road and drive four miles to the park on the left, on the beach.

CAMPING

Contact: Crescent Beach RV Park, 360/928-3344, www.olypen.com/crescent.

⑩ SALT CREEK RECREATION AREA

🏕🏊🛶🐴🎣🚤♿🚐⛺

Scenic rating: 8

near the Strait of Juan de Fuca

The former site of Camp Hayden, a World War II–era facility, Salt Creek Recreation Area is a great spot for gorgeous ocean views, fishing, and hiking near Striped Peak, which overlooks the campground. Only a small beach area is available because of the rugged coastline, but there is an exceptionally good spot for tidepool viewing on the park's west side. The park covers 196 acres and overlooks the Strait of Juan de Fuca. It is known for its Tongue Point Marine Life Sanctuary. Recreation options include nearby hiking trails, swimming, fishing, horseshoes, and field sports. It's a good layover spot if you're planning to take the ferry out of Port Angeles to Victoria, British Columbia. The camp fills up quickly most summer weekends. Note that the gate closes at dusk.

Campsites, facilities: There are 92 sites, including 39 with partial hookups (30 and 50 amps) for tents or RVs of any length. Picnic tables and fire rings are provided. A restroom with flush toilets and coin showers, dump station, firewood, a playground, basketball and volleyball courts, and a covered picnic shelter that can be reserved are available. Some facilities are wheelchair accessible. Leashed pets are permitted.

Reservations, fees: Reservations are accepted only by downloading a reservation form at www.clallam.net/CountyParks. Sites are $18–24 per night, $5 per extra vehicle per night. Discount for Clallam County residents. Credit cards are not accepted. Open year-round.

Directions: From U.S. 101 in Port Angeles, drive north five miles to a fork with Highway 112. Turn right (west) on Highway 112 and drive 13 miles to Camp Hayden Road. Turn right (north) near Mile Marker 54 and drive 3.5 miles to the park entrance on the left.
Contact: Salt Creek Recreation Area, Clallam County, 360/928-3441, www.clallam.net/CountyParks.

⑪ PEABODY CREEK RV PARK

🚴🛶🚐🐴🚐⛺

Scenic rating: 5

in Port Angeles

This three-acre RV park is right in the middle of town but offers a wooded, streamside setting. Nearby recreation options include salmon fishing, an 18-hole golf course, marked biking trails, a full-service marina, and tennis courts. The park is within walking distance of shopping and ferry services.

Campsites, facilities: There is a grassy area for tents and 11 sites with full hookups (30 and 50 amps) for RVs of any length. Restrooms with flush toilets and coin showers, cable TV, ice, and a coin laundry are available. No open fires are allowed. A store and a café are located within one block. Boat docks and launching facilities are located within one mile. Leashed pets are permitted.

Reservations, fees: Reservations are accepted. RV sites are $25 per night, tent sites are $12 per night, $2 per person per night for more than two people. Credit cards are not accepted. Open year-round.

Directions: From U.S. 101 in Port Angeles, bear left on Lincoln Street and drive 0.5 mile to 2nd Street and the park entrance on the right.
Contact: Peabody Creek RV Park, tel./fax 360/457-7092 or 800/392-2361, www.peabodyrv.com.

12 AL'S RV PARK

Scenic rating: 8

near Port Angeles

This campground is a good choice for RV owners. The campground is set in the country at about 1,000 feet elevation yet is centrally located and not far from the Strait of Juan de Fuca. Nearby recreation options include an 18-hole golf course and a full-service marina. Olympic National Park and the Victoria ferry are a short drive away.

Campsites, facilities: There are 31 sites with full hookups (20, 30, and 50 amps) for RVs up to 40 feet long and a grassy area for tents. No open fires are allowed. Picnic tables are provided. Restrooms with flush toilets and showers, drinking water, cable TV, modem access, and a coin laundry are available. A store, café, propane gas, and ice are located within 0.5 mile. Boat docks and launching facilities are located within two miles. Some facilities are wheelchair accessible. Leashed pets are permitted.

Reservations, fees: Reservations are not accepted. RV sites are $26 per night, tent sites are $18 per night, $3 per person per night for more than two people. Weekly and monthly rates available. Credit cards are not accepted. Open year-round.

Directions: From Port Angeles, take U.S. 101 east for two miles to North Brook Avenue. Turn left (north) on North Brook Avenue, then left (almost immediately) on Lees Creek Road, and drive 0.5 mile to the park on the right.

Contact: Al's RV Park, 360/457-9844.

13 KOA PORT ANGELES-SEQUIM

Scenic rating: 5

near Port Angeles

This is a private, developed camp covering 13 acres in a country setting. A pleasant park, it features the typical KOA offerings, including a pool, recreation hall, and playground. Horseshoe pits and a sports field are also available. Hayrides are available in summer. Nearby recreation options include miniature golf, an 18-hole golf course, marked hiking trails, and tennis courts, and nearby side trips include Victoria, Butchart Gardens, and whale-watching tours.

Campsites, facilities: There are 24 tent sites, 82 sites with full and partial hookups (20, 30, and 50 amps) for tents or RVs of any length, 12 cabins, and one lodge. Some sites are pull-through. Picnic tables and fire pits are provided. Restrooms with flush toilets and showers, drinking water, cable TV, Wi-Fi and modem access, propane gas, firewood, dump station, convenience store, coin laundry, ice, a playground, miniature golf, organized activities, bicycle rentals, a recreation room, and a seasonal heated swimming pool and spa are available. A café is located within two miles. Some facilities are wheelchair accessible. Leashed pets are permitted.

Reservations, fees: Reservations are accepted at 800/562-7558. Sites are $25–90 per night, $6 per person per night for more than two people (ages six and older), and $6 per extra vehicle per night. Some credit cards are accepted. Open March–October.

Directions: In Port Angeles, go east on Highway 101 for seven miles to O'Brien Road. Turn right on O'Brien Road and drive half a block to the campground on the right.

Contact: KOA Port Angeles-Sequim, 360/457-5916, fax 360/452-4248, www.portangeles koa.com.

CAMPING

14 DUNGENESS RECREATION AREA

Scenic rating: 5

near the Strait of Juan de Fuca

This 216-acre park overlooks the Strait of Juan de Fuca and is set near the Dungeness National Wildlife Refuge. Quite popular, it fills up on summer weekends. A highlight, the refuge sits on a seven-mile spit with a historic lighthouse at its end. Bird-watchers often spot bald eagles in the wildlife refuge. There is a one-mile bluff trail, and equestrian trails are available. A 100-acre upland hunting area is open during season. Nearby recreation options include marked hiking trails, fishing, and golfing. The toll ferry at Port Angeles can take you to Victoria, British Columbia.

Campsites, facilities: There are 64 sites, including five pull-through sites, for tents or RVs of any length (no hookups) and eight hike-in/bike-in sites. Picnic tables and fire grills are provided. Restrooms with flush toilets and coin showers, drinking water, firewood, dump station, a playground, and a picnic area are available. A camp host is on-site. Some facilities are wheelchair accessible. Leashed pets are permitted.

Reservations, fees: Reservations are accepted only by downloading a reservation form at www.clallam.net/CountyParks. Sites are $18 per night, $5 per extra vehicle per night. Discount for Clallam County residents. Open February–September, with facilities limited to day use in the winter. Entrance gates close at dusk year-round.

Directions: From Sequim, drive north on U.S. 101 for four miles to Kitchen-Dick Road. Turn right (north) on Kitchen-Dick Road and drive three miles to the park on the left.

Contact: Dungeness Recreation Area, Clallam County, 360/683-5847, www.clallam.net/CountyParks/.

15 SEQUIM WEST INN & RV PARK

Scenic rating: 5

near the Dungeness River

This two-acre camp is near the Dungeness River and within 10 miles of Dungeness National Wildlife Refuge. It's located in town and is a pleasant spot with full facilities and an urban setting. An 18-hole golf course and a full-service marina at Sequim Bay are close by.

Campsites, facilities: There are 27 pull-through sites for tents or RVs of any length (30 and 50 amp full hookups), 17 cabins, and 21 motel rooms. Picnic tables are provided. No open fires are allowed. Restrooms with flush toilets and showers, drinking water, cable TV, coin laundry, a pay phone, and ice are available. Propane gas, gasoline, a store, and a café are located within one mile. Leashed pets are permitted.

Reservations, fees: Reservations are accepted. Sites are $29–34 per night, $1 per person per night for more than two adults. Some credit cards are accepted. Open year-round.

Directions: From Sequim and U.S. 101, take the Washington Street exit and drive west on Washington Street for 2.7 miles to the park on the left.

Contact: Sequim West Inn & RV Park, 360/683-4144 or 800/528-4527, fax 360/683-6452, www.sequimwestinn.com

16 RAINBOW'S END RV PARK

Scenic rating: 6

on Sequim Bay

This park on Sequim Bay is pretty and clean and features a pond (no fishing) and a creek running through the campground. There is a weekly potluck dinner in the summer, with free hamburgers and hot dogs, and a special landscaped area available for reunions, weddings, and other gatherings. Nearby recreation opportunities include an 18-hole golf course, marked bike trails, a full-service marina, and tennis courts.

Campsites, facilities: There are 10 tent sites and 42 sites with full hookups (30 and 50 amps), including some pull-through sites, for RVs of any length. Picnic tables are provided at all sites, and fire pits are provided at tent sites. Restrooms with flush toilets and showers, drinking water, dump station, cable TV, Wi-Fi and modem access, propane gas, firewood, coin laundry, and a clubhouse are available. A store, café, and ice are located within one mile. Leashed pets are permitted.

Reservations, fees: Reservations are accepted. RV sites are $30–35 per night, tent sites are $17–20 per night, $2 per person per night for more than two people, $2 per extra vehicle per night. Weekly and monthly rates are available. Some credit cards are accepted. Open year-round.

Directions: From Sequim, drive west on U.S. 101 for one mile past the River Road exit to the park on the right (along the highway).

Contact: Rainbow's End RV Park, 360/683-3863, fax 360/683-2150, www.rainbowsendrvpark.com.

🔢 SEQUIM BAY RESORT

Scenic rating: 5

on Sequim Bay

This is Sequim Bay headquarters for salmon anglers. The camp is set in a wooded, hilly area, close to many activity centers and with an 18-hole golf course nearby.

Campsites, facilities: There are 42 sites with full hookups (15 and 30 amps) for RVs of any length (30 sites are pull-through) and eight cabins. Picnic tables are provided. Restrooms with flush toilets and showers, drinking water,

cable TV, a community fire ring, Wi-Fi, and coin laundry are available. Boat docks and launching facilities are located across the street from the resort. Leashed pets are permitted, but not in cabins.

Reservations, fees: Reservations are accepted. Sites are $27–30 per night, $3 per person per night for more than two people. Credit cards are not accepted. Open year-round.

Directions: In Sequim, drive north 2.5 miles on U.S. 101 to Whitefeather Way (located between Mileposts 267 and 268). Turn right (north) on Whitefeather Way and drive 0.5 mile to West Sequim Bay Road. Turn left (west) and drive one block to the resort on the left.

Contact: Sequim Bay Resort, 360/681-3853, www.sequimbayresort.com.

🔢 SEQUIM BAY STATE PARK

Scenic rating: 8

on Sequim Bay

Sequim translates to "quiet waters," which is an appropriate description of this area. Set in the heart of Washington's rain shadow, a region with far less rainfall than the surrounding areas, Sequim averages only 17 inches of rainfall a year. The 92-acre park features 4,909 feet of saltwater shoreline; two sandbars shield the park from the Strait of Juan de Fuca's rough waters. There is one mile of hiking trails.

Campsites, facilities: There are 60 sites for tents or RVs (no hookups), 16 sites with full hookups (30 amps) for RVs up to 40 feet long, three primitive tent sites, and one tent-only group site for up to 50 people (available mid-May–mid-September). Picnic tables and fire grills are provided. Restrooms with flush toilets and coin showers, drinking water, a dump station, a picnic area with kitchen shelters, an amphitheater, athletic fields, a basketball court, tennis courts, horseshoe pits, playground, and interpretive center are

CAMPING

available. Boat docks, launching facilities, and boat mooring are also available. Some facilities are wheelchair accessible. Leashed pets are permitted.

Reservations, fees: Reservations are accepted at 888/CAMP-OUT (888/226-7688) or www.parks.wa.gov/reservations ($6.50–8.50 reservation fee). Sites are $21–28 per night, $14 per night for hike-in/bike-in sites, $10 per extra vehicle per night, and the group camp is $2.25 per person per night. Boat moorage is $0.50 per foot with a $10 minimum. Some credit cards are accepted. Open year-round.

Directions: From Olympia on I-5, turn north on U.S. 101 and drive 100 miles (near Sequim) to the park entrance on the right (along the highway). The park is located 3.5 miles southeast of the town of Sequim.

Contact: Sequim Bay State Park, 360/683-4235; state park information, 360/902-8844, www.parks.wa.gov.

19 FAIRHOLME

Scenic rating: 9

on Lake Crescent in Olympic National Park

This camp is set on the shore of Lake Crescent, a pretty lake situated within the boundary of Olympic National Park, at an elevation of 580 feet. The campsites lie along the western end of the lake, in a cove with a boat ramp. Located less than one mile off U.S. 101, Fairholme gets heavy use during tourist months; some highway noise is audible at some sites. A naturalist program is often available in the summer. Waterskiing is permitted at Lake Crescent, but personal watercraft are prohibited.

Campsites, facilities: There are 88 sites for tents or RVs up to 21 feet long. Picnic tables and fire grills are provided. A dump station, restrooms with flush toilets (summer season), drinking water, and garbage bins are available. A store and café are located within one mile. Boat-launching facilities and rentals are nearby

on Lake Crescent. Some facilities are wheelchair accessible. Leashed pets are permitted.

Reservations, fees: Reservations are not accepted. Sites are $12 per night, plus a $15 per vehicle national park entrance fee. Open April–October, weather permitting.

Directions: From Port Angeles, drive west on U.S. 101 for about 26 miles and continue along Lake Crescent to North Shore Road. Turn right and drive 0.5 mile to the camp on North Shore Road on the right.

Contact: Olympic National Park, 360/565-3130, fax 360/565-3147, www.nps.gov/olym.

20 LOG CABIN RESORT

Scenic rating: 10

on Lake Crescent in Olympic National Park

Log Cabin Resort is one of my wife's favorite spots. This pretty camp along the shore of Lake Crescent is a good spot for boaters, as it features many sites near the water with excellent views. Fishing and swimming are two options at this family-oriented resort. It is home to a strain of Beardslee trout. Note the fishing is catch-and-release. Waterskiing is permitted, but no personal watercraft are allowed. A marked hiking trail traces the lake's 22-mile shoreline. This camp is extremely popular in the summer months; you may need to make reservations 6–12 months in advance.

Campsites, facilities: There are 38 sites with full hookups (20 and 30 amps) for RVs of any length, four tent sites, and 28 cabins. Some sites are pull-through. Picnic tables and fire barrels are provided. A dump station, restrooms with flush toilets and coin showers, a store, café, gift shop, coin laundry, Wi-Fi, firewood, ice, and a recreation field are available. Boat docks, launching facilities, and boat rentals and hydrobikes are available. Some facilities are wheelchair accessible. Leashed pets are permitted.

Reservations, fees: Reservations are accepted. RV sites are $40 per night, tent sites are $20 per night, $5 per person per night for more than two people, $2 per extra vehicle per night, $15 per pet per night. Some credit cards are accepted. Open Memorial Day weekend–September.

Directions: In Port Angeles, drive 18 miles north on U.S. 101 to East Beach Road. Turn right and drive three miles (along Lake Crescent) to the camp on the left.

Contact: Log Cabin Resort, 360/928-3325, fax 360/928-2088, www.logcabinresort.net.

21 ELWHA

Scenic rating: 7

on the Elwha River in Olympic National Park

The Elwha River is the backdrop for this popular camp with excellent hiking trails close by in Olympic National Park. The elevation is 390 feet. Fishing is good in season at nearby Lake Mills; check regulations. Check at one of the visitors centers for maps and backcountry information.

Campsites, facilities: There are 40 sites for tents or RVs up to 21 feet long. Picnic tables and fire grills are provided. Restrooms with flush toilets, drinking water, and garbage bins are available. Some facilities are wheelchair accessible. Leashed pets are permitted.

Reservations, fees: Reservations are not accepted. Sites are $12 per night, plus a $15 national park entrance fee per vehicle. Open year-round.

Directions: From Port Angeles, drive west on U.S. 101 for about nine miles (just past Lake Aldwell) to the signed entrance road on the left. Turn left at the entrance road and drive three miles south along the Elwha River to the campground on the left.

Contact: Olympic National Park, 360/565-3130, fax 360/565-3147, www.nps.gov/olym.

22 ALTAIRE

Scenic rating: 8

on the Elwha River in Olympic National Park

A pretty and well-treed camp with easy highway access, this camp is set on the Elwha River about one mile from Lake Mills. Fishing is good in season; check regulations. The elevation is 450 feet. Altaire also makes for a nice layover spot before taking the ferry at Port Angeles to Victoria, British Columbia.

Campsites, facilities: There are 30 sites for tents or RVs up to 21 feet long. Picnic tables and fire grills are provided. Restrooms with flush toilets, drinking water, and garbage bins are available. Some facilities are wheelchair accessible. Leashed pets are permitted.

Reservations, fees: Reservations are not accepted. Sites are $12 per night, plus a $15 national park entrance fee per vehicle. Open late May–October.

Directions: From Port Angeles, drive west on U.S. 101 for about nine miles (just past Lake Aldwell) to the signed entrance road on the left. Turn left at the signed entrance road and drive four miles south along the Elwha River.

Contact: Olympic National Park, 360/565-3130, fax 360/565-3147, www.nps.gov/olym.

23 HEART O' THE HILLS

Scenic rating: 9

in Olympic National Park

Heart O' the Hills is nestled on the northern edge of Olympic National Park at an elevation of 1,807 feet. You can drive into the park on Hurricane Ridge Road and take one of numerous hiking trails. Little Lake Dawn is less than 0.5 mile to the west, but note that most of the property around this lake is privately owned. Naturalist programs are available in summer months.

Campsites, facilities: There are 105 sites for tents or RVs up to 21 feet long. Picnic tables and fire grills are provided. Restrooms with flush toilets, drinking water, and garbage bins are available. Some facilities are wheelchair accessible. Leashed pets are permitted.

Reservations, fees: Reservations are not accepted. Sites are $12 per night, plus a $15 national park entrance fee per vehicle. Open year-round, weather permitting.

Directions: From U.S. 101 in Port Angeles at Hurricane Ridge Road, turn left and drive five miles to the camp on the left. (Access roads can be impassable in severe weather.)

Contact: Olympic National Park, 360/565-3130, fax 360/565-3147, www.nps.gov/olym.

24 FORT WORDEN STATE PARK

Scenic rating: 9

in Port Townsend

This park is set on the northeastern tip of the Olympic Peninsula, at the northern end of Port Townsend, on a high bluff with views of Puget Sound. Highlights here include great lookouts and two miles of beach trails over the Strait of Juan de Fuca as it feeds into Puget Sound. The park covers 433 acres at historic Fort Worden (on which construction was begun in 1897 and decommissioned in 1953) and includes buildings from the turn of the 20th century. It has 11,020 feet of saltwater shoreline. Recreation options include 12 miles of marked hiking and biking trails, including five miles of wheelchair-accessible trails. The Coast Artillery Museum, Rothschild House, Commanding Officers Quarters, and the Marine Science Center and Natural History

Museum are open during the summer season. A ferry at Port Townsend will take you across the strait to Whidbey Island. Special note on reservations: This is an extremely popular park and campground and reservations are required online up to five months in advance or in person up to 11 months in advance.

Campsites, facilities: There are 80 sites with full or partial hookups (30 and 50 amps) for tents or RVs up to 75 feet long, including some pull-through sites, five hike-in/bike-in sites, one non-motorized boat-in site, and one group camp for up to 400 people. Other lodging includes 33 Victoria-era houses and three dormitories. Picnic tables and fire grills are provided. Restrooms with flush toilets and coin showers, drinking water, coin laundry, a store, dump station, and firewood are available. A restaurant, conference facilities, a sheltered amphitheater, athletic fields, and interpretive activities are available nearby. Boat docks, buoys, floats, and launching facilities are also nearby, as are several golf courses. Some facilities are wheelchair accessible. Leashed pets are permitted.

Reservations, fees: Reservations are accepted at 360/344-4431 or www.fortworden.net ($8 reservation fee). Sites are $36–42 per night, $13–22 per night for hike-in/bike-in and boat-in sites, $10 per extra vehicle per night, the group camp is $2.25 per person per night, and the dorms and houses are $135–408 per night. Boat moorage is $0.50 per foot with a $10 minimum. Open year-round.

Directions: From Port Townsend, take Highway 20 north through town to Kearney Street. Turn left on Kearney Street and drive to the first stop sign, at Blaine Street. Turn right on Blaine Street and drive to the next stop sign, on Cherry Street. Turn left at Cherry Street and drive 1.75 miles to the park entrance at the end of the road.

Contact: Fort Worden State Park, 360/344-4400, fax 360/385-7248; state park information, 360/902-8844, www.parks.wa.gov.

25 POINT HUDSON MARINA & RV PARK

Scenic rating: 5

in Port Townsend

Point Hudson RV Park is located on the site of an old Coast Guard station near the beach in Port Townsend. This public facility is owned by the Port of Port Townsend. The park features ocean views and 2,000 feet of beach frontage. Known for its Victorian architecture, Port Townsend is called Washington's Victorian seaport. Fishing and boating are popular here, and nearby recreation opportunities include an 18-hole municipal golf course, a full-service marina, Old Fort Townsend State Park, Fort Flagler State Park, and Fort Worden State Park.

Campsites, facilities: There are 43 sites with full hookups (30 amps) for RVs of any length and two sites with no hookups. Some sites are pull-through. Picnic tables are provided at some sites. No fires are allowed. Restrooms with flush toilets and coin showers, drinking water, cable TV, Wi-Fi and modem access, three restaurants, and coin laundry are available. A 100-plus-slip marina is on-site. Leashed pets are permitted.

Reservations, fees: Reservations are accepted. Sites are $27–42 per night, $5 per extra vehicle per night. Some credit cards are accepted. Open year-round.

Directions: From Port Townsend on State Route 20, take the Water Street exit. Turn left (north) and continue (the road becomes Sims Way and then Water Street) to the end of Water Street at the marina. Turn left for registration.

Contact: Point Hudson Marina & RV Park, 360/385-2828 or 800/228-2803, fax 360/385-7331, www.portofpt.com.

26 OLD FORT TOWNSEND STATE PARK

Scenic rating: 10

near Quilcene

This 367-acre park features a thickly wooded landscape, nearly 4,000 feet of saltwater shoreline on Port Townsend Bay, and 6.5 miles of hiking trails. Built in 1856, the historic fort is one of the oldest remaining in the state. The scenic campground has access to a good clamming beach (check regulations), and visitors can take two different short, self-guided walking tours. Note that the nearest boat ramps are at Port Townsend, Fort Flagler, and Hadlock. Mooring buoys are located just offshore of the park on the west side of Port Townsend Bay.

Campsites, facilities: There are 40 sites for tents or RVs up to 40 feet long, four hike-in/bike-in sites, and one group site for up to 80 people. Picnic tables and fire grills are provided. Restrooms with flush toilets and coin showers, drinking water, a playground, ball fields, boat buoys, firewood, a dump station, and a picnic area with a kitchen shelter are available. Some facilities are wheelchair accessible. Leashed pets are permitted.

Reservations, fees: Reservations are accepted at 360/344-4431 ($8.50 reservation fee). Sites are $19 per night, $10 per extra vehicle per night, hike-in/bike-in sites are $12 per night, and the group camp is $2.25 per person per night with a minimum of 20 people, plus $25 reservation fee. Open mid-April–mid-October, weather permitting.

Directions: From Port Townsend and State Route 20, drive south on State Route 20 for two miles to Old Fort Townsend Road. Turn left and drive 0.5 mile to the park entrance road.

Contact: Old Fort Townsend State Park, 360/344-4431 or 360/385-3595; state park information, 360/902-8844, www.parks.wa.gov.

27 FORT FLAGLER STATE PARK

🏃 🚴 ⛵ 🛶 🐴 🎣 ♿ 🚐 ⛺

Scenic rating: 10

near Port Townsend

BEST (

Historic Fort Flagler is a pretty and unique state park, set on Marrowstone Island east of Port Townsend. The camp overlooks Puget Sound and offers 19,100 feet of gorgeous saltwater shore. The park's 784 acres include five miles of trails for hiking and biking, an interpretive trail, and a military museum featuring gun batteries that are open in the summer. The RV sites are situated right on the beach, with views of the Olympic and Cascade Mountains. Anglers like this spot for year-round rockfish and salmon fishing, and crabbing and clamming are good in season (check regulations). Fort Flagler, under construction on some level from 1897 until its closure in 1953, offers summer tours. There is a youth hostel in the park.

Campsites, facilities: There are 116 tent sites, 57 sites with full hookups (30 amps) for RVs up to 50 feet long, two hike-in/bike-in sites, a vacation house, a group tent site for up to 40 people, and a group site for tents or RVs of any length for up to 100 people. Picnic tables and fire grills are provided. Restrooms with flush toilets and coin showers, drinking water, interpretive activities, a dump station, playground, picnic shelters that can be reserved, a camp store, boat buoys, moorage dock, and a launch are available. Some facilities are wheelchair accessible. Leashed pets are permitted.

Reservations, fees: Reservations are accepted at 888/CAMP-OUT (888/226-7688) or www.parks.wa.gov/reservations ($6.50–8.50 reservation fee). Sites are $21–28 per night, $10 per extra vehicle per night, $14 per night for hike-in/bike-in sites. The group sites are $2.25 per person per night, with a minimum of 20 people. The vacation house is $79–105 for up to four people and available year-round.

Some credit cards are accepted. Open mid-May–October, weather permitting.

Directions: From Port Townsend at Highway 20, drive to Highway 19 (Airport cutoff) and make a slight left turn on Highway 19. Drive 3.5 miles to the traffic light at Ness Corner Road and turn left. Drive about one mile on Ness Corner Road to Oak Bay Road/Highway 116. Continue one mile on Highway 116 and turn left at Flagler Road to stay on Highway 116. Remain on Flagler Road and drive about 6.5 miles to the end of the road and the park and campground.

Contact: Fort Flagler State Park, 360/385-1259, fax 360/379-1746; state park information, 360/902-8844, www.parks.wa.gov.

28 KINNEY POINT STATE PARK

🏃 ⛵ 🛶 🐴 ⛺

Scenic rating: 10

on Marrowstone Island

Kinney Point is located on the south end of Marrowstone Island, part of Washington's Cascade Marine Trail. You'll need a non-motorized boat to reach the campsites at this 76-acre park; once you do, 683 feet shoreline await.

Campsites, facilities: There are three primitive sites. A vault toilet and kayak rack are available. There is no drinking water. All garbage must be packed out. Leashed pets are permitted.

Reservations, fees: Reservations are not accepted. Sites are $14 per night. Open year-round.

Directions: From Fort Flagler or Mystery Bay state parks, head south down Marrowstone Island to Kinney Point.

Contact: Kinney Point State Park, 360/385-1259; state park information, 360/902-8844, www.parks.wa.gov.

29 MORA

Scenic rating: 8

in Olympic National Park

At an elevation of 50 feet, this is a good out-of-the-way choice near the Pacific Ocean and the Olympic Coast Marine Sanctuary. The Quillayute River feeds into the ocean near the camp, and upstream lies the Bogachiel, a prime steelhead river in winter months. A naturalist program is available during the summer. This camp includes eight sites that require short walks, and several of them are stellar.

Campsites, facilities: There are 94 sites for tents or RVs up to 21 feet long and one walk-in site. Picnic tables and fire grills are provided. Restrooms with flush toilets, drinking water, garbage bins, and a dump station are available. Some facilities are wheelchair accessible. Leashed pets are permitted.

Reservations, fees: Reservations are not accepted. Sites are $12 per night, plus a $15 national park entrance fee per vehicle. Open year-round.

Directions: From Aberdeen, drive north on U.S. 101 for 108 miles to Forks. Continue past Forks for two miles to La Push Road/Highway 110. Turn left (west) and drive 12 miles to the campground on the left (well marked along the route).

Contact: Olympic National Park, 360/565-3130, fax 360/565-3147, www.nps.gov/olym.

30 LONESOME CREEK RV RESORT

Scenic rating: 8

near Forks

This private, developed park is set along the Pacific Ocean and the coastal Dungeness National Wildlife Refuge. It has some of the few ocean sites available in the area and offers such recreation options as fishing, surfing, beachcombing, boating, whale-watching, and sunbathing.

Campsites, facilities: There are 42 sites for tents or RVs of any length (30 and 50 amp full hookups) and five tent sites; some sites are pull-through. Picnic tables and fire rings are provided. Restrooms with flush toilets and coin showers, a coin laundry, gasoline and propane gas, and a convenience store with a deli and ice are available. Boat docks, a marina, and launching facilities are located within one mile. Leashed pets are permitted.

Reservations, fees: Reservations are accepted and are recommended for the 18 oceanfront sites. Tent sites are $18 per night, and RV sites are $30–35 per night, with reduced rates in winter. Some credit cards are accepted. Open year-round.

Directions: From the town of Forks, drive north on U.S. 101 for two miles to La Push Road/Highway 110. Turn left (west) and drive 14 miles to the resort on the left.

Contact: Lonesome Creek RV Resort, 360/374-4338.

31 THREE RIVERS RESORT

Scenic rating: 8

on the Quillayute River

Three Rivers Resort is a small, private camp is set at the junction of the Quillayute, Sol Duc, and Bogachiel Rivers. Situated above this confluence, about six miles upstream from the ocean, this pretty spot features wooded, spacious sites. Hiking and fishing are popular here, and there is a fishing guide service. Salmon and steelhead migrate upstream, best on the Sol Duc and Bogachiel Rivers; anglers should check regulations. The coastal Dungeness National Wildlife Refuge and Pacific Ocean, which often offer good whale-watching in the spring, are a short drive to the west. Hoh

Rain Forest, a worthwhile side trip, is about 45 minutes away.

Campsites, facilities: There are 10 sites for tents or RVs of any length (no hookups), two sites with full or partial hookups (30 and 50 amps) for tents or RVs of any length, and six rental cabins. Picnic tables and fire rings are provided. Restrooms with flush toilets and coin showers, a convenience store, gas station, firewood, a café, coin laundry, firewood, and ice are available. Leashed pets are permitted.

Reservations, fees: Reservations are accepted. Tent sites are $14 per night, RV sites are $16–18 per night, $5 per pet per night. Some credit cards are accepted. Open year-round.

Directions: From Aberdeen, drive north on U.S. 101 for 108 miles to Forks. Continue past Forks for two miles to La Push Road/Highway 110. Turn left (west) and drive eight miles to the resort on the right.

Contact: Three Rivers Resort, 360/374-5300, www.northolympic.com/threerivers.

32 KLAHANIE

Scenic rating: 8

on the North Fork Klahanie River

This camp was closed for several years, but it is now open again. That means it is likely off the radar of many travelers, so it is worth checking in on. Sites nestle amid large, old-growth spruce and lots of ferns. It is quite pretty, set along a riparian zone on the North Fork Klahanie River, and features a hiking trail that hugs the river for 0.25 mile.

Campsites, facilities: There are eight sites for tents or RVs up to 21 feet. Picnic tables and fire grills are provided. Drinking water and vault toilets are available. Garbage must be packed out. Leashed pets are permitted.

Reservations, fees: Reservations are not accepted. Sites are $5 per night. Open May–late September, weather permitting.

Directions: From Aberdeen, drive north on U.S. 101 to Forks. Continue past Forks for one mile to Forest Road 29. Turn right (east) and drive five miles to the campground on the right.

Contact: Olympic National Forest, Pacific Ranger District, 360/374-6522, fax 360/374-1250, www.fs.fed.us.

33 BOGACHIEL STATE PARK

Scenic rating: 6

on the Bogachiel River

A good base camp for salmon or steelhead fishing trips, this 123-acre park is set on the Bogachiel River, with marked hiking trails in the area. It can be noisy at times because a logging mill is located directly across the river from the campground. Also note that there is highway noise, and you can see the highway from some campsites. A one-mile hiking trail is nearby, and opportunities for wildlife-viewing are outstanding in the park. Hunting is popular in the adjacent national forest. This region is heavily forested, with lush vegetation fed by an average of 140–160 inches of rain each year. This park was established in 1931.

Campsites, facilities: There are 36 sites for tents or RVs (no hookups), six sites with partial hookups (30 amps) for RVs up to 40 feet long, one hike-in/bike-in site, and one group tent camp with a covered shelter for up to 20 people. Picnic tables and fire grills are provided. Restrooms with flush toilets and coin showers, drinking water, dump station, and a picnic area are available. A primitive boat ramp is nearby. Some facilities are wheelchair accessible. Leashed pets are permitted.

Reservations, fees: Reservations are not accepted for individual sites but are required for the group camp at 360/374-6356. Sites are $19–25 per night, the hike-in/bike-in site is

$12 per night, $10 per extra vehicle per night. The group site is $2.25 per person per night. Open year-round, with some sites closed in winter.

Directions: From Olympia on I-5, take Exit 104 and drive north on U.S. 101 to the Aberdeen/Highway 8 exit. Turn west on Highway 8 and drive 36 miles to Aberdeen. Continue through Aberdeen four miles to U.S. 101. Turn north on U.S. 101 and drive 102 miles to the park (six miles south of Forks) on the left side of the road.

Contact: Bogachiel State Park, Northwest Region, 360/374-6356; state park information, 360/902-8844, www.parks.wa.gov.

34 HOH RIVER RESORT
Scenic rating: 6

on the Hoh River

This camp along U.S. 101 features a choice of grassy or graveled, shady sites and is most popular as a fishing camp. Although the Hoh River is nearby, you cannot see the river from the campsites. Marked hiking trails are in the area. This pleasant little park offers steelhead and salmon fishing in season as well as elk hunting in the fall. Horseshoe pits and a recreation field are available for campers.

Campsites, facilities: There are 23 sites with full or partial hookups for tents or RVs of any length and two cabins. Some sites are pull-through. Picnic tables and fire pits are provided. Restrooms with flush toilets and coin showers, a general store, propane gas, a gas station, firewood, and ice are available. A boat launch is available nearby. Leashed pets are permitted.

Reservations, fees: Reservations are accepted. RV sites are $15–25 per night, tent sites are $15 per night, $5 per person per night for more than two people. Some credit cards are accepted. Open year-round.

Directions: From Aberdeen, drive north on U.S. 101 for 90 miles to the resort (15 miles south of Forks) on the left.

Contact: Hoh River Resort, 360/374-5566, www.hohriverresort.com.

35 COTTONWOOD
Scenic rating: 8

on the Hoh River

This primitive camp is set along the Hoh River, providing an alternative to Hoh Oxbow, Willoughby Creek, and Minnie Peterson campgrounds. Like Hoh Oxbow, Cottonwood offers the bonus of a boat launch. Its distance from the highway makes it quieter here. The camp is popular for anglers and hunters (in season).

Campsites, facilities: There are nine sites for tents or RVs up to 16 feet long. Picnic tables, fire grills, and tent pads are provided. There is no drinking water, and garbage must be packed out. Vault toilets and a boat launch are available. Some facilities are wheelchair accessible. Leashed pets are permitted.

Reservations, fees: Reservations are not accepted. There is no fee for camping. Open year-round.

Directions: From Olympia on I-5, take Exit 104 and drive north on U.S. 101 to the Aberdeen/Highway 8 exit. Turn west on Highway 8 and drive 36 miles to Aberdeen. Continue through Aberdeen four miles to U.S. 101. Turn north on U.S. 101 and drive 92 miles to Oil City Road between Mileposts 177 and 178. Turn left (west) on Oil City Road and drive 2.3 miles. Turn left on Road H4060 (gravel) and drive one mile to the camp at the end of the road.

Contact: Department of Natural Resources, Olympic Region, 360/374-6131, fax 360/374-5446, www.dnr.wa.gov.

36 HOH OXBOW

Scenic rating: 7

on the Hoh River

This is the most popular of the five camps on the Hoh River. It's primitive and close to the highway, and the price is right. The adjacent boat launch makes this the camp of choice for anglers, best in fall and winter for salmon and steelhead; check regulations. It is also a popular hunters' camp in the fall. One downer: there is some highway noise within range of the campsites. You can't see the traffic, but you can hear it, which can be irritating for those who want perfect quiet.

Campsites, facilities: There are eight sites for tents or small RVs. Picnic tables, fire grills, and tent pads are provided. Vault toilets and a hand boat launch are available. There is no drinking water, and garbage must be packed out. Some facilities are wheelchair accessible. Leashed pets are permitted.

Reservations, fees: Reservations are not accepted. There is no fee for camping. Open year-round.

Directions: From Aberdeen, drive north on U.S. 101 for 90 miles to the campground (15 miles south of Forks). Exit between Mileposts 176 and 177 and look for the campground on the right, next to the river. Note: The road in is narrow and not advised for RVs or trailers.

Contact: Department of Natural Resources, Olympic Region, 360/374-6131, fax 360/374-5446, www.dnr.wa.gov.

37 WILLOUGHBY CREEK

Scenic rating: 9

in Hoh Clearwater State Forest

This little-known camp along Willoughby Creek and the Hoh River is tiny and rustic, with good fishing nearby for steelhead and salmon during peak migrations in season. The area gets heavy rainfall. Other campground options in the vicinity include Hoh Oxbow, Cottonwood, and Minnie Peterson.

Campsites, facilities: There are three campsites for tents or RVs up to 16 feet long. Picnic tables, fire grills, and tent pads are provided. Vault toilets are available. There is no drinking water, and garbage must be packed out. Leashed pets are permitted.

Reservations, fees: Reservations are not accepted. There is no fee for camping. Open year-round.

Directions: From Olympia on I-5, take Exit 104 and drive north on U.S. 101 to the Aberdeen/Highway 8 exit. Turn west on Highway 8 and drive 36 miles to Aberdeen. Continue through Aberdeen four miles to U.S. 101. Turn north on U.S. 101 and drive about 90 miles. Exit between Mileposts 178 and 179. At Hoh Rain Forest Road/Upper Hoh Valley Road, turn east and drive 3.5 miles to the campground on the right.

Contact: Department of Natural Resources, Olympic Region, 360/374-6131, fax 360/374-5446, www.dnr.wa.gov.

38 MINNIE PETERSON

Scenic rating: 9

on the Hoh River

If location is everything, then it's why this campground has become popular. Minnie Peterson is set on the Hoh River on the edge of the Hoh Rain Forest. It's quite pretty, forested with Sitka spruce and western hemlock, and offers nice riverside sites. Bring your rain gear.

Campsites, facilities: There are eight sites for tents or RVs up to 16 feet long. Picnic tables, fire grills, and tent pads are provided. Vault toilets are available. There is no drinking water, and garbage must be packed out. Firing guns is prohibited. Some facilities are wheelchair accessible. Leashed pets are permitted.

Reservations, fees: Reservations are not accepted. There is no fee for camping. Open year-round.

Directions: From Olympia on I-5, take Exit 104 and drive north on U.S. 101 to the Aberdeen/Highway 8 exit. Turn west on Highway 8 and drive 36 miles to Aberdeen. Continue through Aberdeen four miles to U.S. 101. Turn north on U.S. 101 and drive about 90 miles. Exit between Mileposts 178 and 179. At Hoh Rain Forest Road/Upper Hoh Valley Road, turn east and drive 4.5 miles to the campground on the left.

Contact: Department of Natural Resources, Olympic Region, 360/374-6131, fax 360/374-5446, www.dnr.wa.gov.

39 UPPER CLEARWATER

Scenic rating: 8

on the Clearwater River

One of the three primitive camps set along the Clearwater River, Upper Clearwater is a great camp: It's very pretty, is unused by most tourists, and—best of all—it's free. Campsites sit amid a forest of western hemlock, red alder, and big leaf maple.

Note that there was considerable damage from the river in 2008 and 2009. Also, the camp is fairly small and is not suited for RVs.

Campsites, facilities: There are six sites for tents and small self-contained RVs (pickups And truck campers). Picnic tables, fire grills, and tent pads are provided. Vault toilets are available. There is no drinking water, and garbage must be packed out. There are unimproved boat-launching facilities for small crafts, such as river dories, rafts, canoes, and kayaks. Leashed pets are permitted.

Reservations, fees: Reservations are not accepted. There is no fee for camping. Open year-round.

Directions: From Olympia on I-5, take Exit 104

and drive north on U.S. 101 to the Aberdeen/Highway 8 exit. Turn west on Highway 8 and drive 36 miles to Aberdeen. Continue through Aberdeen four miles to U.S. 101. Turn north on U.S. 101 and drive about 60 miles to Milepost 147. Turn north on Clearwater Mainline Road and drive about 13 miles to C-3000 Road (a gravel one-lane road). Turn right and drive 3.3 miles to the camp entrance on the right.

Contact: Department of Natural Resources, Olympic Region, 360/374-6131, fax 360/374-5446, www.dnr.wa.gov.

40 YAHOO LAKE

Scenic rating: 10

on Yahoo Lake

Yahoo Lake is the most primitive and remote campground in the Olympic Region. A rustic trail surrounds the beautifully scenic and tranquil lake.

Campsites, facilities: There are three lakeside sites for tents or RVs up to 16 feet long. Picnic tables and fire grills are provided. A vault toilet is available. There is no drinking water. All garbage must be packed out. Leashed pets are permitted.

Reservations, fees: Reservations are not accepted. There is no fee for camping. Open year-round.

Directions: From Olympia on I-5, take Exit 104 and drive north on U.S. 101 to the Aberdeen/Highway 8 exit. Turn west on Highway 8 and drive 36 miles to Aberdeen. Continue through Aberdeen four miles to U.S. 101. Turn north on U.S. 101 and drive about 60 miles to Milepost 147. Turn north on Clearwater Mainline Road and drive about 13 miles to C-3000 Road (a gravel one-lane road). Turn right and drive 0.8 mile to C-3100 Road. Turn right on C-3100 Road (paved one-lane, then gravel one-lane). Continue 6.1 miles to trailhead. This road is not recommended for motor home travel.

CAMPING

Contact: Department of Natural Resources, Olympic Region, 360/374-6131, www.dnr.wa.gov.

41 KALALOCH

👫 🛶 🛖 ♿ 🚐 ⛺

Scenic rating: 10

in Olympic National Park

`BEST (`

This camp, located on a bluff above the beach, offers some wonderful oceanview sites—which explains its popularity. It can fill quickly. Like other camps set on the coast of the Olympic Peninsula, heavy rain in winter and spring is common, and it's often foggy in the summer. A naturalist program is offered in the summer months. There are several good hiking trails in the area; check out the visitors center for maps and information.

Campsites, facilities: There are 170 sites for tents or RVs up to 35 feet long, and one double site. The nearby Kalaloch Lodge offers a group site for tents or RVs that can accommodate up to 30 people. Picnic tables and fire grills are provided at Kalaloch Campground and the Kalaloch Lodge group camp. Restrooms with flush toilets, drinking water, garbage bins, and a dump station are available at Kalaloch Campground. A water tap and a pit toilet are available at the Kalaloch Lodge group site. A store and a restaurant are located within one mile of both campgrounds. Some facilities are wheelchair accessible. Leashed pets are permitted in the campground.

Reservations, fees: Reservations are accepted for the group site at 360/962-2271. Reservations are accepted June–September at 877/444-6777 or www.recreation.gov ($10 reservation fee). Single sites are $14–18 per night, the double site is $28–36 per night, and the national park entrance fee is $15 per vehicle. The group site is $20 per night for the first 10 people and $2 per person per night for each additional person, plus a $20 reservation fee. Open year-round.

Directions: From Aberdeen, drive north on U.S. 101 for 83 miles to the campground on the left. It is located near the mouth of the Kalaloch River five miles north of the U.S. 101 bridge over the Queets River.

Contact: Olympic National Park, 360/565-3130, fax 360/565-3147, www.nps.gov/olym.

42 COPPERMINE BOTTOM

👫 🛶 🛥 🛖 🚐 ⛺

Scenic rating: 9

on the Clearwater River

`BEST (`

Few tourists ever visit this primitive, hidden campground set on the Clearwater River, a tributary of the Queets River, which runs to the ocean. The river dory–launching facility is a bonus and makes this a perfect camp for anglers and river runners who want to avoid the usual U.S. 101 crowds. Salmon fishing is popular here during the migratory journey of the anadromous fish.

Campsites, facilities: There are nine campsites for tents or RVs up to 16 feet long. Picnic tables, fire grills, and tent pads are provided. Vault toilets, a group shelter, and a hand boat launch are available. There is no drinking water, and garbage must be packed out. Leashed pets are permitted.

Reservations, fees: Reservations are not accepted. There is no fee for camping. Open year-round.

Directions: From Olympia on I-5, take Exit 104 and drive north on U.S. 101 to the Aberdeen/Highway 8 exit. Turn west on Highway 8 and drive 36 miles to Aberdeen. Continue through Aberdeen four miles to U.S. 101. Turn north on U.S. 101 and drive about 60 miles to Milepost 147. Turn north on Clearwater Mainline Road and drive about 14 miles to C-3000 Road. Turn right (east) on C-3000 Road (a gravel one-lane road) and drive two miles to C-1010 Road. Turn right on C-1010 Road and drive one mile. The camp is on the left.

Contact: Department of Natural Resources, Olympic Region, 360/374-6131, fax 360/374-5446, www.dnr.wa.gov.

43 SOUTH BEACH

Scenic rating: 6

in Olympic National Park

Little South Beach campground is located in an open field with little shade or privacy, but the payoff is that it is just a stone's throw from the ocean.

Campsites, facilities: There are 50 sites for tents or RVs up to 21 feet long. Picnic tables and fire grills are provided. Drinking water and non-accessible restrooms with flush toilets are available during summer. In winter, only pit toilets are available, and there is no drinking water. Leashed pets are permitted in the campground.

Reservations, fees: Reservations are not accepted. Sites are $10 per night, plus a $15 national park entrance fee per vehicle. Open late May–mid-September.

Directions: From Aberdeen, drive north on U.S. 101 for 65 miles to the campground.

Contact: Olympic National Park, 360/565-3130, fax 360/565-3147, www.nps.gov/olym.

44 PACIFIC BEACH STATE PARK

Scenic rating: 10

near Pacific Beach

This is the only state park campground in Washington where you can see the ocean from your campsite. Set on just nine acres, within the town of Pacific Beach, it boasts 2,300 feet of beachfront. This spot is great for long beach walks, although it can be windy, especially in the spring and early summer. Because of those winds, this is a great place for kite-flying. Clamming (for razor clams) is permitted only in season. Note that rangers advise against swimming or body surfing because of strong riptides. Vehicle traffic is allowed seasonally on the uppermost portions of the beach, but ATVs are not allowed in the park, on the beach, or on sand dunes. This camp is popular and often fills up quickly.

Campsites, facilities: There are 32 developed tent sites and 32 sites with partial hookups (30 amps) for RVs up to 60 feet long. Picnic tables are provided. Restrooms with flush toilets and coin showers, drinking water, a dump station, and a picnic area are available. No fires are permitted, except on the beach; charcoal and propane barbecues are allowed in campsites. Some facilities are wheelchair accessible. Leashed pets are permitted.

Reservations, fees: Reservations are accepted at 888/CAMP-OUT (888/226-7688) or www.parks.wa.gov/reservations ($6.50–8.50 reservation fee). Sites are $21–27 per night, $10 per night for hike-in/bike-in sites, and $10 per extra vehicle per night. Some credit cards are accepted. Open year-round.

Directions: From Hoquiam, drive north on State Route 109 for 37 miles to Pacific Beach and Main Street. Turn left on Main Street and drive 0.5 mile to 2nd Street. Turn left on 2nd Street and continue to the park entrance.

Contact: Pacific Beach State Park, 360/276-4297; state park information, 360/902-8844, www.parks.wa.gov.

45 DRIFTWOOD ACRES OCEAN CAMPGROUND

Scenic rating: 7

in Copalis Beach

Driftwood Acres spreads over some 150 acres and features secluded tent sites and large RV sites. It is located along a tidal river basin, out

CAMPING

of the wind. Most find the rustic camp family friendly, with its beach access, old-growth forest, and marked hiking trails. A bundle of firewood is provided for each night's stay. Clamming in season is often good in the area. Additional facilities within seven miles include an 18-hole golf course and a riding stable.

Campsites, facilities: There are 20 tent sites and 17 sites with partial hookups (20 and 30 amps) for tents or RVs of any length. Restrooms with flush toilets and coin showers, drinking water, a free bundle of firewood per day, a recreation hall, and dump station are available. A clam-cleaning station is nearby. Propane gas, a store, café, and ice are located within one mile. Leashed pets are permitted with certain restrictions.

Reservations, fees: Reservations are accepted. Sites are $30 per night, $5 per extra vehicle per night. Some credit cards are accepted. Open year-round.

Directions: From Hoquiam, drive west on State Route 109 for 21 miles to Copalis Beach. Continue 0.5 mile north to the camp on the left, between Mileposts 21 and 22.

Contact: Driftwood Acres Ocean Campground, 360/289-3484 or 877/298-1916, www.driftwoodacres.com.

46 SURF AND SAND RV PARK

🏊 🛶 🐕 🚐 ⛺

Scenic rating: 4

in Copalis Beach

Although not particularly scenic, this five-acre park is a decent layover for an RV vacation and will do the job if you're tired and ready to get off U.S. 101. It has beach access, possible with a 15-minute walk; the surrounding terrain is flat and grassy. Facilities are serviceable, but in need of updating.

Campsites, facilities: There are 16 tent sites and 50 sites with full or partial hookups (30 amps) for RVs of any length. Some sites are pull-through. Picnic tables and fire grills are provided. Restrooms with flush toilets and showers, drinking water, cable TV, coin laundry, a recreation room with kitchen facilities, and ice are available. Propane gas is available within one mile. Leashed pets are permitted.

Reservations, fees: Reservations are accepted. RV sites are $27–40 per night, tent sites are $15 per night, $4 per extra vehicle per night. Some credit cards are accepted. Open year-round.

Directions: From Hoquiam, drive west on State Route 109 for 21 miles to Copalis Beach and Heath Road. Turn left (west) on Heath Road and drive 0.2 mile to the park.

Contact: Surf and Sand RV Park, 360/289-2707 or 866/787-2751.

47 RIVERSIDE RV RESORT

🏊 🛶 🚻 🐕 🚐 ⛺

Scenic rating: 8

near Copalis Beach

River access is a bonus at this nice and clean six-acre resort. Most sites have a river view. Salmon fishing can be good in the Copalis River, and a boat ramp is available nearby for anglers. Other options include swimming and beachcombing.

Campsites, facilities: There are 56 sites with full hookups (30 amps) for RVs of any length and 15 tent sites. Some sites are pull-through. Picnic tables and fire grills are provided. Restrooms with flush toilets and coin showers, drinking water, a dump station, a spa, modem access, firewood, and a recreation hall are available. A café is located within one mile. A boat dock, launching facilities, and boat rentals are nearby. Leashed pets are permitted.

Reservations, fees: Reservations are accepted. Tent sites are $16 per night, RV sites are $21 per night, $2 per person per night for more than two people. Some credit cards are accepted. Open year-round.

Directions: From Hoquiam, drive west on State Route 109 for 22 miles to Copalis Beach. The park is off the highway on the left.
Contact: Riverside RV Resort, 360/289-2111 or 800/500-2111, www.riversidervresort.net.

48 TIDELANDS RESORT

Scenic rating: 7

near Copalis Beach

This flat, wooded resort covers 47 acres and provides beach access and a great ocean view. It's primarily an RV park, and the sites are pleasant. Ten sites are set on sand dunes, while the rest are in a wooded area. In the spring, azaleas and wildflowers abound. Horseshoe pits and a sports field offer recreation possibilities. Though more it's remote than at the other area campgrounds, clamming is an option in season. Various festivals are held in the area from spring through fall.

Campsites, facilities: There are 25 sites for tents or RVs (no hookups), 35 sites with full or partial hookups (20 and 30 amps) for tents or RVs of any length, one rental trailer, and three cottages. Some sites are pull-through. Picnic tables and fire pits are provided. Restrooms with flush toilets and coin showers, drinking water, a dump station, firewood, ice, cable TV, and a playground are available. A café is located within one mile. A casino and horseback riding are within five miles. A golf course is within six miles. Leashed pets are permitted.

Reservations, fees: Reservations are accepted. RV sites are $26–30 per night, tent sites are $20–21. Some credit cards are accepted. Open year-round.

Directions: From Hoquiam, drive west on State Route 109 for about 20 miles to the resort on the left. It is located between Mileposts 20 and 21, about one mile south of Copalis Beach.

Contact: Tidelands Resort, 360/289-8963, www.tidelandsresort.com.

49 OCEAN MIST RESORT

Scenic rating: 9

on Conners Creek

Always call to determine whether space is available before planning a stay here. This is a membership resort RV campground, and members always come first. If space is available, they will rent sites to the public. Surf fishing is popular in the nearby Pacific Ocean, while the Copalis River offers salmon fishing and canoeing opportunities. It's about a one-block walk to the beach. There's a golf course within five miles.

Campsites, facilities: There are 107 sites for RVs up to 40 feet long, most with full hookups (30 amps), a grassy area for tents, and two trailers. Picnic tables are provided. Restrooms with flush toilets and showers, drinking water, cable TV, modem access, dump station, two community fire pits, a spa, clubhouse, and coin laundry are available. A grocery store is within one mile in Ocean City. Leashed pets are permitted.

Reservations, fees: Reservations are accepted in the summer. Tent sites are $15 per night, and RV sites are $35 per night. Some credit cards are accepted. Open year-round.

Directions: From Hoquiam, drive west on State Route 109 for 19 miles to the resort on the left (one mile north of Ocean City).

Contact: Ocean Mist Resort, 360/289-3656, fax 360/289-2807, www.kmresorts.com.

50 OCEAN CITY STATE PARK

Scenic rating: 9

near Hoquiam

BEST (

This 170-acre oceanfront camp, an excellent example of coastal wetlands and dune succession, features ocean beach, dunes, and dense thickets of pine surrounding freshwater

CAMPING

marshes. The Ocean Shores Interpretive Center is located on the south end of Ocean Shores near the marina (open summer season only). This area is part of the Pacific Flyway, and the migratory route for gray whales and other marine mammals lies just offshore. Spring wildflowers are excellent and include lupine, buttercups, and wild strawberry. This is also a good area for surfing and kite-flying, with springs typically windy. Beachcombing, clamming, and fishing are possibilities at this park. An 18-hole golf course is nearby.

Campsites, facilities: There are 149 sites for tents or self-contained RVs (no hookups), 29 sites with full hookups (30 amps) for RVs up to 50 feet long; some sites are pull-through. There are also three hike-in/bike-in sites, and two group camps for tents only for 20–30 people each. Picnic tables and fire rings are provided. Restrooms with flush toilets and coin showers, drinking water, dump station, sheltered picnic area, and firewood are available. A ball field and amphitheater are available nearby. A camp host is on-site. Some facilities are wheelchair accessible. Leashed pets are permitted.

Reservations, fees: Reservations are accepted at 888/226-7688 (CAMP-OUT) or www.parks.wa.gov/reservations ($6.50–8.50 reservation fee). Sites are $21–28 per night, $10 per extra vehicle per night, hike-in/bike-in sites are $14 per night, and group sites are $2.25 per person, plus $25 for reservations. Some credit cards are accepted. Open year-round.

Directions: From Hoquiam, drive northwest on State Route 109 for 16 miles to State Route 115. Turn left and drive 1.2 miles south to the park on the right (1.5 miles north of Ocean Shores).

Contact: Ocean City State Park, 360/289-3553, fax 360/289-9405; state park information, 360/902-8844, www.parks.wa.gov.

51 SOL DUC

Scenic rating: 10

on the Sol Duc River in Olympic National Park

This site is a nice hideaway, with nearby Sol Duc Hot Springs a highlight. The problem is that this camp is very popular. It fills up quickly on weekends, and a fee is charged to use the hot springs, which have been fully developed since the early 1900s. The camp is set at 1,680 feet along the Sol Duc River.

Campsites, facilities: There are 82 sites for tents or RVs up to 21 feet long, and one group site for up to 24 people. Picnic tables and fire grills are provided. Restrooms with flush toilets and drinking water are available in the summer season; there is no water in the winter season, but pit toilets are available. A dump station is available nearby, and a store and café are within one mile. Some facilities are wheelchair accessible. Leashed pets are permitted.

Reservations, fees: Reservations accepted for the group site only at 360/327-3534 (Apr. 16–Oct. 31) and at 360/928-3380 (Mar. 1–Apr. 15). Sites are $14 per night, plus a $15 national park entrance fee per vehicle. The group site is $1 per person per night, plus a $20 reservation fee. Open May–late October, with limited facilities in winter.

Directions: From Port Angeles, continue on U.S. 101 for 27 miles, just past Lake Crescent. Turn left at the Sol Duc turnoff and drive 12 miles to the camp.

Contact: Olympic National Park, 360/565-3130, fax 360/565-3147, www.nps.gov/olym.

52 DEER PARK

Scenic rating: 9

near Blue Mountain in Olympic National Park

This camp is set in the Olympic Peninsula's high country at an elevation of 5,400 feet, just below 6,000-foot Blue Mountain. There are numerous trails in the area, including a major trailhead into the backcountry of Olympic National Park and the Buckhorn Wilderness.

Campsites, facilities: There are 14 tent sites. Picnic tables and fire grills are provided. Pit toilets are available. There is no drinking water. At times, garbage must be packed out. Some facilities are wheelchair accessible. Leashed pets are permitted.

Reservations, fees: Reservations are not accepted. Sites are $10 per night, plus a $15 per vehicle park entrance fee. Open mid-June–late September.

Directions: From Port Angeles, drive east on U.S. 101 for about five miles to Deer Park Road. Turn right (south) and drive 18 miles to the campground at the end of the road. Note that the last six miles are gravel, steep and narrow, closed to RVs and trailers, and often closed to all vehicles in winter.

Contact: Olympic National Park, 360/565-3132, fax 360/565-3147, ww.nps.gov/olym.

53 DUNGENESS FORKS

Scenic rating: 7

on the Dungeness and Gray Wolf Rivers in Olympic National Forest

This pretty, wooded spot is nestled at the confluence of the Dungeness and Gray Wolf Rivers at an elevation of 1,000 feet. It offers seclusion, yet easy access from the highway. The campsites are set in the forest. If you want quiet, you'll often find it here. The Upper Dungeness Trailhead, located about seven miles south of camp, provides access to Buckhorn Wilderness and Olympic National Park. The trailhead for Gray Wolf Trail is four miles from camp, but note that portions of this trail are sometimes closed due to slides; check with rangers before embarking on a long trip. The Gray Wolf River is closed to fishing year-round to protect salmon. Fishing

is permitted on the Dungeness River. Check regulations.

Campsites, facilities: There are 10 tent sites. Picnic tables and fire rings are provided. Vault toilets are available. There is no drinking water, and garbage must be packed out. Leashed pets are permitted.

Reservations, fees: Reservations are not accepted. Sites are $14 per night, $5 per extra vehicle per night. Open May–September, weather permitting.

Directions: From Olympia on I-5, turn north on U.S. 101 and drive approximately 100 miles to Palo Alto Road, located 1.5 miles north of Sequim Bay State Park and three miles southeast of Sequim. Turn left (south) on Palo Alto Road and drive about seven miles to Forest Road 2880. Turn right (west) and drive one mile (after crossing Dungeness River Bridge) to the campground on the right. Obtaining a U.S. Forest Service map is advised. Trailers and RVs are not recommended because of the steep, narrow, and unpaved access road.

Contact: Olympic National Forest, Hood Canal Ranger District, Quilcene Office, 360/765-2200, fax 360/765-2202, www.fs.fed.us.

54 HOH

Scenic rating: 10

in Olympic National Park

This camp at a trailhead leading into the interior of Olympic National Park is located in the beautiful heart of a temperate, old-growth rainforest. Hoh Oxbow, Cottonwood, Willoughby Creek, and Minnie Peterson campgrounds are nearby, set downstream on the Hoh River, outside national park boundaries. In the summer, there are naturalist programs, and a visitors center is nearby. This is one of the most popular camps in the park. The elevation is 578 feet.

Campsites, facilities: There are 88 sites for

tents or RVs up to 21 feet long. Picnic tables and fire grills are provided. Garbage bins and restrooms with flush toilets and drinking water are available. A dump station is nearby. Some facilities are wheelchair accessible. Leashed pets are permitted.

Reservations, fees: Reservations are not accepted. Sites are $12 per night, plus a $15 national park entrance fee per vehicle. Open year-round.

Directions: From Aberdeen, drive north on U.S. 101 for about 90 miles to Milepost 176. Turn east on Hoh River Road and drive 19 miles to the campground on the right (near the end of the road).

Contact: Olympic National Park, 360/565-3130, fax 360/565-3147, www.nps.gov/olym.

55 SOUTH FORK HOH

Scenic rating: 10

in Hoh Clearwater State Forest

This rarely used, beautiful camp set along the cascading South Fork of the Hoh River is way out there. It's tiny and primitive but offers a guarantee of peace and quiet, something many U.S. 101 cruisers would cheerfully give a limb for after a few days of fighting crowds. The South Fork Trailhead in Olympic National Park is two miles away. When conditions are right, fishing for steelhead can be excellent (check regulations).

Campsites, facilities: There are three sites for tents or RVs up to 16 feet long. Picnic tables, fire grills, and tent pads are provided. Vault toilets are available. There is no drinking water, and garbage must be packed out. Leashed pets are permitted.

Reservations, fees: Reservations are not accepted. There is no fee for camping. Open year-round.

Directions: From Olympia on I-5, take Exit 104 and drive north on U.S. 101 to the Aberdeen/Highway 8 exit. Turn west on Highway

8 and drive 36 miles to Aberdeen. Continue through Aberdeen four miles to U.S. 101. Turn north on U.S. 101 and drive about 94 miles. Exit at Milepost 176. At Hoh Mainline Road turn east and drive 6.5 miles. Turn left on Road H1000 and drive 7.5 miles to the campground on the right. Obtaining a Department of Natural Resources (DNR) map is advised.

Contact: Department of Natural Resources, Olympic Region, 360/374-6131, fax 360/374-5446, www.dnr.wa.gov.

56 DOSEWALLIPS WALK-IN

Scenic rating: 7

on the Dosewallips River in Olympic National Park

This road is closed to vehicles due to a road washout at Milepost 10. You can still get to the campground on foot or mountain bike, but it requires a 5.5-mile hike or bike ride. Set on the Dosewallips River at an elevation of 1,500 feet, the camp provides a major trailhead into the backcountry of Olympic National Park. The trail follows the Dosewallips River over Anderson Pass, proceeds along the Quinault River, and ultimately reaches Quinault Lake. Other hiking trails are available nearby. Dosewallips is a more remote option to Collins.

Campsites, facilities: There are 30 tent sites. Picnic tables and fire grills are provided. Pit toilets are available. There is no drinking water. Leashed pets are permitted.

Reservations, fees: Reservations are not accepted. There is no fee for camping. Open mid-May–late September.

Directions: From Olympia on I-5, drive north on U.S. 101 for 60 miles to a signed turnoff near Brinnon (located about one mile north of Dosewallips State Park) for Forest Road 2610 (County Road 2500). Turn left (west) and drive 15 miles along the Dosewallips River to the washout. Note that the access road is not paved and is not recommended for RVs or trailers.

Contact: Olympic National Park, 360/565-3132, fax 360/565-3147, www.nps.gov/olym.

57 COLLINS

Scenic rating: 7

on the Duckabush River in
Olympic National Forest

Most vacationers cruising U.S. 101 don't have a clue about this quiet spot set on a great launch point for adventure, yet it's only five or six miles from the highway. This four-acre camp is located on the Duckabush River at 200 feet elevation. It has small, shaded sites, river access nearby, and plenty of fishing and hiking; check fishing regulations. Just one mile from camp is Duckabush Trail, which connects to trails in Olympic National Park. Murhut Falls Trail starts about three miles from the campground, providing access to a 0.8-mile trail to the falls. It's a 1.5-mile drive to Dosewallips State Park and a 30- to 35-minute drive to Olympic National Park.

Campsites, facilities: There are six tent sites and 10 sites for RVs up to 21 feet long. Picnic tables and fire rings are provided. Vault toilets are available, but there is no drinking water. Garbage must be packed out. Leashed pets are permitted.

Reservations, fees: Reservations are not accepted. Sites are $14 per night. Open May–September, weather permitting.

Directions: From Olympia on I-5, drive north on U.S. 101 for 59 miles to Forest Road 2510 (near Duckabush). Turn left on Forest Road 2510 and drive six miles west to the camp on the left.

Contact: Olympic National Forest, Hood Canal Ranger District, Quilcene Office, 360/765-2200, fax 360/765-2202, www.fs.fed.us.

58 QUEETS WALK-IN

Scenic rating: 9

on the Queets River in Olympic National Park

This primitive camp on the shore of the Queets River is a gem. You must plan ahead to bring your own water or purify river water. A trailhead leads into the interior of Olympic National Park. The elevation is 290 feet.

Campsites, facilities: There are 20 primitive tent sites. Picnic tables and fire grills are provided. Pit toilets are available. There is no drinking water, and garbage must be packed out. Leashed pets are permitted.

Reservations, fees: Reservations are not accepted. Sites are $10 per night and there's a $15 national park entrance fee per vehicle. Open year-round.

Directions: From Aberdeen, drive north on U.S. 101 for 38 miles to Lake Quinault, and continue for 19 miles to a signed turnoff for the campground at Forest Road 21. Turn right (northeast) on Forest Road 21 (an unpaved road) and drive 14 miles (along the Queets River) to the campground at the end of the road; not recommended for RVs or trailers.

Contact: Olympic National Park, 360/565-3130, fax 360/565-3147, www.nps.gov/olym.

59 GRAVES CREEK HIKE-IN

Scenic rating: 6

near the Quinault River in
Olympic National Park

A road washout now requires a hike of 4.5 miles to reach this spot. This camp is located at an elevation of 540 feet and is a short distance from a trailhead leading into the backcountry of Olympic National Park. The East Fork Quinault River is nearby, and there are lakes in the area.

CAMPING

Campsites, facilities: There are 30 sites for tents. Picnic tables and fire grills are provided. Drinking water and restrooms with flush toilets are available in summer; off season, pit toilets are available, and there is no drinking water. Leashed pets are permitted.

Reservations, fees: Reservations are not accepted. Sites are $12 per night, plus a $15 national park entrance fee per vehicle. Open year-round.

Directions: From Aberdeen, drive north on U.S. 101 for 38 miles to the Lake Quinault turnoff and South Shore Road. Turn east on South Shore Road and drive 15 miles to the road washout. Park and hike 4.5 miles to the campground. The Graves Creek Ranger Station is located nearby.

Contact: Olympic National Park, 360/565-3130, fax 360/565-3147, www.nps.gov/olym.

60 LENA LAKE HIKE-IN

Scenic rating: 8

near the Hamma Hamma River in
Olympic National Forest

BEST (

Lena Lake is one of the most popular lakes on the Olympic Peninsula. Though it is comparatively crowded in the summer, you can usually get a site. The 55-acre lake is nestled along the Hamma Hamma drainage, between rugged peaks and adjacent to the Brothers Wilderness. It takes a three-mile hike-in from the trailhead at Lena Creek to reach this camp. This adventure is suitable for the entire family—an outstanding way to turn youngsters on to backpacking. It's a lovely setting, too, with a pleasantly mild climate in summer. The lake is good for swimming and fishing for rainbow trout. The elevation is 1,800 feet.

Campsites, facilities: There are 29 primitive sites at this hike-in campground. There is no drinking water. A compost toilet and fire rings are available. Garbage must be packed out. Leashed pets are permitted.

Reservations, fees: Reservations are not accepted. There is no fee for camping, but you must obtain a $30 annual Trail Park Pass or pay $5 per day to park at the trailhead. Open May–September, weather permitting.

Directions: From Olympia on I-5, turn north on U.S. 101 and drive about 37 miles to Hoodsport. Continue north on U.S. 101 for 14 miles to Forest Road 25. Turn left (west) on Forest Road 25 and drive eight miles to the Lena Creek Camp and the trailhead. Hike 3.2 miles north to Lena Lake. Campsites are scattered around the lake.

Contact: Olympic National Forest, Hood Canal Ranger District, 360/877-5254, fax 360/352-2569, www.fs.fed.us.

61 LENA CREEK

Scenic rating: 7

on the Hamma Hamma River in
Olympic National Forest

This seven-acre camp, set amid both conifers and hardwoods, is located where Lena Creek empties into the Hamma Hamma River. A popular trailhead camp, Lena Creek features a three-mile trail from camp to Lena Lake, with four additional miles to Upper Lena Lake. A map of Olympic National Forest details the trail and road system. The camp is rustic with some improvements.

Campsites, facilities: There are 13 sites for tents or RVs to 21 feet. Picnic tables and fire rings are provided. Vault toilets and drinking water are available. Garbage must be packed out. Leashed pets are permitted.

Reservations, fees: Reservations are not accepted. Sites are $14 per night, $5 per extra vehicle per night. Open mid-May–September.

Directions: From Olympia on I-5, turn north on U.S. 101 and drive about 37 miles to Hoodsport. Continue north on U.S. 101 for 14 miles to Forest Road 25. Turn left (west) on Forest Road 25 and drive eight miles to the camp on the left.

Contact: Olympic National Forest, Hood Canal Ranger District, Quilcene Office, 360/765-2200, fax 360/765-2202, www. fs.fed.us.

62 HAMMA HAMMA

Scenic rating: 7

on the Hamma Hamma River in
Olympic National Forest

This camp is set on the Hamma Hamma River at an elevation of 600 feet. It's small and primitive, but it can be preferable to some of the developed camps on the U.S. 101 circuit. The Civilian Conservation Corps is memorialized in a wheelchair-accessible interpretive trail that begins in the campground and leads 0.25 mile along the river. The sites are set among conifers and hardwoods.

Campsites, facilities: There are 15 sites for tents or RVs up to 22 feet long. Picnic tables and fire rings are provided. Vault toilets are available. There is no drinking water, and garbage must be packed out. (In season, drinking water is available two miles away at Lena Creek Campground.) Some facilities are wheelchair accessible. Leashed pets are permitted.

Reservations, fees: Reservations are not accepted. Sites are $10 per night, $5 per night per additional vehicle. Open May–September, weather permitting.

Directions: From Olympia on I-5, turn north on U.S. 101 and drive 37 miles to Hoodsport. Continue on U.S. 101 for 14 miles north to Forest Road 25. Turn left on Forest Road 25 and drive seven miles to the camp on the left side of the road.

Contact: Olympic National Forest, Hood Canal Ranger District, Quilcene Office, 360/765-2200, fax 360/765-2202, www. fs.fed.us.

63 WILLABY

Scenic rating: 8

on Lake Quinault in Olympic National Forest

This pretty, 14-acre wooded camp is set on the shore of Lake Quinault, which covers about six square miles. Part of the Quinault Indian Reservation, the camp is at 200 feet elevation, adjacent to where Willaby Creek empties into the lake. A boating permit and fishing license are required before fishing on the lake. The campsites vary, with some open and featuring lake views, while others are more private, with no views. The tree cover consists of Douglas fir, western red cedar, western hemlock, and big leaf maple. The forest floor is covered with wall-to-wall greenery, with exceptional moss growth. Quinault Rain Forest Nature Trail and the Quinault National Recreation Trail System are nearby. This camp is operated by a concessionaire.

Campsites, facilities: There are 32 sites for tents or RVs up to 16 feet long and two walk-in sites. Picnic tables and fire pits are provided. Drinking water, garbage bins, and restrooms with flush toilets are available. Launching facilities and rentals are available at nearby Lake Quinault. Some facilities are wheelchair accessible. Leashed pets are permitted.

Reservations, fees: Reservations are not accepted. Sites are $14 per night, $5 per extra vehicle per night. Open Memorial Day weekend–September.

Directions: From Aberdeen, drive north on U.S. 101 for 42 miles to the Lake Quinault-South Shore turnoff. Turn right (northeast) on South Shore Road and drive 1.5 miles to the camp on the southern shore of the lake.

Contact: Olympic National Forest, Pacific Ranger District, Quinault Office, 360/288-2525, fax 360/288-0286, www.fs.fed.us.

CAMPING

64 FALLS CREEK

Scenic rating: 8

on Lake Quinault in Olympic National Forest

This scenic, wooded three-acre camp is set where Falls Creek empties into Quinault Lake. A canopy of lush big leaf maple hangs over the campground. The campground features both drive-in and walk-in sites, with the latter requiring about a 125-yard walk. Quinault Rain Forest Nature Trail and the Quinault National Recreation Trail System are nearby. The camp is located adjacent to the Quinault Ranger Station and historic Lake Quinault Lodge at an elevation of 200 feet.

Campsites, facilities: There are 10 walk-in sites and 21 sites for tents or RVs up to 16 feet long. Picnic tables and fire pits are provided. Drinking water and restrooms with flush toilets are available. A camp host has firewood for sale nearby. A picnic area, boat launching facilities, and boat rentals are available at Lake Quinault. Some facilities are wheelchair accessible. Leashed pets are permitted.

Reservations, fees: Reservations are not accepted. Sites are $12–15 per night, $5 per extra vehicle per night. Open Memorial Day weekend–Labor Day weekend.

Directions: From Aberdeen, drive north on U.S. 101 for 42 miles to the Lake Quinault-South Shore turnoff. Turn right (northeast) on South Shore Road and drive 2.5 miles to the camp on the southeast shore of Lake Quinault. Make a very sharp left turn into the campground.

Contact: Olympic National Forest, Pacific Ranger District, Quinault Office, 360/288-2525, fax 360/288-0286, www.fs.fed.us.

65 GATTON CREEK WALK-IN

Scenic rating: 9

on Lake Quinault in Olympic National Forest

This five-acre wooded camp is set on the shore of Lake Quinault (elevation 200 feet), where Gatton Creek empties into it. Reaching the campsites requires about a 100-yard walk from the parking area. The camp features great views across the lake to the forested slopes of Olympic National Park. The lake is part of the Quinault Indian Nation, which has jurisdiction here. Rules allow a 24-mph speed limit on the lake, but no towing and no personal watercraft. Salmon fishing is catch-and-release only, and fishing opportunities vary from year to year—always check regulations. Lake Quinault covers about six square miles. Quinault Rain Forest Nature Trail and the Quinault National Recreation Trail System are nearby. About nine miles of loop trails are accessible here. This camp, like the others on the lake, is concessionaire operated.

Campsites, facilities: There are 15 walk-in sites for tents and 10 overflow sites for RVs up to 24 feet long. Picnic tables and fire pits are provided at the tent sites. Vault toilets, firewood, and a picnic area are available. Some facilities are wheelchair accessible. Leashed pets are permitted.

Reservations, fees: Reservations are not accepted. Sites are $12 per night. Open late May–early October, weather permitting.

Directions: From Aberdeen, drive north on U.S. 101 for 42 miles to the Lake Quinault-South Shore turnoff. Turn right (northeast) on South Shore Road and drive three miles to the camp on the southeast shore of Lake Quinault.

Contact: Olympic National Forest, Pacific Ranger District, Quinault Office, 360/288-2525, fax 360/288-0286, www.fs.fed.us.

66 CAMPBELL TREE GROVE
🏕 🏊 🏠 ♿ 🚐 ⛰

Scenic rating: 8

on the Humptulips River in
Olympic National Forest

BEST (

This 14-acre camp is set amid dense, old-growth forest featuring stands of both conifers and hardwoods, with licorice ferns growing on the trunks and branches of the big leaf maples. The camp is a favorite for hikers, with trailheads nearby that provide access to the Colonel Bob Wilderness. One of the best, the 3,400-foot climb to the Colonel Bob Summit provides an 8.5-mile round-trip accessible from the Pete's Creek Trailhead, which is located a couple of miles south of camp on Forest Road 2204. Note that much of this summit hike is a great butt-kicker. The West Fork of the Humptulips River runs near the camp, and Humptulips Trail provides access. Fishing is an option here as well; check state regulations.

Campsites, facilities: There are eight tent sites and three sites for RVs up to 16 feet long. Picnic tables and fire grills are provided. Vault toilets, garbage bins and drinking water (well water) are available. Some facilities are wheelchair accessible. Leashed pets are permitted.

Reservations, fees: Reservations are not accepted. There is no fee for camping. Open May–October, weather permitting.

Directions: From Aberdeen, drive north on U.S. 101 for 22 miles to Humptulips and continue for another five miles to Forest Road 22 (Donkey Creek Road). Turn right and drive eight miles to Forest Road 2204. Turn left (north) and drive nine miles to the campground.

Contact: Olympic National Forest, Pacific Ranger District, Quinault Office, 360/288-2525, fax 360/288-0286, www.fs.fed.us.

67 STAIRCASE
🏕 🏊 🏠 ♿ 🚐 ⛰

Scenic rating: 9

on the North Fork of the Skokomish River in
Olympic National Park

This camp is located near the Staircase Rapids of the North Fork of the Skokomish River, about one mile from where it empties into Lake Cushman. The elevation is 765 feet. A major trailhead at the camp leads to the backcountry of Olympic National Park, and other trails are nearby. Hiking trails along the river can be accessed nearby. Stock facilities are also available nearby. Note that Staircase Road is closed in winter.

Campsites, facilities: There are 47 sites for tents or RVs up to 21 feet long. Picnic tables and fire grills are provided. Restrooms with flush toilets and drinking water are available during the summer season. In winter, pit toilets are available, but there is no drinking water. Leashed pets are permitted in camp.

Reservations, fees: Reservations are not accepted. Sites are $12 per night, plus a $15 national park entrance fee per vehicle. Open year-round, with limited winter services.

Directions: From Olympia on I-5, take U.S. 101 and drive north about 37 miles to the town of Hoodsport and Lake Cushman Road (County Road 119). Turn left (west) and drive 17 miles to the camp at the end of the road (set about one mile above the inlet of Lake Cushman). The last several miles of the road are unpaved.

Contact: Olympic National Park, 360/565-3130, fax 360/565-3147, www.nps.gov/olym.

CAMPING

68 COHO

Scenic rating: 10

on Wynoochee Lake in Olympic National Forest

BEST (

This eight-acre camp sits on the shore of Wynoochee Lake, which is 4.4 miles long and covers 1,140 acres. The camp is set at an elevation of 900 feet. The fishing season opens June 1 and closes October 31. Powerboats, waterskiing, and personal watercraft are permitted. Points of interest include Working Forest Nature Trail, Wynoochee Dam Viewpoint and exhibits, and 12-mile Wynoochee Lake Shore Trail, which circles the lake. This is one of the most idyllic drive-to settings you could hope to find.

Campsites, facilities: There are 46 sites for tents or RVs up to 36 feet long and 10 walk-in sites. Picnic tables are provided. Vault toilets are available. There is no drinking water. A dump station is nearby. Boat docks and launching facilities are available at Wynoochee Lake. Leashed pets are permitted.

Reservations, fees: Reservations are not accepted. Sites are $18 per night, $14 per night for walk-in sites, $5 extra vehicle per night. Open May–November, weather permitting.

Directions: From Olympia on I-5, take Exit 104 and drive north on U.S. 101 to the Aberdeen/Highway 8 exit. Turn west on Highway 8 and drive 36 miles (it becomes Highway 12 at Elma) to Montesano. Continue two miles on Highway 12 to Wynoochee Valley Road. Turn right (north) on Wynoochee Valley Road and drive 12 miles to Forest Road 22. Continue north on Forest Road 22 (a gravel road) for 23 miles to Wynoochee Lake. Just south of the lake, bear left and drive on Forest Road 2294 (which runs along the lake's northwest shore) for one mile to the camp on the west shore of Wynoochee Lake. Obtaining a U.S. Forest Service map is helpful.

Contact: Olympic National Forest, Hood Canal Ranger District, Quilcene Office, 360/765-2200, fax 360/765-2202, www.fs.fed.us.

69 BROWN CREEK

Scenic rating: 9

on Brown Creek in Olympic National Forest

Brown Creek is little known among out-of-town visitors. While this camp is accessible to two-wheel-drive vehicles, the access road connects to a network of primitive, backcountry forest roads. The campground was moved out of the riparian habitat and expanded to 60 sites. It is situated within the vast Olympic National Forest, which offers many opportunities for outdoor recreation. Wheelchair-accessible Brown Creek Nature Trail begins at the hand pump and makes a one-mile loop around the camp, featuring views of an active beaver pond. Obtain a U.S. Forest Service map to expand your trip.

Campsites, facilities: There are 20 sites for tents or RVs up to 20 feet long. Picnic tables and fire rings are provided. Drinking water and vault toilets are available. Garbage must be packed out. Some facilities are wheelchair accessible. Leashed pets are permitted.

Reservations, fees: Reservations are not accepted. Sites are $14 per night, $5 per extra vehicle per night. Open May–September, weather permitting.

Directions: From Olympia on I-5, take Exit 104 for U.S. 101/Highway 8. Drive north on U.S. 101 for 31 miles (about six miles past Shelton) to Skokomish Valley Road. Turn left (west) and drive 5.3 miles to Forest Road 23. Turn right on Forest Road 23 and drive nine miles to Forest Road 2353. Turn right on Forest Road 2353 and drive one mile to the South Fork Skokomish River Bridge. Cross the bridge, turn right sharply onto Forest Road 2340 and drive 0.25 mile to the camp. Obtaining a U.S. Forest Service map is advisable.

Contact: Olympic National Forest, Hood Canal Ranger District, Quilcene Office, 360/765-2200, fax 360/765-2202, www.fs.fed.us.

70 LEBAR HORSE CAMP

Scenic rating: 9

in Olympic National Forest

This camp is exclusively for people with horses or pack animals, such as mules, mollies, llamas, and goats. The camp provides access to Lower South Fork Skokomish Trail, a 10.9-mile trip, one-way. The camp features beautiful old-growth forest, with western hemlock and Douglas fir.

Campsites, facilities: There are 13 sites for tents or RVs up to 28 feet long for the exclusive use of campers with pack animals. Picnic tables, fire grills, hitching posts, and high lines are provided. Vault toilets are available. There is no drinking water, and garbage must be packed out. A day-use area with a picnic shelter is available nearby. Leashed pets are permitted.

Reservations, fees: Reservations are not accepted. Sites are $10 per night, $5 per extra vehicle per night. Open May–September, weather permitting.

Directions: From Olympia on I-5, take Exit 104 for U.S. 101/Highway 8. Drive north on U.S. 101 for 31 miles (about six miles past Shelton) to Skokomish Valley Road. Turn left (west) and drive 5.3 miles to Forest Road 23. Turn right on Forest Road 23 and drive nine miles to Forest Road 2353. Turn right on Forest Road 2353 and drive one mile to the South Fork Skokomish River Bridge. Cross the bridge, turn left sharply to remain on Forest Road 2353, and drive 0.5 mile to the camp. Obtaining a U.S. Forest Service map is advisable.

Contact: Olympic National Forest, Hood Canal Ranger District, 360/765-2200, fax 360/765-2202, www.fs.fed.us.

71 BIG CREEK

Scenic rating: 7

near Lake Cushman in Olympic National Forest

Big Creek is an alternative to Staircase camp on the North Fork of Skokomish River and Camp Cushman and Recreation Park, both of which get heavier use. The sites here are large and well spaced for privacy over 30 acres, primarily of second-growth forest. Big Creek runs adjacent to the campground. A four-mile loop trail extends from camp and connects to Mount Eleanor Trail. A bonus: two walk-in sites are located along the creek.

Campsites, facilities: There are 23 sites for tents or RVs up to 30 feet long. Picnic tables and fire grills are provided. Drinking water, vault toilets, and a sheltered picnic area are available. A boat dock and ramp are located at nearby Lake Cushman. Garbage must be packed out. Leashed pets are permitted.

Reservations, fees: Reservations are not accepted. Sites are $14 per night, $5 per extra vehicle per night. Open May–September, weather permitting.

Directions: From Olympia on I-5, take Exit 104 for U.S. 101/Highway 8. Drive north on U.S. 101 for 37 miles to Hoodsport and Lake Cushman Road (Highway 119). Turn left on Lake Cushman Road and drive nine miles (two miles north of Camp Cushman) to the T intersection with Forest Road 24. Turn left and the campground is on the right.

Contact: Olympic National Forest, Hood Canal Ranger District, Quilcene Office, 360/765-2200, www.fs.fed.us; visitors center, 360/877-2021.

CAMPING

CAMPING

72 CAMP CUSHMAN AND RECREATION PARK

Scenic rating: 10

on Lake Cushman

BEST (

Set in the foothills of the Olympic Mountains on the shore of Lake Cushman, this 500-acre park features a 10-mile-long blue-water mountain lake, eight miles of park shoreline, forested hillsides, and awesome views of snowcapped peaks. Beach access and good trout fishing are other highlights. The park has eight miles of hiking trails. Windsurfing, waterskiing, and swimming are all popular here. A nine-hole golf course is nearby.

Campsites, facilities: There are 50 sites for tents or RVs up to 30 feet long (no hookups), 30 sites with full hookups (30 amps) for RVs up to 30 feet long, two hike-in/bike-in sites, and one group camp for up to 72 people. Picnic tables and fire grills are provided. Restrooms with flush toilets and coin showers, drinking water, a camp store, picnic area, amphitheater, horseshoe pits, badminton, ice, and firewood are available. A restaurant is within three miles. Boat docks and launching facilities are located nearby on Lake Cushman. Some facilities are wheelchair accessible. Leashed pets are permitted.

Reservations, fees: Reservations are accepted. Sites are $20–26 per night, $6 per extra vehicle per night, $10 per pet per stay. The group camp is a minimum of $135 per night. Some credit cards are accepted. Open mid-April–October, weather permitting.

Directions: From Olympia on I-5, take the U.S. 101 exit and drive north 37 miles to Hoodsport and Highway 119 (Lake Cushman Road). Turn left (west) on Lake Cushman Road and drive 7.5 miles to the park on the left.

Contact: Camp Cushman and Recreation Park, 360/877-6770 or 866/259-2900, fax 360/877-6550, www.lakecushman.com.

73 LAKE CUSHMAN RESORT

Scenic rating: 10

on Lake Cushman

This campground on Lake Cushman has full facilities for water sports, including boat launching and rentals. Waterskiing and fishing are popular. Lake Cushman Dam makes a good side trip. A nine-hole golf course is nearby.

Campsites, facilities: There are 50 sites for tents or RVs up to 22 feet long (no hookups), 21 sites with partial hookups (20 amps) for RVs up to 40 feet long, and 11 cabins. Picnic tables and fire grills are provided. Drinking water, flush and portable toilets, firewood, a convenience store, boat docks and launching facilities, mooring, and boat rentals are available. Groups can be accommodated. Some facilities are wheelchair accessible. Leashed pets are permitted.

Reservations, fees: Reservations are accepted. Tent sites are $15–25.50 per night, RV sites are $20–29.50 per night, $10 per pet per stay, and mooring is $10–15 per day. Some credit cards are accepted. Open year-round.

Directions: From Olympia on I-5, take the U.S. 101 exit and drive north 37 miles to Hoodsport and Highway 119/Lake Cushman Road. Turn left (west) on Lake Cushman Road and drive 4.5 miles to the resort on the left.

Contact: Lake Cushman Resort, 360/877-9630 or 800/588-9630, fax 360/877-9356, www.lakecushman.com.

74 REST-A-WHILE RV PARK

Scenic rating: 5

on Hood Canal

This seven-acre park, located at sea level on Hood Canal, offers waterfront sites and a private beach for clamming and oyster gathering, not to mention plenty of opportunities to fish, boat, and scuba dive. It's an alternative to Potlatch State Park and Glen-Ayr RV Park.

Campsites, facilities: There are 80 sites for tents or RVs of any length (30 amp full hookups), two tent sites, two rental trailers, and a bunkhouse. Some sites are pull-through. Picnic tables and fire rings are provided. Restrooms with flush toilets and showers, drinking water, cable TV, modem access, propane gas, firewood, a clubhouse, convenience store, drive-in restaurant, coin laundry, and ice are available. A café is within walking distance. Boat docks, launching facilities, a scuba diving shop, seasonal boat and kayak rentals, and a private beach for clamming and oyster gathering (in season) are also available. Leashed pets are permitted.

Reservations, fees: Reservations are accepted. Sites are $30–35 per night, $2 per extra vehicle per night, and $4 per person per night for more than two people. Some credit cards are accepted. Open year-round.

Directions: From Olympia on I-5, take Exit 104 for U.S. 101/Highway 8. Drive north on U.S. 101 for 37 miles to Hoodsport. Continue 2.5 miles north on U.S. 101 to the park located at Milepost 329.

Contact: Rest-A-While RV Park, 360/877-9474 or 866/637-9474, www.restawhile.com.

75 GLEN-AYR RV PARK & MOTEL

Scenic rating: 5

on Hood Canal

This fully developed, nine-acre park is located at sea level on Hood Canal, where there are opportunities to fish and scuba dive. Salmon fishing is especially excellent. Swimming and boating round out the options. The park has a spa, moorage, horseshoe pits, recreation field, and a motel.

Campsites, facilities: There are 38 sites with full hookups (five with 50 amps and 33 with 30 amps) for RVs of any length, 18 motel rooms, a townhouse, and two suites with kitchens. Some sites are pull-through. No open fires are allowed. Picnic tables are provided. Restrooms with flush toilets and showers, drinking water, cable TV, Wi-Fi, propane gas, a spa, recreation hall, horseshoe pits, seasonal organized activities, and coin laundry are available. A store, café, and ice are within one mile. A boat dock is located across the street from the park. Leashed pets are permitted.

Reservations, fees: Reservations are accepted. Sites are $30–40 per night, $5 per person per night for more than two people, $5 per extra vehicle per night. Some credit cards are accepted. Open year-round.

Directions: From Olympia on I-5, take Exit 104 for U.S. 101/Highway 8. Drive north on U.S. 101 for 37 miles to Hoodsport. Continue one mile north on U.S. 101 to the park on the left.

Contact: Glen-Ayr RV Park & Motel, 360/877-9522 or 866/877-9522, www.glen-ayr.com.

76 POTLATCH STATE PARK

Scenic rating: 8

on Hood Canal

This state park features good shellfish harvesting in season. The park has 9,570 feet of shoreline on Hood Canal. There are 1.5 miles of trails for hiking and biking, but the shoreline and water bring people here for the good kayaking, windsurfing, scuba diving, clamming, and fishing. The park is named for the potlatch, a Skyhomish gift-giving ceremony. There are four major rivers, the Skokomish, Hamma Hamma, Duckabush, and Dosewallips, within a 30-mile radius of the park. The park receives an annual rainfall of 64 inches.

Campsites, facilities: There are 18 sites with full hookups (30 and 50 amps) for RVs up to 60 feet long, 19 developed tent sites, and two hike-in/bike-in sites. Picnic tables and fire grills are provided. Restrooms with flush toilets and coin showers, drinking water, a dump station, firewood, an amphitheater, a picnic area, and seasonal interpretive programs are available. Five mooring buoys are located at the park, and a boat launch and dock are available nearby. Groceries, gas, and propane are available three miles away. Some facilities are wheelchair accessible. Leashed pets are permitted.

Reservations, fees: Reservations are accepted in summer at 888/226-7688 or www.parks. wa.gov. Sites are $19–26 per night, $12 per night for hike-in/bike-in sites, $10 per extra vehicle per night. Open year-round.

Directions: From Olympia on I-5, take Exit 104 for U.S. 101/Highway 8. Drive north on U.S. 101 for 22 miles to Shelton. Continue north on U.S. 101 for 12 miles to the park on the right (located along the shoreline of Annas Bay on Hood Canal).

Contact: Potlatch State Park, 360/877-5361, fax 360/877-6346; state park information, 360/902-8844, www.parks.wa.gov.

77 SCHAFER STATE PARK

Scenic rating: 8

on the Satsop River

This unique destination boasts many interesting features, including buildings constructed from native stone. A heavily wooded, rural camp, Schafer State Park covers 119 acres along the East Fork of the Satsop River. The river is well known for fishing and rafting. Fish for sea-run cutthroat in summer, salmon in fall, and steelhead in late winter. There are good canoeing and kayaking spots, some with Class II and III rapids, along the Middle and West Forks of the Satsop. Three miles of hiking

trails are also available. At one time, this park was the Schafer Logging Company Park and was used by employees and their families.

Campsites, facilities: There are 32 developed tent sites, 10 sites with partial hookups (30 amps) for RVs up to 40 feet long, two hike-in/bike-in sites, and two group camps for up to 50 and 100 people. Picnic tables and fire grills are provided. Restrooms with flush toilets and coin showers, drinking water, picnic shelters that can be reserved, a dump station, and horseshoe pits are available. Some facilities are wheelchair accessible. Leashed pets are permitted.

Reservations, fees: Reservations are not accepted for individual sites but are required for the group camp at 360/482-3852. Sites are $19–25 per night, $10 per extra vehicle per night; hike-in/bike-in sites are $12 per night. The group area is $2.25 per person per night with a $25 reservation fee. Open late April–early October, weather permitting.

Directions: From Olympia on I-5, take Exit 104 to U.S. 101. Drive west on U.S. 101 for six miles to Highway 8. Turn west on Highway 8 and drive to Elma (Highway 8 becomes Highway 12). Continue west on Highway 12 for five miles to the Brady exit/West Satsop Road (four miles east of Montesano). Turn right (north) on West Satsop Road and drive eight miles to Schafer Park Road. Turn right and drive two miles to the park.

Contact: Schafer State Park, tel./fax 360/482-3852; state park information, 360/902-8844, www.parks.wa.gov.

78 LAKE SYLVIA STATE PARK

Scenic rating: 8

on Lake Sylvia

BEST (

This 234-acre state park on the shore of Lake Sylvia features nearly three miles of freshwater shoreline. The park is located in a former logging camp in a wooded area set midway between Olympia and the Pacific Ocean. Expect plenty of rustic charm, with displays of old logging gear, a giant ball carved out of wood from a single log, and some monstrous stumps. The lake is good for fishing and ideal for canoes, prams, or small boats with oars or electric motors; no gas motors are permitted. Five miles of hiking trails and a 0.5-mile wheelchair-accessible trail meander through the park. Additional recreation options include trout fishing and swimming.

Campsites, facilities: There are 35 sites for tents or RVs up to 30 feet long (no hookups), two hike-in/bike-in sites, and one group site for up to 60 people and 10 vehicles. Picnic tables and fire grills are provided. Restrooms with flush toilets and coin showers, drinking water, a dump station, boat launch, picnic area, a kitchen shelter that can be reserved, firewood, and a playground are available. A coin laundry and grocery store are located within two miles. Some facilities are wheelchair accessible. Leashed pets are permitted.

Reservations, fees: Reservations are accepted for individual sites and are required for the group site at 888/CAMP-OUT (888/226-7688) or www.parks.wa.gov/reservations ($6.50–8.50 reservation fee). Sites are $21 per night, $10 per extra vehicle per night; hike-in/bike-in sites are $14 per night. The group site is $2.25 per person, with a 20-person minimum. Open early April–mid-October, weather permitting.

Directions: From Olympia on I-5, take Exit 104 to U.S. 101. Drive west on U.S. 101 six miles to Highway 8. Turn west on Highway 8 (becomes Highway 12) and drive 26 miles to Montesano and West Pioneer Street (the only stoplight in town). Turn left on West Pioneer Street and drive three blocks to 3rd Street. Turn right and drive two miles to the park entrance (route is well signed).

Contact: Lake Sylvia State Park, 360/249-3621, fax 360/249-5571; state park information, 360/902-8844, www.parks.wa.gov.

79 TRAVEL INN RESORT

Scenic rating: 7

on Lake Sylvia

This is a membership campground, which means sites for RV travelers are available only if there is extra space. It can be difficult to get a spot May–September, but the park opens up significantly in the off-season. There are five major rivers or lakes within 15 minutes of this camp (Satsop, Chehalis, Wynoochee, Black River, and Lake Sylvia). Nearby Lake Sylvia State Park provides multiple marked hiking trails. Additional recreation options include trout fishing, swimming, and golf (three miles away).

Campsites, facilities: There are 200 sites with full or partial hookups (30 and 50 amps) for RVs of any length and three tent sites. Picnic tables are provided. Restrooms with flush toilets and showers, drinking water, coin laundry, two community fire pits, a gazebo, a seasonal heated swimming pool, game room, cable TV, Wi-Fi and modem access, seasonal organized activities, and a clubhouse are available. A grocery store, gas station, propane, and restaurant are available within one mile. Some facilities are wheelchair accessible. Leashed pets are permitted.

Reservations, fees: Reservations are accepted May–September. Sites are $35 per night. No credit cards are accepted. Open year-round.

Directions: From Olympia on I-5, take Exit 104 to U.S. 101. Drive west on U.S. 101 for six miles to Highway 8. Turn west on Highway 8 and drive to Elma (Highway 8 becomes Highway 12). Take the first Elma exit and drive to the stop sign and Highway 12/East Main Street. Turn right and drive about 200 yards to the end of the highway and a stop sign. Turn right and drive another 200 yards to the resort on the right.

Contact: Travel Inn Resort, 360/482-3877 or 800/871-2888, www.kmresorts.com.

CAMPING

80 FALLS VIEW

Scenic rating: 8

on the Big Quilcene River in
Olympic National Forest

BEST (

A viewing area to a pretty waterfall on the Big Quilcene River, where you see a narrow, 100-foot cascade, is only a 150-foot walk from the campground. That explains why, despite the rustic setting, this spot on the edge of the Olympic National Forest has a host of facilities and is popular. Enjoy the setting of mixed conifers and rhododendrons along a one-mile scenic loop trail, which overlooks the river and provides views of the waterfall. A picnic area is also located near the waterfall.

Campsites, facilities: There are 30 sites for tents or RVs up to 35 feet long. Picnic tables and fire pits are provided. Vault toilets are available. There is no drinking water. Leashed pets are permitted.

Reservations, fees: Reservations are not accepted. Sites are $10 per night, $5 per extra vehicle per night. Open May–September, weather permitting.

Directions: From Olympia on I-5, turn north on U.S. 101 and drive approximately 70 miles to the campground entrance on the left (located about four miles south of Quilcene).

Contact: Olympic National Forest, Hood Canal Ranger District, Quilcene Office, 360/765-2200, fax 360/765-2202, www.fs.fed.us.

81 KITSAP MEMORIAL STATE PARK

Scenic rating: 10

on Hood Canal

BEST (

Kitsap Memorial State Park is a beautiful spot for campers along Hood Canal. The park covers only 58 acres but features sweeping views of Puget Sound and 1,797 feet of shoreline. The park has 1.5 miles of hiking trails and two open grassy fields for family play. Note that the nearest boat launch is four miles away, north on State Route 3 at Salisbury County Park. An 18-hole golf course and swimming, fishing, and hiking at nearby Anderson Lake Recreation Area are among the activities available. A short drive north will take you to historic Old Fort Townsend, which makes an excellent day trip.

Campsites, facilities: There are 21 sites for tents or RVs up to 30 feet long, 18 sites with partial hookups (30 amps) for RVs, three hike-in/bike-in sites, a group camp for 20 to 56 people, four cabins, and a vacation house. Picnic tables and fire grills are provided. Restrooms with flush toilets and showers, drinking water, a dump station, sheltered picnic area, firewood, a playground, ball fields, and a community meeting hall are available. Two gas stations with mini-marts are located just outside the park. Two boat buoys are available. Some facilities are wheelchair accessible. Leashed pets are permitted.

Reservations, fees: Reservations are not accepted for individual campsites but are required for the group camp at 888/CAMP-OUT (888/226-7688) or www.parks.wa.gov/reservations ($6.50–8.50 reservation fee). Sites are $21–27 per night, $14 per night for hike-in/bike-in sites, $10 per extra vehicle per night. The group camp is $102 per night. Cabins are $60 per night, and the vacation house is $117–156 per night. Open year-round.

Directions: From Tacoma on I-5, turn north on Highway 16 and drive 44 miles (Highway 16 turns into Highway 3). Continue north on Highway 3 and drive six miles to Park Street. Turn left and drive 200 yards to the park entrance on the right (well marked). The park is located four miles south of the Hood Canal Bridge.

Contact: Kitsap Memorial State Park, 360/779-3205, fax 360/779-3161; state park information, 360/902-8844, www.parks.wa.gov.

82 RAINBOW GROUP CAMP

Scenic rating: 7

near Quilcene in Olympic National Forest

Rainbow Group Camp is in a rugged, primitive setting on the edge of Olympic National Forest. This area is heavily wooded with old-growth and new-growth forest, a variety of wildflowers, and spring-blooming rhododendrons. The Rainbow Canyon Trailhead, located at the far side of the campground, provides a short hike to the Big Quicene River and a waterfall. It is fairly steep, but it's not a butt-kicker. Forest roads provide considerable backcountry access (obtaining a U.S. Forest Service map is advisable). The nearest is Forest Road 2730, just 0.10 mile away, which leads to spectacular scenery at the Mount Walker Observation Area. Olympic National Park is also just a short drive away.

Campsites, facilities: This is a group campground only. There are nine sites for tents or pickup campers that can accommodate up to 50 people. Picnic tables and fire grills are provided. Vault toilets are available. There is no drinking water. A store, café, coin laundry, and ice are within five miles. Leashed pets are permitted.

Reservations, fees: Reservations are accepted at 360/765-2200. The camp is $50 per night. Open May–September, weather permitting.

Directions: From I-5 at Olympia, drive north on U.S. 101 and drive approximately 69 miles to the campground (about six miles past Dosewallips State Park) on the left (near Walker Pass).

Contact: Olympic National Forest, Hood Canal Ranger District, Quilcene Office, 360/765-2200, fax 360/765-2202, www.fs.fed.us.

83 COVE RV PARK

Scenic rating: 5

near Dabob Bay

This five-acre private camp enjoys a rural setting close to the shore of Dabob Bay, yet it is fully developed. Sites are grassy and graveled with a few trees. Scuba diving is popular in this area, and the park sells air for scuba tanks. Dosewallips State Park is a short drive away and a possible side trip.

Campsites, facilities: There are 32 sites with full hookups (30 and 50 amps) for RVs up to 40 feet long and six tent sites. Some sites are pull-through. Picnic tables and fire rings are provided. Restrooms with flush toilets and coin showers, drinking water, cable TV, modem access, propane gas, a convenience store, bait and tackle, coin laundry, a sheltered picnic area, and ice are available. Boat docks and launching facilities are on Hood Canal 2.2 miles from the park. Leashed pets are permitted.

Reservations, fees: Reservations are accepted. Tent sites are $17 per night; RV sites are $27 per night. Some credit cards are accepted. Open year-round.

Directions: From Olympia on I-5, drive north on U.S. 101 for 60 miles to Brinnon (located about one mile north of Dosewallips State Park). Continue three miles north on U.S. 101 to the park on the right (before Milepost 303).

Contact: Cove RV Park, 360/796-4723 or 866/796-4723, fax 360/796-3452.

84 SEAL ROCK

Scenic rating: 9

on Dabob Bay in Olympic National Forest

Seal Rock is a 30-acre camp set along the shore near the mouth of Dabob Bay. This is

CAMPING

one of the few national forest campgrounds anywhere located on saltwater. It brings with it the opportunity to harvest oysters and clams in season, and it is an outstanding jumping-off point for scuba diving. Most campsites are set along the waterfront, spaced among trees. Carry-in boats, such as kayaks and canoes, can be launched from the north landing. Native American Nature Trail and Marine Biology Nature Trail begin at the day-use area. These are short walks, each less than 0.5 mile. This camp is extremely popular in the summer, often filling up quickly.

Campsites, facilities: There are 41 sites for tents or RVs up to 21 feet long. Picnic tables and fire rings are provided. Restrooms with flush toilets, drinking water, garbage bins, and a picnic area are available. A camp host is on-site in summer. Boat docks and launching facilities are nearby on Hood Canal and in Dabob Bay. Some facilities, including viewing areas and trails, are wheelchair accessible. Leashed pets are permitted.

Reservations, fees: Reservations are not accepted. Sites are $18 per night. Open May–September, weather permitting.

Directions: From Olympia on I-5, drive north on U.S. 101 for 62 miles to Brinnon (located about one mile north of Dosewallips State Park). Continue two miles north on U.S. 101 to Seal Rock and the camp on the right.

Contact: Olympic National Forest, Hood Canal Ranger District, Quilcene Office, 360/765-2200, fax 360/765-2202, www.fs.fed.us.

85 DOSEWALLIPS STATE PARK

Scenic rating: 8

on Dosewallips Creek

This 425-acre park is set on the shore of Hood Canal at the mouth of Dosewallips River. It features 5,500 feet of saltwater shoreline on Hood Canal and 5,400 feet of shoreline on both sides of the Dosewallips River. Most campsites are grassy and located in scenic, rustic settings. Mushrooming is available in season. Check regulations for fishing and clamming, which fluctuate according to time, season, and supply. The park hosts an annual "Shrimp Fest," often in April. This camp is popular because it's set right off a major highway; reservations or early arrival are advised. Access is not affected by the nearby slide area.

Campsites, facilities: There are 140 sites for tents or RVs up to 60 feet long (no hookups), 40 sites with full hookups (30 amps) for RVs up to 60 feet long, two hike-in/bike-in sites, three platform tent rentals, two group camps for up to 50 and 80 people, and three cabins. Picnic tables and fire rings are provided. Restrooms with flush toilets and coin showers, drinking water, a sheltered picnic area, interpretive activities, and a summer Junior Ranger Program are available. A wildlife-viewing platform, horseshoe pits, and saltwater boat-launching facilities are available within the park. A store and café are available nearby. Some facilities are wheelchair accessible. Leashed pets are permitted.

Reservations, fees: Reservations are accepted at 888/CAMP-OUT (888/226-7688) or www.parks.wa.gov/reservations ($6.50–8.50 reservation fee). Sites are $21–27 per night, $10 per extra vehicle per night; hike-in/bike-in sites are $14 per night, platform tent rentals are $50–55 per night, group camps are $2.25 per person per night with a $25 reservation fee, and cabins are $60 per night. Some credit cards are accepted. Open year-round.

Directions: From Olympia on I-5, drive north on U.S. 101 for 61 miles (one mile south of Brinnon) to the state park entrance on the left.

Contact: Dosewallips State Park, 360/796-4415; state park information, 360/902-8844, www.parks.wa.gov.

86 SCENIC BEACH STATE PARK

🏃 🚣 �－ 🎣 🐴 👫 ♿ 🚐 ⛺

Scenic rating: 10

on Hood Canal

Scenic Beach is an exceptionally beautiful state park with beach access and superb views of the Olympic Mountains. It features 1,500 feet of saltwater beachfront on Hood Canal. The park is also known for its wild rhododendrons in spring. Wheelchair-accessible paths lead to a country garden, gazebo, rustic bridge, and large trees. Many species of birds and wildlife can often be seen here. This camp is also close to Green Mountain Forest, where there is extensive hiking. A boat ramp is 0.5 mile east of the park. A nice touch here is that park staff will check out volleyballs and horseshoes during the summer.

Campsites, facilities: There are 52 sites for tents or RVs up to 60 feet long (some pull-through), two hike-in/bike-in sites, and a group camp for 20–50 people. Picnic tables and fire grills are provided. Restrooms with flush toilets and coin showers, drinking water, and a dump station are available. A sheltered picnic area, playground, horseshoe pits, and volleyball fields are nearby. A boat ramp, dock, and moorage are available within one mile. Some facilities are wheelchair accessible. Leashed pets are permitted.

Reservations, fees: Reservations are accepted at 888/CAMP-OUT (888/226-7688) or www. parks.wa.gov/reservations ($6.50–8.50 reservation fee). Sites are $21 per night, $10 per extra vehicle per night, hike-in/bike-in sites are $14 per night, and the group site is $2.25 per person per night plus a $25 reservation fee. Open year-round, weather permitting.

Directions: From the junction at Highway 16 and Highway 3 in Bremerton, turn north on Highway 3 and drive about nine miles and take the first Silverdale exit (Newberry Hill Road). Turn left and drive approximately three miles to the end of the road. Turn right on Seabeck Highway and drive six miles to Scenic Beach Road. Turn right and drive one mile to the park.

Contact: Scenic Beach State Park, 360/830-5079, fax 360/830-2970; state park information, 360/902-8844, www.parks.wa.gov.

87 FAY BAINBRIDGE STATE PARK

🏃 🚣 �－ 🎣 🐴 👫 ♿ 🚐 ⛺

Scenic rating: 10

on Bainbridge Island

BEST (

A beach park that offers beauty and great recreation, this camp is set on the edge of Puget Sound. The park covers just 17 acres but features 1,420 feet of saltwater shoreline on the northeast corner of the island. You can hike several miles along the beach at low tide; the water temperature is typically about 55°F in summer. The primitive walk-in sites are heavily wooded, and the developed sites have great views of the sound. On clear days, campers can enjoy views of Mount Rainier and Mount Baker to the east, and at night the park provides beautiful vistas of the lights of Seattle. Clamming, diving, picnicking, beachcombing, and kite-flying are popular here. In the winter months, there is excellent salmon fishing just offshore of the park.

Campsites, facilities: There are 26 sites for tents or RVs up to 40 feet long (no hookups), 10 sites for tents only, and four hike-in/bike-in sites. Picnic tables and fire grills are provided. Restrooms with flush toilets and coin showers, drinking water, a dump station, sheltered picnic areas, firewood, horseshoes, and playground are available. Mooring buoys are available nearby. A store and café are located within three miles. Some facilities are wheelchair accessible. Leashed pets are permitted.

Reservations, fees: Reservations are not accepted. Sites are $17 per night, $10 per extra vehicle per night, hike-in/bike-in sites are $14 per night, and moorage is $0.50 per foot, with a $10 per night minimum. Open year-round, weather permitting.

Directions: From Tacoma at I-5, turn north on Highway 16 and drive 30 miles to Bremerton to the junction with Highway 3. Turn north on Highway 3 and drive 18 miles to Highway 305. Turn south on Highway 305 and drive over the bridge to Bainbridge Island and continue three miles to Day Road. Turn left and drive 1.5 miles to Sunrise Drive. Turn left and drive two miles to the park on the right.

Note: From Seattle, this camp can be more easily accessed by taking the Bainbridge Island ferry and then Highway 305 north to Day Road at the northeast end of the island. From there, follow the directions above.

Contact: Fay Bainbridge State Park, 206/842-3931; state park information, 360/902-8844, www.parks.wa.gov.

88 GREEN MOUNTAIN HIKE-IN

Scenic rating: 7

in Green Mountain State Forest

This is a prime spot. Operated by the Department of Natural Resources, the campground is located in Green Mountain State Forest. The Backcountry Horsemen of Washington hosts the camp, which features facilities for horses. Hand-pumped water is available, a plus for such a primitive site. Note that if the gate is closed, a four-mile hike is required to reach the sites.

Campsites, facilities: There are 12 hike-in sites for tents only. Picnic tables and fire grills are provided. Vault toilets, a group shelter, and facilities for horses, including horse corrals, are available. There is no drinking water, and garbage must be packed out. Some facilities are wheelchair accessible. Leashed pets are permitted.

Reservations, fees: Reservations are not accepted. There is no fee for camping. Open year-round, but a gate limits vehicular access to the

camp 9 A.M.–6 P.M. weekdays April–September; walk-in access is available when the gate is closed. A free map and brochure are available.

Directions: From Tacoma on I-5, turn north on Highway 16 and drive 30 miles to Bremerton and the junction with Highway 3. Turn north on Highway 3 and drive to Newberry Hill Road. Turn left onto Seabeck Highway and drive two miles to Holly Road. Turn right on Holly Road and drive 2.2 miles to Tahuya Lake Road. Turn left and drive one mile to Green Mountain Road and the Department of Natural Resources (DNR) parking lot and trailhead. If the gate is closed, hike four miles to the campground.

Contact: Department of Natural Resources, South Puget Sound Region, 360/825-1631, fax 360/825-1672, www.dnr.wa.gov.

89 ILLAHEE STATE PARK

Scenic rating: 9

near Bremerton

This 75-acre park, named for a Native American word for earth or country, features the last stand of old-growth forest in Kitsap County, including one of the largest yew trees in America. The park also features 1,785 feet of saltwater frontage. The campsites are located in a pretty, forested area, and some are grassy. The shoreline is fairly rocky, set on the shore of Port Orchard Bay, although there is a small sandy area for sunbathers. Clamming is popular here. A fishing pier is available for anglers. Note that large vessels can be difficult to launch at the ramp here.

Campsites, facilities: There are 23 sites for tents or RVs up to 40 feet long (no hookups), two sites for tents or RVs up to 35 feet long (50 amp full hookups), and two hike-in/bike-in sites. Picnic tables and fire grills are provided. Restrooms with flush toilets and coin showers, drinking water, firewood, dump station, and a pier are available. Boat docks, launching facilities, five mooring buoys, and 356 feet of moorage float space are also available. A sheltered picnic area, horseshoes, volleyball, a field, and a playground are nearby. A coin laundry and ice are located within one mile. Some facilities are wheelchair accessible. Leashed pets are permitted.

Reservations, fees: Reservations are not accepted. Sites are $19–26 per night, $12 per night for hike-in/bike-in sites, $10 per extra vehicle per night. Moorage is a $0.50 per foot, with a $10 per night minimum. Open year-round.

Directions: On Highway 3, drive to Bremerton and the East Bremerton exit. Drive east for 7.5 miles to Sylvan Way. Turn left and drive 1.5 miles to the park entrance road.

Contact: Illahee State Park, 360/478-6460; state park information, 360/902-8844, www.parks.wa.gov.

90 MANCHESTER STATE PARK

Scenic rating: 9

near Port Orchard

Manchester State Park is set on the edge of Port Orchard, providing excellent lookouts across Puget Sound. The park covers 111 acres, with 3,400 feet of saltwater shoreline on Rich Passage in Puget Sound. The landscape is filled with fir maple, hemlock, cedar, alder, and ash, which are very pretty in the fall. There are approximately 2.5 miles of hiking trails, including an interpretive trail. Group and day-use reservations are available. Note that the beach is closed to shellfish harvesting. In the early 1900s, this park site was used as a U.S. Coast Guard defense installation. A gun battery remains from the park's early days, along with two other buildings that are on the register of National Historical Monuments.

Campsites, facilities: There are 35 tent sites, 15 sites with partial hookups (30 amps) for tents or RVs up to 60 feet long, three hike-in/ bike-in sites, and one group site with hookups (30 amps) for tents or RVs for up to 130 people. Picnic tables and fire grills are provided. Restrooms with flush toilets and coin showers, drinking water, dump station, firewood, sheltered picnic area, volleyball field, and horseshoe pit are available. Some facilities are wheelchair accessible. Leashed pets are permitted.

Reservations, fees: Reservations are accepted for individual sites (mid-May–mid-Sept.) and the group site at 888/CAMP-OUT (888/226-7688) or www.parks.wa.gov/reservations ($6.50–8.50 reservation fee). Sites are $21–28 per night, $10 per extra vehicle per night, and hike-in/bike-in sites are $14 per night. The group site is $2.25 per person per night with a minimum of 20 people and a $25 reservation fee. Some credit cards are accepted. Open year-round, with limited winter facilities.

Directions: From Tacoma on I-5, turn north on Highway 16 and drive to the Port Orford/ Sedgwick Road exit and Highway 160. Turn right (east) and drive one mile to Long Lake Road. Turn left and drive six miles to Milehill. Turn right on Milehill and drive about one mile to Colchester Road. Turn left on Colchester Road and drive through Manchester, continuing for two miles to the park.

Note: Directions to this park are flawed on most website maps and in other books. Use the directions above, and when nearing the camp, you will note the route is signed.

Contact: Manchester State Park, 360/871-4065; state park information, 360/902-8844, www.parks.wa.gov.

91 BLAKE ISLAND BOAT-IN STATE PARK

Scenic rating: 10

near Seattle

Blake Island offers a boat-in camp on a small island in the middle of the massive Seattle

CAMPING

metropolitan area. At night, it can seem almost surreal. The park covers 475 acres and features magnificent views of the Seattle skyline and Olympic Mountains. It boasts five miles of saltwater shoreline, a 0.75-mile nature trail, and 15.5 miles of hiking and biking trails. Good bottom fishing is available off the reef. The tidelands make up an underwater park. Blake Island was an ancestral camping ground of the Suquamish tribe, and according to legend, the renowned Chief Seattle was born here. Native American–style dinners and dancing are available at Tillicum Village, a concession on the island. A bonus: primitive sites on the west side of the island available only by canoe or kayak.

Campsites, facilities: There are 48 boat-in sites, four boat-in sites for non-motorized craft, and one group camp for up to 250 people. Picnic tables and fire grills are provided (only charcoal and gas grills are permitted). Drinking water, restrooms with flush toilets and coin showers, firewood, 1,500 feet of mooring with 24 mooring buoys, and two picnic shelters with a fire pit are available. There are also interpretive activities, horseshoe pits, volleyball, and a field. Garbage must be packed out. A store and snack bar are available nearby. Some facilities are wheelchair accessible. Leashed pets are permitted.

Reservations, fees: Reservations are not accepted for individual sites but are required for the group camp at 888/CAMP-OUT (888/226-7688) or www.parks.wa.gov/reservations ($25 reservation fee). Sites are $12–19 per night, and the group camp is $2.25 per person per night with a minimum of 20 people. Moorage is $10 per night. Open year-round.

Directions: Blake Island is located eight miles west of Seattle, between Vashon and Bainbridge Islands. It is best reached by launching from Bremerton, Port Orchard, or Manchester. From Manchester it is a two-mile cruise east to the island. Then trace the shore around to the buoy floats. There are four main camping areas located between Vashon Island and Bainbridge Island. The park can also be reached by

tour boat through Argosy Cruises, 206/623-1445 or 206/622-8687.

Contact: Blake Island Boat-In State Park, 360/731-8330; state park information, 360/902-8844, www.parks.wa.gov.

92 BELFAIR STATE PARK

Scenic rating: 8

on Hood Canal

Belfair State Park is situated along the southern edge of Hood Canal, spanning 65 acres with 3,720 feet of saltwater shoreline. This park is known for its saltwater tidal flats, wetlands, and wind-blown beach grasses. Beach walking and swimming are good. The camp is set primarily amid conifer forest and marshlands on Hood Canal with nearby streams, tideland, and wetlands. A gravel-rimmed pool that is separate from Hood Canal creates a unique swimming area; water level is determined by the tides. Note that the DNR Tahuya Multiple-Use Area is nearby with trails for motorcycles, mountain biking, hiking, horseback riding, and off-road vehicles. Big Mission Creek and Little Mission Creek, both located in the park, are habitat for chum salmon during spawning season in fall.

Campsites, facilities: There are 137 sites for tents, 47 sites with full hookups (30 amps) for RVs up to 60 feet long, three hike-in/bike-in sites, and one water trail site. Picnic tables and fire grills are provided. Restrooms with flush toilets and coin showers, drinking water, firewood, a bathhouse, dump station, swimming lagoon, playground, badminton, volleyball court, and horseshoe pits are available. A store and restaurant are located nearby. Some facilities are wheelchair accessible. Leashed pets are permitted.

Reservations, fees: Reservations are accepted at 888/CAMP-OUT (888/226-7688) or www.parks.wa.gov/reservations ($6.50–8.50 reservation fee). Sites are $21–28 per night, $10 per extra vehicle per night, hike-in/bike-in sites are $14 per night, and the water trail site is $14 per night. Some credit cards are accepted. Open year-round.

Directions: From Tacoma on I-5, drive to the Highway 16 west exit. Take Highway 16 northwest and drive about 27 miles toward Bremerton and Belfair (after the Port Orchard exits, note that the highway merges into three lanes). Get in the left lane for the Belfair/State Route 3 south exit. Take that exit and turn left at the traffic signal. Take State Route 3 eight miles south to Belfair to State Route 300 (at the signal just after the Safeway). Turn right and drive three miles to the park entrance.

Contact: Belfair State Park, 360/275-0668; state park information, 360/902-8844, www.parks.wa.gov.

93 TWANOH STATE PARK

🏃 🏊 🛶 🚣 🏕 🐴 🚴 ♿ 🚗 ⛰

Scenic rating: 8

near Union

This state park is set on the shore of Hood Canal at one of the warmest saltwater bodies in Puget Sound—and likely the warmest saltwater beach in the state. Twanoh, from a Native American word meaning gathering place, covers 182 acres, with 3,167 feet of saltwater shoreline. Swimming and oyster, clam, and crab harvesting are popular here. Winter smelting is also popular; check regulations. In late fall, the chum salmon can be seen heading up the small creek; fishing for them is prohibited. Most of the park buildings are made of brick, stone, and round logs, built by the Civilian Conservation Corps in the 1930s. You'll also see extensive evidence of logging from the 1890s. Amenities include a tennis court, horseshoe pits, and a concession stand.

Campsites, facilities: There are 25 sites for tents or RVs (no hookups), 22 sites with full hookups (30 and 50 amps) for RVs up to 35 feet long, and a group tent camp for up to 50

people. Picnic tables and fire grills are provided. Restrooms with flush toilets and coin showers and drinking water are available. A seasonal snack bar, sheltered picnic area, firewood, boat ramp, boat dock, moorage buoys, marine pump-out station, wading pool, horseshoes, badminton, and volleyball are available nearby. Some facilities are wheelchair accessible. Leashed pets are permitted.

Reservations, fees: Reservations are accepted only for the group site at 888/226-7688 or www.parks.wa.gov. Sites are $21–28 per night, $10 per extra vehicle per night. The group camp is $2.25 per person per night with a minimum of 20 people, plus a $25 reservation fee. Open April–October, weather permitting.

Directions: From Bremerton, take Highway 3 southwest to Belfair and Highway 106. Turn right (west) and drive eight miles to the park. If driving from U.S. 101, turn east on Highway 106 and drive 12 miles to the park.

Contact: Twanoh State Park, 360/275-2222; state park information, 360/902-8844, www.parks.wa.gov.

94 JARRELL COVE STATE PARK

🏃 🚴 🛶 🚣 🏕 🐴 ♿ 🚗 ⛰

Scenic rating: 8

on Harstine Island

Most visitors to this park arrive by boat. Campsites are near the docks, set on a rolling, grassy area. The park covers just 43 acres but boasts 3,500 feet of saltwater shoreline on the northeast end of Harstine Island in South Puget Sound. The park's dense forest presses nearly to the water's edge at high tides—a beautiful setting. At low tides, tideland mud flats are unveiled. The beach is rocky and muddy—not exactly Hawaii. Hiking and biking are limited to just one mile of trail.

Campsites, facilities: There are 22 sites for tents or RVs up to 34 feet long, one boat-in site (non-motorized boats only), and a group camp for up to 64 people. Picnic tables and fire grills are provided. Restrooms with flush toilets and coin showers and drinking water are available. Boat docks, a marine pump-out station, and 14 mooring buoys are available. A picnic area and a horseshoe pit are nearby. Some facilities are wheelchair accessible. Leashed pets are permitted.

Reservations, fees: Reservations are accepted and are required for the group camp at 888/CAMP-OUT (888/226-7688) or www.parks.wa.gov/reservations ($7 reservation fee). Sites are $12–25 per night, $10 per extra vehicle per night, and the group site is $2 per person per night with a 20-person minimum. Open year-round.

Directions: From Olympia on I-5, turn north on U.S. 101 and drive 22 miles to Shelton and Highway 3. Turn north on Highway 3 and drive about eight miles to Pickering Road. Turn right and drive to the Harstine Bridge. Cross the bridge and continue to North Island Drive. Turn left and drive four miles to Wingert Road. Turn left and drive 0.25 mile to the park on the left.

Contact: Jarrell Cove State Park, 360/426-9226; state park information, 360/902-8844, www.parks.wa.gov.

95 JARRELL'S COVE MARINA

Scenic rating: 6

near Shelton

The marina and nearby Puget Sound are the big draws here. This small camp features 1,000 feet of shoreline and 0.5 mile of public beach. Clamming is available in season.

Campsites, facilities: There are three sites with partial hookups for RVs up to 40 feet long. Picnic tables and barbecues are provided. Restrooms with flush toilets and coin showers, drinking water, propane gas, a dump station, a seasonal convenience store, fishing licenses, bait and tackle, coin laundry, gasoline, marine fuel, boat docks, and moorage are available. Leashed pets are permitted.

Reservations, fees: Reservations are accepted. Sites are $26 per night. Some credit cards are accepted. Open year-round, with limited winter facilities.

Directions: From Olympia on I-5, turn north on U.S. 101 and drive 22 miles to Shelton and Highway 3. Turn north on Highway 3 and drive about eight miles to Pickering Road. Turn right and drive to the Harstine Bridge. Cross the bridge and continue to North Island Drive. Turn left on North Island Drive and drive 2.8 miles to Haskell Hill Road. Turn left (west) on Haskell Hill Road and drive one mile to the marina.

Contact: Jarrell's Cove Marina, 360/426-8823 or 800/362-8823.

96 JOEMMA BEACH STATE PARK

Scenic rating: 8

on Puget Sound

This beautiful camp set along the shore of the peninsula provides an alternative to nearby Penrose Point State Park. It covers 122 acres and features 3,000 feet of saltwater frontage on the southeast Kitsap Peninsula. This area is often excellent for boating, fishing, and crabbing. It is a forested park with the bonus of boat-in campsites. Hiking is limited to a trail less than a mile long.

Campsites, facilities: There are 19 sites for tents or RVs up to 40 feet long, two hike-in/bike-in sites, and two boat-in sites (non-motorized boats only). Picnic tables and fire grills are provided. Vault toilets, drinking water, boat-launching facilities, a dock and mooring buoys, and a picnic shelter that can be reserved are available. A grocery store is approximately five miles away. Some facilities are wheelchair accessible. Leashed pets are permitted.

Reservations, fees: Reservations are not

accepted. Sites are $19 per night, $12 per night for hike-in/bike-in and boat-in sites, $10 per extra vehicle per night. Moorage is $0.50 per foot with a $10 per night minimum. Open year-round.

Directions: From Tacoma, drive north on Highway 16 for about 10 miles to Highway 302/Purdy exit. At the light turn left onto Highway 302, which changes into Key Peninsula Highway. Stay on Key Peninsula Highway and drive about 15 miles to Whiteman Road. Turn right on Whiteman Road and drive four miles to Bay Road. Turn right and drive one mile to the park entrance (stay on the asphalt road when entering the park).

Contact: Joemma Beach State Park, 253/884-1944; state park information, 360/902-8844, www.parks.wa.gov.

97 PENROSE POINT STATE PARK
🧍🚴🛶🚤🐕♿🚐⛺

Scenic rating: 8

on Puget Sound

This park on Carr Inlet on Puget Sound, overlooking Lake Bay, has a remote feel, but it's actually not far from Tacoma. The park covers 162 acres, with two miles of saltwater frontage on Mayo Cove and Carr Inlet. The camp has impressive stands of fir and cedars nearby, along with ferns and rhododendrons. The park has 2.5 miles of trails for biking and hiking. Bay Lake is a popular fishing lake for trout and is located one mile away; a boat launch is available there. Penrose is known for its excellent fishing, crabbing, clamming, and oysters. The nearest boat launch to Puget Sound is located three miles away in the town of Home.

Campsites, facilities: There are 82 sites for tents or RVs up to 35 feet (no hookups), one marine trail boat-in site, and a group camp for tents or RVs for 20–50 people. Picnic tables and fire grills are provided. Restrooms with

flush toilets and coin showers, drinking water, a dump station, firewood, horseshoe pits, sheltered picnic areas, an interpretive trail, and a beach are available. Boat docks, a marine pump-out station, and mooring buoys are nearby. Some facilities are wheelchair accessible. Leashed pets are permitted.

Reservations, fees: Reservations are accepted (and required for the group camp) at 888/CAMP-OUT (888/226-7688) or www.parks.wa.gov/reservations ($6.50–8.50 reservation fee). Sites are $21 per night, $10 per extra vehicle per night, and the group site is $2.25 per person per night, with a minimum of 20 people per night. Boat mooring is $0.50 per foot with a $10 minimum. Some credit cards are accepted. Open year-round.

Directions: From Tacoma, drive north on Highway 16 for about 10 miles to Highway 302/Purdy exit. At the light turn left onto Highway 302, which changes into Key Peninsula Highway. Stay on Key Peninsula Highway and drive south nine miles through the towns of Key Center and Home to Cornwall Road KPS (second road after crossing the Home Bridge). Drive 1.25 miles more to 158 Avenue KPS. Turn left and continue on 158 Avenue KPS to the park entrance.

Contact: Penrose Point State Park, 253/884-2514; state park information, 360/902-8844, www.parks.wa.gov.

98 KOPACHUCK STATE PARK
🧍🛶🚤🐕♿🚐⛺

Scenic rating: 8

on Puget Sound

This park is located on Henderson Bay on Puget Sound near Tacoma. Noteworthy are the scenic views and dramatic sunsets across Puget Sound and the Olympic Mountains. The park covers 109 acres, with 5,600 feet of saltwater shoreline. A unique element of this park is Cutts Island (also called Deadman's Island), which is located 0.5 mile from shore and is accessible only by boat. (There is no camping on the island.) The park has sandy beaches, located about 250 yards down the hill from the camp. Two miles of hiking trails are available. Fishing access is by boat only; a boat launch is located not far from camp.

Campsites, facilities: There are 41 sites for tents or RVs up to 35 feet (no hookups), one primitive boat-in site (no motorized boats permitted), and two group sites for up to 20 and 35 people, respectively. Picnic tables and fire grills are provided. Restrooms with flush toilets and coin showers, drinking water, a dump station, covered picnic areas, a Junior Ranger Program (seasonal), interpretive activities, and boat buoys are available. A small store is approximately one mile away. Some facilities are wheelchair accessible. Leashed pets are permitted.

Reservations, fees: Reservations are not accepted for individual sites but are required for the group site at 253/265-3606. Sites are $21 per night, $10 per extra vehicle per night; the boat-in site is $14 per night. The group site is $2.25 per person per night with a 20-person minimum. Open year-round.

Directions: From Tacoma on I-5, turn north on Highway 16. Drive seven miles north to the third Gig Harbor exit (Wollochet Drive NW). Take that exit and follow the signs for about seven miles to Kopachuck State Park. Note: The road changes names several times, but the route is well signed.

Contact: Kopachuck State Park, 253/265-3606; state park information, 360/902-8844, www.parks.wa.gov.

99 GIG HARBOR RV RESORT

Scenic rating: 7

near Tacoma

This is a popular layover spot for folks heading up to Bremerton. Just a short jaunt off the highway, it's pleasant, clean, and friendly. An 18-hole golf course, full-service marina, and tennis courts are located nearby. Look for the great view of Mount Rainier from the end of the harbor.

Campsites, facilities: There are 93 sites, most with full or partial hookups (30 and 50 amps), including some long-term rentals, for tents or RVs of any length and one cabin. Some sites are pull-through. Restrooms with flush toilets and showers, drinking water, cable TV, modem access, propane gas, a dump station, a clubroom, coin laundry, ice, playground, horseshoe pits, sports field, and a seasonal heated swimming pool are available. Leashed pets are permitted.

Reservations, fees: Reservations are accepted. Tent sites are $21–26 per night, and RV sites are $32–35 per night. Some credit cards are accepted. Open year-round.

Directions: From Tacoma, drive northwest on Highway 16 for 12 miles to the Burnham Drive NW exit. Take that exit and enter the roundabout to the first right and Burnham Drive NW. Turn right on Burnham Drive NW and drive 1.25 miles to the resort on the left.

Contact: Gig Harbor RV Resort, 253/858-8138 or 800/526-8311, fax 253/858-8399.

100 AMERICAN SUNSET RV AND TENT RESORT

Scenic rating: 8

near Westport Harbor

If location is everything, then this RV camp, set on a peninsula, is a big winner. It covers 32 acres and is 10 blocks from the ocean; hiking and biking trails are nearby. The park is divided into two areas: one for campers, another for long-term rentals. Nearby are Westhaven and Westport Light State Parks, popular with hikers, rockhounds, scuba divers, and surf anglers. Fishing and crabbing off the docks are also options; you can also swim, but not off the docks. Monthly rentals are available in summer.

Campsites, facilities: There are 120 sites with full hookups (20, 30, and 50 amps) for RVs up to 45 feet long, 50 sites for tents or RVs up to 30 feet (no hookups), one lighthouse unit, one beach house, one cabana, and one rental trailer. Some sites are pull-through. Picnic tables and fire rings are provided. Restrooms with flush toilets and showers, drinking water, satellite TV, Wi-Fi, coin laundry, a convenience store, propane, a seasonal heated swimming pool, horseshoe pits, a playground, fish-cleaning station, and recreation hall are available. A marina is located three blocks away. Leashed pets are permitted.

Reservations, fees: RV Sites are $30–32 per night, and tent sites are $21–22. Some discounts are available. Some credit cards are accepted. Open year-round.

Directions: From Aberdeen, drive south on State Route 105 for 22 miles to Westport and Montesano Street (the first exit in Westport). Turn right (northeast) on Montesano Street and drive three miles to the resort on the left.

Contact: American Sunset RV and Tent Resort, 360/268-0207 or 800/569-2267, www. americansunsetrv.com.

101 TOTEM RV PARK

Scenic rating: 8

in Westport

This 3.2-acre park is set 300 yards from the ocean and features an expanse of sand dunes between the park and the ocean. It has large, grassy sites close to Westhaven State Park, which offers day-use facilities. The owner is a fishing guide and can provide detailed fishing information. The salmon fishing within 10 miles of this park is often excellent in summer. Marked biking trails and a full-service marina are within five miles of the park.

Campsites, facilities: There are 80 sites with full or partial hookups (30 and 50 amps) for tents or RVs of any length. Some sites are pull-through. Restrooms with flush toilets and coin showers, drinking water, cable TV, Wi-Fi, a dump station, coin laundry, and ice are available. A pavilion, barbecue facilities with kitchen, and a fish-cleaning station are also available. Boat docks, launching facilities, and fishing charters are nearby. Propane gas, a store, and café are within 0.5 mile. Some facilities are wheelchair accessible. Leashed pets are permitted.

Reservations, fees: Reservations are accepted. Sites are $24–27 per night. Some credit cards are accepted. Open year-round.

Directions: From Aberdeen, drive south on State Route 105 for 20 miles to the turnoff for Westport. Turn right (north) on the State Route 105 spur and drive 4.3 miles to the docks and Nyhus Street. Turn left on Nyhus Street and drive two blocks to the park on the left.

Contact: Totem RV Park, 360/268-0025 or 888/TOTEM-RV (888/868-3678).

102 HOLAND CENTER

Scenic rating: 6

in Westport

This pleasant, 18-acre RV park is one of several in the immediate area. The sites are graveled or grassy, with ample space and pine trees in between. There is no beach access from the park, but full recreational facilities are available nearby. About half of the sites are long-term rentals.

Campsites, facilities: There are 85 sites with full hookups for RVs up to 40 feet long. Picnic tables are provided. No open fires are allowed. Restrooms with flush toilets and coin showers, cable TV, coin laundry, and storage sheds are available. Propane gas, a store, café, and ice are located within one mile. Boat docks and launching facilities are nearby. Leashed pets are permitted.

Reservations, fees: Reservations are accepted. Sites are $30 per night. Credit cards are not accepted. Open year-round.

Directions: From Aberdeen, drive south on State Route 105 for 22 miles to Westport. Continue on State Route 105 to a Y intersection. Bear right on Montesano Street and drive approximately two miles to Wilson Street. The park is on the left, at the corner of State Route 105 and Wilson Street.

Contact: Holand Center, phone/fax 360/268-9582.

103 PACIFIC MOTEL AND RV PARK

🚶 🚴 🏊 ⛴ 🛶 ⛺ 🐕 🚐 ⛺

Scenic rating: 5

near Twin Harbors

This five-acre park has shaded sites in a wooded setting. It's near Twin Harbors and Westport Light State Park, a day-use park nearby. Both parks have beach access. A full-service marina is located within two miles. About 25 percent of the sites are occupied with long-term rentals.

Campsites, facilities: There are 80 sites with full hookups (20 and 30 amps) for RVs of any length and 12 tent sites. Picnic tables and fire rings are provided. Restrooms with flush toilets and coin showers, drinking water, propane gas, a dump station, fish-cleaning station, recreation hall with a kitchen, cable TV, modem access, pay phone, coin laundry, and a seasonal heated swimming pool are available. A store, café, and ice are located within one mile. Boat-launching and boat docks are nearby in a full-service marina. Leashed pets are permitted.

Reservations, fees: Reservations are accepted. RV sites are $27 per night, tent sites are $20 per night, $2 per person per night for more than two people. Some credit cards are accepted. Open year-round.

Directions: From Aberdeen, drive south on State Route 105 for approximately 21 miles to Westport. Go past the first Westport exit to a stop sign. Turn right onto the State Route 105 spur (becomes Forrest Street in Westport) and drive 1.8 miles to the park on the right.

Contact: Pacific Motel and RV Park, 360/268-9325, fax 360/268-6227, www.pacificmotelandrv.com.

104 TWIN HARBORS STATE PARK

🚶 🛶 🐕 ♿ 🚐 ⛺

Scenic rating: 8

near Westport

The park covers 172 acres and is located four miles south of Westhaven. It was a military training ground in the 1930s. The campsites are close together and often crammed to capacity in the summer. Highlights include beach access and marked hiking trails, including Shifting Sands Nature Trail. The most popular recreation activities are surf fishing, surfing, beachcombing, and kite-flying. Fishing boats can be chartered nearby in Westport.

Campsites, facilities: There are 250 tent sites, 49 sites with for tents or RVs up to 35 feet long (30 amp full hookups), four hike-in/bike-in sites, and one group site for up to 60 people. Picnic tables and fire grills are provided. Restrooms with flush toilets and coin showers, drinking water, a dump station, a picnic area with a kitchen shelter, and horseshoe pits are available. A store, café, and ice are available within one mile. Some facilities are wheelchair accessible. Leashed pets are permitted.

Reservations, fees: Reservations are accepted for individual sites and are required for the group site at 888/CAMP-OUT (888/226-7688) or www.parks.wa.gov/reservations ($6.50–8.50 reservation fee). Sites are $21–28 per night, $10 per extra vehicle per night, and hike-in/bike-in sites are $14 per night. The group site is $2.25 per person per night with a 20-person minimum. Some credit cards are accepted. Open year-round.

Directions: From Aberdeen, drive south on State Route 105 for 17 miles to the park entrance on the left (three miles south of Westport).

Contact: Twin Harbors State Park, 360/268-9717; state park information, 360/902-8844, www.parks.wa.gov.

105 PORTER CREEK

Scenic rating: 7

on Porter Creek in Capitol Forest

This primitive, rustic campground is located about 30 miles from Olympia. It is set in the Capitol Forest along the shore of Porter Creek and is managed by the Department of Natural Resources. It offers trails for hiking, horseback riding, or motorbikes. The camp serves as a launch point for a variety of trips. Most campers take the 0.5-mile trail to Porter Falls, departing from the trailhead just across the road. Within three miles, you can also access trails that lead to a network of 87 miles of off-road vehicle trails and 84 miles of trails for non-motorized use—mountain biking is popular here. With corrals and hitching posts available, this camp is popular among horseback riders.

Note: As of 2010, access from Porter Creek Campground to Capitol Forest was closed because of flood damage and slides; check conditions before attempting a visit.

Campsites, facilities: There are 16 sites for tents or RVs up to 16 feet (no hookups). Picnic tables and fire grills are provided. There is no drinking water, and garbage must be packed out. Vault toilets, corrals, hitching posts, and horse-loading ramps are available. All-terrain vehicles are permitted. Some facilities are wheelchair accessible. Leashed pets are permitted.

Reservations, fees: Reservations are not accepted. There is no fee for camping. Open May–November, weather permitting.

Directions: On I-5, drive to Exit 88 (10 miles north of Chehalis) and U.S. 12. Turn west on U.S. 12 and drive 21 miles to Porter and Porter Creek Road. Turn right (northeast) on Porter Creek Road and drive 3.4 miles (last half mile is gravel) to a junction. Continue straight on B-Line Road for 0.6 mile to the campground on the left.

Contact: Department of Natural Resources, Pacific Cascade Region North, 360/577-2025, fax 360/274-4196, www.dnr.wa.gov.

106 MIDDLE WADDELL

Scenic rating: 7

on Waddell Creek in Capitol Forest

This wooded campground is nestled along Waddell Creek in Capitol Forest. The trails in the immediate vicinity are used primarily for all-terrain vehicles (ATVs), making for some noise. There is an extensive network of ATV trails in the area. Mountain bikers tend to prefer Fall Creek camp.

Campsites, facilities: There are 24 sites for tents or RVs of any length. Picnic tables and fire grills are provided. Vault toilets are available. There is no drinking water, and garbage must be packed out. A camp host is on-site. Some facilities are wheelchair accessible. Leashed pets are permitted.

Reservations, fees: Reservations are not accepted. There is no fee for camping. Open May–November, weather permitting.

Directions: From Olympia on I-5, drive south for about 10 miles to Exit 95 and Highway 121. Turn west on Highway 121 and drive four miles to Littlerock. Continue west for one mile to Waddell Creek Road. Turn right and drive three miles and look for the campground entrance road on the left.

Contact: Department of Natural Resources, Pacific Cascade Region North, 360/577-2025, fax 360/274-4196, www.dnr.wa.gov.

107 FALL CREEK

Scenic rating: 7

on Fall Creek in Capitol Forest

With good access to an 84-mile network of trails for non-motorized use, this camp is something of a mountain-biking headquarters. Although ATVs are allowed in the campground, they are not allowed on the adjacent trails. This wooded camp on Fall Creek in Capitol Forest also provides horse facilities.

Campsites, facilities: There are eight sites for tents or RVs up to 45 feet (no hookups). Picnic tables and fire grills are provided. There is no drinking water, and garbage must be packed out. Vault toilets, corrals, a hitching post, and a horse-loading ramp are available. A day-use staging area is also available. Some facilities are wheelchair accessible. Leashed pets are permitted.

Reservations, fees: Reservations are not accepted. There is no fee for camping. Open May–November, weather permitting.

Directions: From Olympia, take I-5 to exit 95 onto Maytown Road SW and turn west. (If coming from I-5 South, you will cross under I-5.) Drive west on Maytown Road SW to Littlerock, where the road becomes 128th Avenue SW. Continue on 128th Avenue SW until it ends at Waddell Creek Road SW. Turn right (northwest) on Waddell Creek Road SW and drive two miles to the Triangle. Turn left. The road will become Sherman Valley Road SW. Drive one mile on Sherman Valley Road SW; the pavement ends and it becomes the "C-Line" road and enters the Capitol Forest. Drive four miles and turn left at the second turnoff to the left, Road C-6000, signed Fall Creek Campground. Drive three miles to the campground on the right, just beyond a small bridge.

Contact: Department of Natural Resources, Pacific Cascade Region North, 360/577-2025, fax 360/274-4196, www.dnr.wa.gov.

108 SHERMAN VALLEY/ NORTH CREEK

Scenic rating: 8

on Cedar Creek in Capitol Forest

One of several secluded camps located in the Capitol Forest, Sherman Valley is managed by the Department of Natural Resources. Its pleasant, shady campsites are set along the shore of Porter Creek. The forest here is primarily alder and fir trees. Hiking trails can be found at nearby North Creek camp. As with North Creek, this camp is used by hunters in season.

Campsites, facilities: There are four primitive sites for tents or RVs up to 25 feet long and three walk-in sites. Picnic tables and fire grills are provided. Vault toilets are available. There is no drinking water, and garbage must be packed out. Mountain bikes are permitted on the roads only; trails are reserved for hikers. Leashed pets are permitted.

Reservations, fees: Reservations are not accepted. There is no fee for camping. Open May–November, weather permitting.

Directions: From Olympia, take I-5, to Exit 95 onto Maytown Road SW. Take that exit and turn southwest on Maytown Road drive to Littlerock (where the road becomes 128th Ave. SW) and continue on 128th to where it ends at Waddell Creek Road SW. Turn right on Waddell Creek Road SW and drive two miles to the Triangle. Turn left (the road will become Sherman Valley Road SW) and drive one mile (the pavement ends and the road becomes C-Line Road and enters Capitol Forest), and continue four miles to Road C-6000. Turn left (signed Falls Creek Campground) and drive three miles (just beyond a small bridge) to the campground on the right.

Contact: Department of Natural Resources, Pacific Cascade Region North, 360/577-2025, fax 360/274-4196, www.dnr.wa.gov.

109 MARGARET McKENNY

Scenic rating: 7

in Capitol Forest

With trails linked to an extensive network of trails for non-motorized use only, this camp is used primarily as a trailhead for horseback riders and mountain bikers. Most of the campsites are well away from the stream, but seven walk-in sites are available, where a 300- to 400-foot walk down a stairway takes you to pretty streamside campsites.

Campsites, facilities: There are 21 primitive sites for tents or RVs up to 45 feet long and four walk-in sites. Picnic tables, fire pits, and grills are provided. There is no drinking water, and garbage must be packed out. Vault toilets, a campfire circle, and a horse-loading ramp are available. A campground host is on-site during the summer season. Some facilities are wheelchair accessible. Leashed pets are permitted.

Reservations, fees: Reservations are not accepted. There is no fee for camping. Open May–November, weather permitting.

Directions: From Olympia on I-5, drive south for about 10 miles to Exit 95 and Highway 121. Turn west on Highway 121 and drive four miles to Littlerock. Continue west for one mile to Waddell Creek Road. Turn right and drive 2.5 miles and look for the campground entrance road on the left.

Contact: Department of Natural Resources, Pacific Cascade Region North, 360/577-2025, fax 360/274-4196, www.dnr.wa.gov.

110 NORTH CREEK/ SHERMAN VALLEY

Scenic rating: 8

on Cedar Creek

This little-known, wooded campground managed by the Department of Natural Resources is set along Cedar Creek, which offers fishing. There are trails for hikers only (no horses or mountain bikes are allowed). A four-mile loop trail leads to Sherman Valley (a bridge has been out on this trail, with a longer alternative route available; call before planning a hike). Hunters use this camp in the fall. For a side trip, visit the Chehalis River, a five-mile drive to the west. A canoe launch off U.S. 12 is available north of Oakville.

Campsites, facilities: There are five primitive sites for tents or RVs up to 25 feet long. Picnic tables and fire grills are provided. Vault toilets are available. There is no drinking water, and garbage must be packed out. Mountain bikes are permitted on the roads only; trails are reserved for hikers. Some facilities are wheelchair accessible. Leashed pets are permitted.

Reservations, fees: Reservations are not accepted. There is no fee for camping. Open May–November, weather permitting.

Directions: From Olympia, take I-5 to to Exit 95 onto Maytown Road SW. Take that exit and turn southwest on Maytown Road drive to Littlerock (where the road becomes 128th Ave. SW) and continue on 128th to where it ends at Waddell Creek Road SW. Turn right on Waddell Creek Road SW and drive two miles to the Triangle. Turn left (the road will become Sherman Valley Road SW) and drive one mile (the pavement ends and the road become C-Line Road and enters Capitol Forest), and continue four miles to Road C-6000. Turn left (signed Falls Creek Campground) and drive three miles (just beyond a small bridge) to the campgrounds.

Contact: Department of Natural Resources, Pacific Cascade Region North, 360/577-2025, fax 360/274-4196, www.dnr.wa.gov.

CAMPING

111 MIMA FALLS TRAILHEAD

🚶 🏇 ♿ 🚐 ⛺

Scenic rating: 10

near Mima Falls

The highlight here is the five-mile loop trail for hikers and horseback riders that leads to beautiful 90-foot Mima Falls. The campground is quiet and pretty. This spot can be a first-rate choice. One of the unique qualities of this campground is that it provides facilities for both wheelchair users and horseback riders. The trail is not wheelchair accessible, but wheelchair users on horses can access the trip to Mima Falls. The trail runs across the brink of the falls.

Campsites, facilities: There is a primitive, dispersed camping area for about five tents or RVs up to 25 feet long. Picnic tables and fire grills are provided. Vault toilets and a horse-loading ramp are available. There is no drinking water, and garbage must be packed out. Some facilities are wheelchair accessible. Leashed pets are permitted.

Reservations, fees: Reservations are not accepted. There is no fee for camping. Open May–November, weather permitting.

Directions: From Olympia, drive south on I-5 for 10 miles to Highway 121. Turn west on Highway 121 and drive four miles west to Littlerock. Continue west for one mile to Mima Road. Turn left on Mima Road and drive 1.5 miles to Bordeaux Road. Turn right on Bordeaux Road and drive 0.5 mile to Marksman Road. Turn right and drive about 0.6 mile to the campground access road on the left. Turn left and drive 200 yards to the campground.

Contact: Department of Natural Resources, Pacific Cascade Region North, 360/577-2025, fax 360/274-4196, www.dnr.wa.gov.

112 GRAYLAND BEACH STATE PARK

🚶 🏊 🏇 ♿ 🚐 ⛺

Scenic rating: 8

near Grayland

This state park features 7,500 feet of beach frontage. All the campsites are within easy walking distance of the ocean. The campsites are relatively spacious for a state park, but they are not especially private. This park is popular with out-of-towners, especially during summer. Recreation options include fishing, beachcombing, and kite-flying. The best spot for surfing is five miles north at Westhaven State Park.

Campsites, facilities: There are 100 sites, including 58 with full-hookups (30 and 50 amps) for tents and RVs up to 40 feet long, four hike-in/bike-in sites, and 16 yurts. Picnic tables and fire grills are provided. Drinking water and restrooms with flush toilets and coin showers, an amphitheater, and a dump station are available. Some facilities are wheelchair accessible. Leashed pets are permitted.

Reservations, fees: Reservations are accepted at 888/CAMP-OUT (888/226-7688) or www.parks.wa.gov/reservations ($6.50–8.50 reservation fee). Sites are $27–28 per night, $10 per extra vehicle per night, hike-in/bike-in sites are $14 per night, and yurts are $55–60 per night. Some credit cards are accepted. Open year-round.

Directions: From Aberdeen, drive south on State Route 105 for 22 miles to the park entrance. The park is just south of the town of Grayland on the right (west).

Contact: Grayland Beach State Park, 360/267-4301; state park information, 360/902-8844, www.parks.wa.gov.

113 BAY CENTER/ WILLAPA BAY KOA

Scenic rating: 7

on Willapa Bay

This KOA is 200 yards from Willapa Bay, within walking distance of a beach that seems to stretch to infinity. A trail leads to the beach and from here you can walk for miles in either direction. The beach sand is mixed with agates, driftwood, and seaweed. Dungeness crabs, clams, and oysters all live near shore. Another bonus is that herds of Roosevelt elk roam the nearby woods. Believe it or not, there are also black bear, although they are seldom seen here. The park covers five acres, and the campsites are graveled and shaded.

Campsites, facilities: There are 42 sites with full or partial hookups (20, 30, and 50 amps) for RVs of any length, 23 tent sites, and two cabins. Some sites are pull-through. Picnic tables and fire rings are provided. Restrooms with flush toilets and showers, drinking water, propane gas, dump station, cable TV, modem access, a recreation hall, camp store, firewood, coin laundry, and ice are available. A café, boat docks, and launching facilities are nearby. Some facilities are wheelchair accessible. Leashed pets are permitted, with certain restrictions.

Reservations, fees: Reservations are accepted at 800/562-7810. Sites are $30–37 per night, $4 per person per night for more than two people, $4 per extra vehicle per night. Some credit cards are accepted. Open mid-March–late October.

Directions: From Nemah on U.S. 101, drive north for five miles to Bay Center/Dike exit (located between Mileposts 42 and 43, 16 miles south of Raymond). Turn left (west) and drive three miles to the campground.

Contact: Bay Center/Willapa Bay KOA, 360/875-6344, www.koa.com.

114 RAINBOW FALLS STATE PARK

Scenic rating: 8

on the Chehalis River Bay

This 139-acre park is set on the Chehalis River and boasts 3,400 feet of shoreline. The camp features stands of old-growth cedar and fir and is named after a few small cascades with drops of about 10 feet. The park has 10 miles of hiking trails, including an interpretive trail, seven miles of bike trails, and seven miles of horse trails. A pool at the base of Rainbow Falls is excellent for swimming. Another attraction, a small fuchsia garden, has more than 40 varieties. There are also several log structures built by the Civilian Conservation Corps in 1935.

Campsites, facilities: There are 45 sites for tents or RVs up to 32 feet (no hookups), eight sites with partial hookups (30 and 50 amps) for tents or RVs up to 60 feet long, three hike-in/bike-in sites, three equestrian sites with hitching points and stock water, and one group site for up to 60 people. Picnic tables and fire rings are provided. Restrooms with flush toilets and coin showers, drinking water, a dump station, firewood, a picnic area, interpretive activities, a playground, horseshoe pits, and a softball field are available. Some facilities are wheelchair accessible. Leashed pets are permitted.

Reservations, fees: Reservations are accepted for only for group site at 360/291-3767. Sites are $21–27 per night, $10 per extra vehicle per night, and hike-in/bike-in sites are $10 per night. Open year-round.

Directions: From Chehalis on I-5, take Exit 77 to drive west 11.7 miles on Highway 6 to milepost 40. Drive 0.4 miles past the marker to River Road. Turn right (west) on River Road and drive 2.7 miles to the Bailey Bridge. Turn right to cross the bridge and immediately turn left onto Leudinghaus Road. Drive 2.2 miles west on Leudinghaus Road to the park

CAMPING

CAMPING

entrance on the left. Once inside the park, the campground is on the right.

Contact: Rainbow Falls State Park, 360/291-3767 or 360/902-8844, www.parks.wa.gov.

115 OCEAN PARK RESORT

Scenic rating: 5

on Willapa Bay

This wooded, 10-acre campground is located 0.5 mile from Willapa Bay. With grassy, shaded sites, it caters primarily to RVs. Fishing, crabbing, and clamming are popular in season. Ocean Park has several festivals during the summer season. During these festivals, this resort fills up. To the north, Leadbetter Point State Park provides a side-trip option.

Campsites, facilities: There are 70 sites with full hookups for RVs of any length, seven tent sites, and two park-model cottages. Some sites are pull-through. Picnic tables are provided. Fire pits are provided at tent sites. Restrooms with flush toilets and coin showers, drinking water, propane gas, a recreation hall, coin laundry, playground, firewood, a spa, and a seasonal heated swimming pool are available. A store and café are available within one mile. Boat docks and launching facilities are located nearby on Willapa Bay. Leashed pets are permitted, with certain restrictions.

Reservations, fees: Sites are $25–30 per night, plus $3 per person per night for more than two people. Some credit cards are accepted. Open year-round.

Directions: From Kelso/Longview on I-5, turn west on Highway 4 and drive 63 miles to U.S. 101. Turn south on U.S. 101 and drive 13 miles to the junction with Highway 103. Turn right (north) on Highway 103 and drive 11 miles to the town of Ocean Park and 259th Street. Turn right (east) on 259th Street and drive two blocks to the resort at the end of the road.

Contact: Ocean Park Resort, 360/665-4585 or 800/835-4634, www.opresort.com.

116 WESTGATE CABIN & RV PARK

Scenic rating: 9

near Long Beach

Highlights at this pretty and clean four-acre camp include beach access, oceanfront sites, and all the amenities. There are 28 miles of beach that can be driven on. Additional facilities within five miles of the park include an 18-hole golf course.

Campsites, facilities: There are 38 sites with full hookups (30 amps) for RVs up to 50 feet long and six cabins. Some sites are pull-through. Picnic tables are provided. Restrooms with flush toilets and showers, drinking water, cable TV, modem access, coin laundry, gas station, a recreation hall, and ice are available. A store and café are available about four miles away. Boat docks and launching facilities are located nearby on Willapa Bay. Leashed pets are permitted, but not in cabins.

Reservations, fees: Reservations are accepted. Sites are $35–42 per night, plus $2 per person per night for more than two people. Some credit cards are accepted. Open year-round.

Directions: From Kelso/Longview on I-5, turn west on Highway 4 and drive 63 miles to U.S. 101. Turn left (south) on U.S. 101 and drive 13 miles to the junction with Highway 103. Turn right (north) on Highway 103 and drive nine miles to the park on the left (located at the south edge of the town of Ocean Park).

Contact: Westgate Cabin & RV Park, 360/665-4211, fax 360/665-2451.

117 ANDERSEN'S RV PARK ON THE OCEAN

Scenic rating: 7

near Long Beach

Timing is everything here. When the dates are announced for the local festivals, reservations start pouring in and the sites at this park can be booked a year in advance. Located near the city limits of Long Beach, this five-acre camp features a path through the dunes that will get you to the beach in a flash. It is set in a flat, sandy area with gravel sites. Recreation options include beach bonfires, beachcombing, surf fishing, and clamming (seasonal). Additional facilities found within five miles of the park include marked dune trails, a nine-hole golf course, a riding stable, and tennis courts. The park is big-rig friendly.

Campsites, facilities: There are 60 sites for tents or RVs of any length (20, 30, and 50 amp full hookups). Picnic tables and fire pits are provided. Restrooms with flush toilets and showers, drinking water, cable TV, Wi-Fi, modem access, a dump station, coin laundry, ice, propane gas, fax machine, group facilities, a horseshoe pit, and a playground are available. A store and café are available within two miles. Leashed pets are permitted.

Reservations, fees: Reservations are accepted. Sites are $28–36 per night, plus $2 per person per night for more than two people. Some credit cards are accepted. Open year-round.

Directions: From Kelso/Longview on I-5, turn west on Highway 4 and drive 63 miles to U.S. 101. Turn left (south) on U.S. 101 and drive 13 miles to the junction with Highway 103. Turn right (north) on Highway 103 and drive five miles to the park on the left.

Contact: Andersen's RV Park on the Ocean, 360/642-2231 or 800/645-6795, www.andersensrv.com.

118 OCEANIC RV PARK

Scenic rating: 3

in Long Beach

This two-acre park is located in the heart of downtown, within walking distance of restaurants and stores. It is also within five miles of an 18-hole golf course, marked bike trails, and a full-service marina.

Campsites, facilities: There are 18 pull-through sites with full hookups (30 and 50 amps) for RVs of any length. No open fires are allowed. Restrooms with flush toilets and showers, cable TV, a restaurant, and propane gas are available. A store, coin laundry, and ice are located within one mile. Boat docks, launching facilities, and boat rentals are nearby. Leashed pets are permitted.

Reservations, fees: Reservations are accepted. Sites are $35 per night, plus $2 per person per night for more than two people. Some credit cards are accepted. Open year-round.

Directions: From Kelso/Longview on I-5, turn west on Highway 4 and drive 63 miles to U.S. 101. Turn left (south) on U.S. 101 and drive 13 miles to the junction with Highway 103. Turn right (north) on Highway 103 and drive two miles to Long Beach. Continue to the park at the south junction of Pacific Highway (Highway 103) and 5th Avenue on the right.

Contact: Oceanic RV Park, 360/642-3836.

119 MERMAID INN AND RV PARK

Scenic rating: 3

near Long Beach

Situated along the highway, this three-acre park is within four blocks of the beach. It is also within five miles of an 18-hole golf course, a full-service marina, and a riding stable.

Campsites, facilities: There are 11 sites with

CAMPING

full hookups (20 and 30 amps) for RVs of any length and 10 motel rooms. Picnic tables are provided. Restrooms with flush toilets and showers, drinking water, cable TV, a picnic area, and coin laundry are available. Propane gas, a gas station, store, restaurant, and ice are located within one mile.

Reservations, fees: Reservations are accepted. Sites are $21–30, plus $1.50 per person per night for more than two people. Some credit cards are accepted. Open year-round.

Directions: From Kelso/Longview on I-5, turn west on Highway 4 and drive 63 miles to U.S. 101. Turn left (south) on U.S. 101 and drive 13 miles to the junction with Highway 103. Turn right (north) on Highway 103 and drive three miles to the park on the right.

Contact: Mermaid Inn and RV Park, 360/642-2600, www.mermaidinnatlongbeachwa.com.

120 DRIFTWOOD RV PARK
🚴 🛶 ⛺ 🐕 🚐

Scenic rating: 2

near Long Beach

This two-acre park features grassy, shaded sites and beach access close by. A fenced pet area is a bonus. Additional facilities within five miles of the park include a nine-hole golf course and a full-service marina.

Campsites, facilities: There are 56 sites with full hookups (30 amps) for RVs of any length. Many sites are pull-through. Picnic tables are provided and portable fire pits can be rented. Restrooms with flush toilets and showers, drinking water, coin laundry, cable TV, Wi-Fi, modem access, group facilities, and a fenced pet area are available. Propane gas, a gas station, store, and restaurant are available within one mile. Leashed pets are permitted, with certain restrictions.

Reservations, fees: Reservations are accepted. Sites are $25–33 per night, plus $3 per person per night for more than two people. Some credit cards are accepted. Open year-round.

Directions: From Kelso/Longview on I-5, turn

west on Highway 4 and drive 63 miles to U.S. 101. Turn left (south) on U.S. 101 and drive 13 miles to the junction with Highway 103. Turn right (north) on Highway 103 and drive 2.25 miles to the park on the right, at 14th Street North and Pacific Avenue.

Contact: Driftwood RV Park, 360/642-2711 or 888/567-1902, www.driftwood-rvpark.com.

121 SAND CASTLE RV PARK
🚴 🛶 ⛺ 🐕 🚐

Scenic rating: 3

in Long Beach

This park is set across the highway from the ocean. Although not particularly scenic, it is clean and does provide nearby beach access. The park covers two acres, has grassy areas, and is one of several in the immediate area. Additional facilities found within five miles of the park include a nine-hole golf course, marked bike trails, a full-service marina, and two riding stables.

Campsites, facilities: There are 38 sites with full hookups (30 and 50 amps) for RVs of any length. Some sites are pull-through. Tents are permitted only with RVs. Picnic tables are provided. Restrooms with flush toilets and coin showers, drinking water, cable TV, Wi-Fi, a dump station, coin laundry, and pay phone are available. Propane gas, a gas station, a store, ice, and a café are available within one mile. Boat docks, launching facilities, and rentals are within five miles. Leashed pets are permitted.

Reservations, fees: Reservations are accepted. Sites are $28.50–30.50 per night, $2 per person per night for more than two people, $2 per extra vehicle per night. Some credit cards are accepted. Open year-round.

Directions: From Kelso/Longview on I-5, turn west on Highway 4 and drive 63 miles to U.S. 101. Turn left (south) on U.S. 101 and drive 13 miles to the junction with Highway 103. Turn right (north) on Highway 103 and drive two miles to the park on the right.

Contact: Sand Castle RV Park, 360/642-2174, www.sandcastlerv.com.

122 WESTERN LAKES

Scenic rating: 9

near Naselle

You want quiet and solitude? You found it. This tiny, primitive jewel of a campground sits near two lakes—Snag Lake and Western Lake (the lower lake)—in a wooded area near Western Lakes, just outside of Naselle. Snag Lake, the area's feature, provides fishing for rainbow trout, brook trout, and cutthroat trout. No gas motors are permitted, so it is ideal for float tubes, prams, rowboats, or canoes (with electric motors permitted). There are some good hiking trails nearby, including a route that connects the two lakes. The lake and campground offer good views of Radar Ridge. It's a prime camp for travelers heading to the coast who want a day or two of privacy before they hit the crowds.

Campsites, facilities: There are five tent sites. Picnic tables and fire grills are provided. Vault toilets are available. There is no drinking water, and garbage must be packed out. Some facilities are wheelchair accessible. Leashed pets are permitted.

Reservations, fees: Reservations are not accepted. There is no fee for camping. Open May–November.

Directions: From Kelso/Longview on I-5, turn west on Highway 4 and drive 60 miles (near Naselle) to Milepost 3 and C-Line Road. Turn right (north) and head uphill on C-Line Road (two-lane gravel road), take the left fork at Naselle Youth Camp entrance, and drive 2.9 miles to C-2600 (gravel one-lane road). Turn left on Road C-2600 and drive 0.9 mile (after 0.4 mile it becomes C-Line Road) to C-2650. Turn right and drive 0.3 miles to the campground on the right at Western Lake.

Contact: Department of Natural Resources,

Pacific Cascade Region North, 360/577-2025, fax 360/274-4196, www.dnr.wa.gov.

123 SNAG LAKE

Scenic rating: 9

near Naselle

This is a classic little DNR camp on small Snag Lake—the kind of place time forgot. Any other clichés? No, seriously, time did forget this place. Very few people know about this spot.

Campsites, facilities: There are five tent sites. Picnic tables and fire grills are provided. Vault toilets are available. There is no drinking water, and garbage must be packed out. Some facilities are wheelchair accessible. Leashed pets are permitted.

Reservations, fees: Reservations are not accepted. There is no fee for camping. Open year-round.

Directions: From Kelso/Longview on I-5, turn west on Highway 4 and drive 60 miles (near Naselle) to Milepost 3 and C-Line Road. Turn right (north) and head uphill on C-Line Road (two-lane gravel road). Take the left fork at Naselle Youth Camp entrance, and drive 2.9 miles to C-2600 (gravel one-lane road). Turn left on Road C-2600 and drive 0.6 mile to C-2650. Turn right and drive 0.2 mile to the campground.

Contact: Department of Natural Resources, Pacific Cascade Region North, 360/577-2025, fax 360/274-4196, www.dnr.wa.gov.

124 SOU'WESTER LODGE

Scenic rating: 7

in Seaview on the Long Beach Peninsula

This one-of-a-kind place features a lodge that dates back to 1892, vintage trailers available for rent, and cottages. Various cultural events are held at the park throughout the year, including fireside evenings with theater and chamber music. The park covers three acres, provides beach access, and is one of the few sites in the immediate area that provides spots for tent camping. This park often attracts creative people such as musicians and artists, and some arrive for vacations in organized groups. It is definitely not for Howie and Ethel from Iowa. Fishing is a recreation option. The area features the Lewis and Clark Interpretive Center, a lighthouse, museums, fine dining, bicycle and boat rentals, bicycle and hiking trails, and bird sanctuaries. Additional facilities found within five miles of the park include an 18-hole golf course, a full-service marina, and a riding stable. The lodge was originally built for U.S. Senator Henry Winslow Corbett. Two side notes: Tch-Tch stands for "trailers, classic, hodge-podge." The park owners also boast of a "t'ink tank," which they say is not quite a think tank. Like I said, the place is unique—and management has a great sense of humor.

Campsites, facilities: There are 60 sites with full hookups (20 and 30 amps) for RVs of any length, 10 tent sites, a historic lodge, four cottages, and 12 1950s-style trailers in vintage condition. Some RV sites are pull-through. Picnic tables are provided at some sites. Restrooms with flush toilets and showers, drinking water, cable TV, modem access, coin laundry, a classic video library, picnic area with pavilion, and community fire pits and grills are available. Propane gas, dump station, a store, gas station, café, and ice are located within one mile. Boat-launching facilities are nearby. Leashed pets are permitted.

Reservations, fees: Reservations are accepted. Sites are $25.75–42.75 per night, plus $3–4 per person per night for more than two people. Some credit cards are accepted. Open year-round.

Directions: From Kelso/Longview on I-5, turn west on Highway 4 and drive 63 miles to U.S. 101. Turn left (south) on U.S. 101 and drive 13 miles to the junction with Highway 103

(flashing light). Turn left to stay on U.S. 101 and drive one block to Seaview Beach Access Road (38th Place). Turn right and drive toward the ocean. Look for the campground on the left.

Contact: Sou'Wester Lodge, 360/642-2542, www.souwesterlodge.com.

125 ILWACO KOA

Scenic rating: 5

near Fort Canby State Park

This 17-acre camp is about nine miles from the beach and includes a secluded area for tents. You'll find a boardwalk nearby, as well as the Lewis and Clark Museum, lighthouses, an amusement park, and fishing from a jetty or charter boats. The Washington State International Kite Festival is held in Long Beach the third week of August. The World Kite Museum and Hall of Fame, also in Long Beach, is open year-round. Additional facilities found within five miles of the campground include a maritime museum, hiking trails, and a nine-hole golf course. In my experience, attempts to phone this park were thwarted by a busy signal for weeks.

Campsites, facilities: There are 114 sites with full hookups for RVs of any length, a tent area for up to 50 tents, and four cabins. Some sites are pull-through. Picnic tables are provided. Restrooms with flush toilets and showers, drinking water, cable TV, propane gas, a dump station, recreation hall, seasonal organized activities and tours, a camp store, coin laundry, ice, and a playground are available. Leashed pets are permitted.

Reservations, fees: Reservations are accepted at 800/562-3258. Sites are $26–40 per night, plus $5 per person per night for more than two people, and $6.50 per extra vehicle per night. Some credit cards are accepted. Open mid-May–mid-October.

Directions: From Kelso/Longview on I-5, turn

west on Highway 4 and drive 63 miles to U.S. 101. Turn left (south) on U.S. 101 and drive 13 miles to the junction with Highway 103. The campground is located at the junction.
Contact: Ilwaco KOA, phone/fax 360/642-3292, www.koa.com.

126 FISHERMAN'S COVE RV PARK

Scenic rating: 7

near Fort Canby State Park

This five-acre park is located by the docks, near where the Pacific Ocean and the Columbia River meet. It has fishing access nearby and caters to anglers. Fish- and clam-cleaning facilities are available in the park. Beach access is approximately one mile away. A maritime museum, hiking trails, a full-service marina, and a riding stable are located within five miles of the park. About 15 percent of the sites are taken by monthly renters.

Campsites, facilities: There are 53 sites with full hookups (30 and 50 amps) for RVs of any length and two tent sites. Picnic tables are provided. Restrooms with flush toilets and coin showers, drinking water, cable TV, modem access, a dump station, and coin laundry are available. Propane gas, a gas station, store, and café are located within one mile. Boat docks, launching facilities, and rentals are nearby. Leashed pets are permitted.

Reservations, fees: Reservations are accepted. RV sites are $30 per night, tent sites are $15 per night. Credit cards are not accepted. Open year-round.

Directions: From Kelso/Longview on I-5, turn west on Highway 4 and drive 63 miles to U.S. 101. Turn left (south) on U.S. 101 and drive 13 miles to the junction with Highway 103. Turn right (north) on Highway 103 and drive two miles to Highway 100/Spruce Street exit. Turn right (south) and drive into the town of Ilwaco. At the junction of Spruce Street SW and 1st

Street, turn right (west) on Spruce Street and drive one block to 2nd Avenue SW. Turn left (south) on 2nd Avenue SW and drive four blocks south to the park on the right.
Contact: Fisherman's Cove RV Park, 360/642-3689.

127 CAPE DISAPPOINTMENT STATE PARK

Scenic rating: 10

near Ilwaco

This park covers 1,882 acres on the Long Beach Peninsula and is fronted by the Pacific Ocean. There is access to 27 miles of ocean beach and two lighthouses. The park contains old-growth forest, lakes, both freshwater and saltwater marshes, streams, and tidelands. It is the choice spot in the area for tent campers. There are two places to camp: a general camping area and the Lake O'Neil area, which offers sites right on the water. Highlights at the park include hiking trails and opportunities for surf, jetty, and ocean fishing. An interpretive center highlights the Lewis and Clark expedition as well as maritime and military history. North Head Lighthouse is open for touring. Colbert House Museum is open during the summer.

Campsites, facilities: There are 83 sites with full or partial hookups (20 and 30 amps) for tents or RVs of any length, 152 sites for tents or RVs of any length (no hookups), five primitive tent sites, three cabins, 14 yurts, and three vacation homes. Picnic tables and fire grills are provided. Restrooms with flush toilets and coin showers, drinking water, a dump station, boat ramp, dock (135 feet), a picnic area, interpretive activities, a horseshoe pit, athletic fields, a small store, and firewood are available. Some facilities are wheelchair accessible. Leashed pets are permitted.

Reservations, fees: Reservations are accepted at 888/CAMP-OUT (888/226-7688) or www.parks.wa.gov/reservations ($6.50–8.50 reservation fee). Sites are $21–28 per night, primitive tent sites are $14 per night, cabins and yurts are $55–60 per night, and vacation homes are $206–388 per night. Some credit cards are accepted. Open year-round.

Directions: From the junction of Highway 4 and Highway 103 (a flashing light, south of Nemah), turn west on Highway 103 (toward Ilwaco) and drive two miles to Ilwaco and Highway 100. Turn right and drive three miles to the park entrance on the right.

Contact: Cape Disappointment State Park, 360/642-3078; state park information, 360/902-8844, www.parks.wa.gov.

128 RIVER'S END RV PARK

Scenic rating: 6

near Fort Columbia State Park

This wooded park spreads over five acres and has riverside access. Salmon fishing is available here. Additional facilities found within five miles of the campground include marked bike trails and a full-service marina. Also nearby is Fort Columbia State Park.

Campsites, facilities: There are 75 sites with full or partial hookups (30 amps) for tents or RVs of any length. Some sites are pull-through. Picnic tables are provided, and fire pits are available at some sites. Restrooms with flush toilets and coin showers, drinking water, cable TV, a dump station, a recreation hall, coin laundry, firewood, a fish-cleaning station, and ice are available. Propane gas, a gas station, store, and café are located within one mile. Boat docks and launching facilities are nearby on the Columbia River. Leashed pets are permitted.

Reservations, fees: Reservations are accepted. Sites are $26 per night, plus $5 per person per night for more than two people. Credit cards are not accepted. Open April–late October.

Directions: From Kelso/Longview on I-5, turn west on Highway 4 and drive 60 miles to Highway 401. Turn left (south) on Highway 401 and drive 14 miles to the park entrance (just north of Chinook) on the left.

Contact: River's End Campground and RV Park, 360/777-8317.

129 MAUCH'S SUNDOWN RV PARK

Scenic rating: 5

near Fort Columbia State Park

This park has about 50 percent of the sites rented monthly, usually throughout the summer. The park covers four acres, has riverside access, and is in a wooded, hilly setting with grassy sites. Nearby fishing from shore is available. It's near Fort Columbia State Park.

Campsites, facilities: There are 44 sites with full or partial hookups (30 amps) for tents or RVs of any length. Some sites are pull-through. Small pets are permitted. Picnic tables are provided. No open fires are allowed. Restrooms with flush toilets and coin showers, drinking water, a dump station, cable TV, coin laundry, a convenience store, propane gas, and ice are available. A café is located within three miles. Boat docks and launching facilities are nearby on the Columbia River.

Reservations, fees: Reservations are accepted. Sites are $10–25 per night, plus $2 per person per night for more than two people. Credit cards are not accepted. Open year-round.

Directions: From Kelso/Longview on I-5, turn west on Highway 4 and drive 60 miles to Highway 401. Turn left (south) on Highway 401 and drive to U.S. 101. Take U.S. 101 to the right and continue for 0.5 mile (do not go over the bridge) to the park on the right.

Contact: Mauch's Sundown RV Park, 360/777-8713.

130 SKAMOKAWA VISTA PARK

🚶 🚲 🏊 🛶 🚤 ⛺ 🐎 🎣 🚐 ⛰️

Scenic rating: 7

near the Columbia River

This public camp covers 70 acres and features a half mile of sandy beach and a Lewis and Clark interpretive site. A short hiking trail is nearby. The camp also has nearby access to the Columbia River, where recreational options include fishing, swimming, and boating. Additional facilities found within five miles of the park include a full-service marina and tennis courts. In Skamokawa, River Life Interpretive Center stays open year-round.

Campsites, facilities: There are seven RV sites with full hookups, 24 sites with partial hookups for RVs of any length, nine sites for tents or RVs of any length (no hookups), four tent sites, and five yurts. Picnic tables and fire grills are provided. Restrooms with flush toilets and coin showers, drinking water, a dump station, firewood, tennis courts, basketball courts, and a playground are available. A café and ice are located within one mile. Boat docks, launching facilities, and canoe and kayak rentals are nearby. Leashed pets are permitted, with some restrictions.

Reservations, fees: Reservations are accepted. Tent sites are $18 per night, and RV sites are $21–28 per night. Some credit cards are accepted. Open year-round.

Directions: From Kelso/Longview on I-5, turn west on Highway 4 and drive 35 miles to Skamokawa. Continue west on Highway 4 for 0.5 mile to the park on the left.

Contact: Skamokawa Vista Park, Port of Wahkiakum No. 2, 360/795-8605, fax 360/795-8611.

OLYMPIC PENINSULA HIKING

© SCOTT LEONARD

BEST HIKES

There may be drier regions of Washington – the

Olympic Mountains get more than 200 inches a year – but the Olympic Peninsula is one of the United States' most unique places. Three distinct and beautiful environments grace this isolated and lightly inhabited peninsula.

On the west side is the Pacific Ocean and the Olympic Coast Wilderness, where picturesque sea stacks and tidal pools bless one of the West Coast's finest stretches of coastline. Protected by wilderness and wildlife designations, the Olympic Coast is environmentally rich. Bald eagles patrol the skies, while sea otters play in the surf. Trails run the length of the Olympic Coast: good day hikes, overnighters, and longer trips.

Farther inland are the area's famous rainforests: giant trees, and moss seemingly blanketing anything that will sit still for a minute. If you've never visited the Olympic rainforest, you're in for a treat. One of the country's few rainforests, the west side of the peninsula grows some of the earth's largest trees. Western hemlock, Sitka spruce, and western red cedar tower some 200-300 feet overhead, forming giant canopies over dense understories of vine maple, elderberry, devil's club, and salmonberry. On the rare dry spring or fall day, humidity hangs in the air, wetting everything it touches – even Gore-Tex. The Bogachiel, Hoh, and Quinault River Valleys are full of trails that explore this great area.

Finally, the wild and beautiful Olympic Mountains, with their subalpine meadows and flowing glaciers, which spread down the valleys for miles, producing distinctive U-shaped valleys. The Olympics are profoundly unique in that they have a circular shape, known as a radial formation. The river drainages start in the center of the range and flow outward. The mountains got their start as deposits of lava and sedimentation under the Pacific Ocean. Gradually they were bent out of shape by the Juan de Fuca plate colliding offshore with the continental plate. The light sedimentary rocks, driven below the heavier continental plate, eventually broke through and sprang like a cork to the surface, creating the circular shape. More recently, the Ice Age left its mark on the range. The Cordilleran ice sheet scraped past and around the mountains, creating the picturesque Hood Canal. To say the least, the Olympics are a great place to geek out on geology.

Several unique species call these forests home, including Roosevelt elk, Olympic salamanders, and Olympic marmots. Late summer in the high country is practically a bear mecca, when the sedate creatures gorge themselves into a stupor on ripe huckleberries. Of the Olympics' many rivers, the longest is the glacier-fed Elwha River, which once bore populations of all five Northwest salmon species. Also on the north peninsula are trails out of Hurricane Ridge, an outstanding visitors center at 6,000 feet.

The northeastern portion of the range is distinguishable by its relatively light rainfall: The mountains receive as little as 20 inches of annual rainfall – an anomaly in this rainy region. Most fronts move off the Pacific in a southwest to northeast direction, and as wet air from the ocean crosses the range, the water is squeezed out over the western side. By the time the air reaches the east side, much of the rain has fallen already, leaving the "rain shadow" dry. All of the retirees flocking to Sequim couldn't be happier. While this region is noticeably drier (tell that to someone hiking here in October), it has some extraordinary richness in landscape and forests.

Moving southward, the rest of the eastern side of the range is comprised of rivers dropping quickly from high mountain crests to the Hood Canal, including the Dosewallips, Duckabush, Hamma Hamma, and Skokomish Rivers. This area receives its fair share of rain, certainly more than the rain shadow.

Whether you're looking for a quiet stroll among tidal pools or a long, satisfying climb to an alpine summit, the Olympic Peninsula satisfies.

HIKING

HIKING

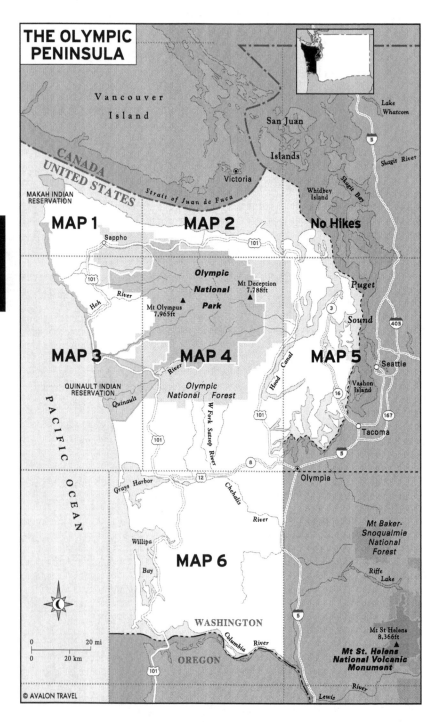

THE OLYMPIC
PENINSULA

Vancouver
Island

San Juan

Islands

Lake
Whatcom

CANADA
UNITED STATES

Strait of Juan de Fuca

Victoria

Whidbey
Island

Skagit Bay

Skagit River

5

MAKAH INDIAN
RESERVATION

MAP 1

MAP 2

No Hikes

Sappho

101

Olympic

National

Park

Mt Deception
7,788ft

Puget

3

Sound

405

River

Hoh

Mt Olympus
7,965ft

MAP 3

River

QUINAULT INDIAN
RESERVATION

Quinault

Olympic
National

Forest

MAP 4

W Fork Satsop River

101

MAP 5

Seattle

Vashon
Island

16

167

101

Hood Canal

Tacoma

5

PACIFIC

101

8

12

Grays Harbor

Chehalis

River

Olympia

OCEAN

Willipa

Bay

MAP 6

Mt Baker-
Snoqualmie
National
Forest

Riffe
Lake

WASHINGTON

5

0   20 mi
0   20 km

Columbia

River

OREGON

101

Mt St Helens
8,366ft

Mt St. Helens
National Volcanic
Monument

Lewis

River

© AVALON TRAVEL

Map 1

Hikes 1-4

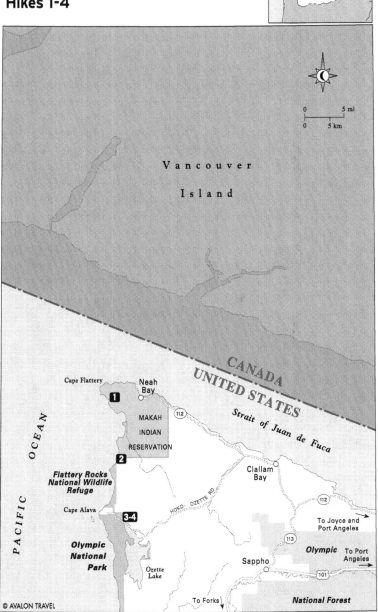

Map 2

Hikes 5-10

HIKING

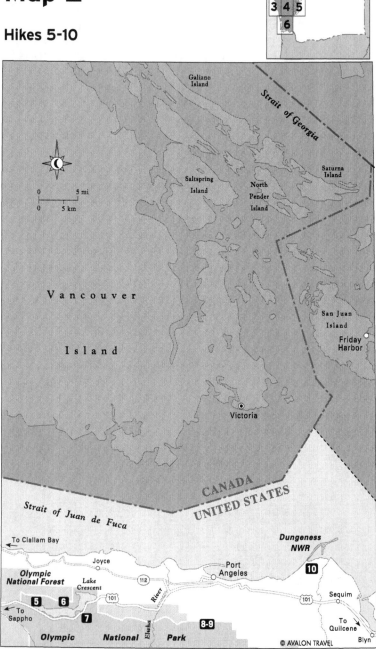

Map 3

Hikes 11-14

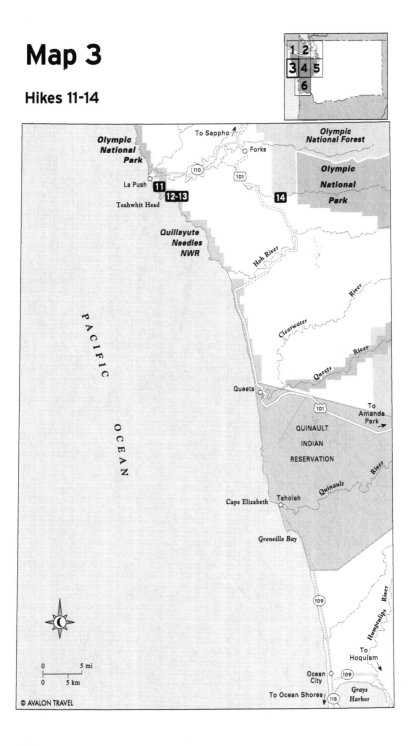

Map 4

Hikes 15-57

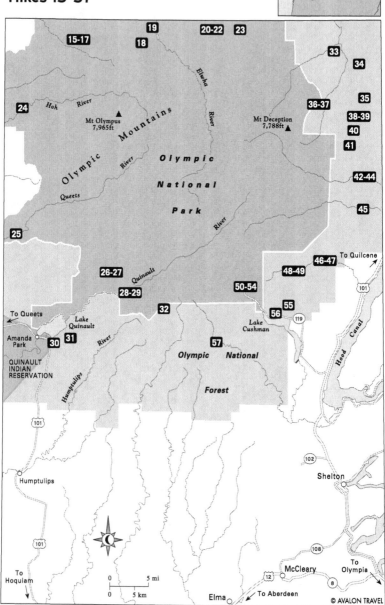

Map 5

Hike 58

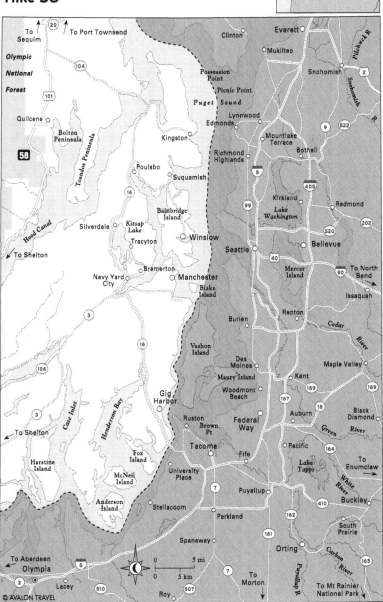

Map 6

Hikes 59-61

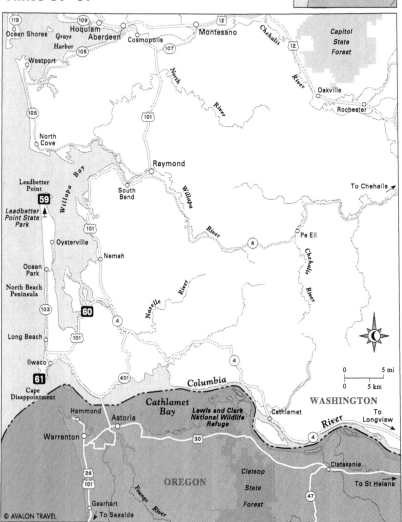

1 CAPE FLATTERY

1.5 mi/1.0 hr

northwest of Neah Bay on the Makah Indian
Reservation

A newly refurbished trail leads through great
coastal forest to one of the Washington Coast's
most scenic places. The Makah Nation rebuilt
Cape Flattery Trail several years back, taking
a dangerous, muddy trail to near perfection.
Four observation decks hover above sea cliffs
overlooking the cape, providing views of ocean
and wildlife. Birds and sea creatures flock to
the area year-round. During the spring and
fall, it's possible to sight gray whales.

Cape Flattery Trail works its way through
a coastal forest of large old-growth cedars and
firs. Many boardwalks and bridges along the
way keep feet dry on this once infamously
muddy trail. The trail pops out of the forest at
the cape, above the Olympic Coast National
Marine Sanctuary. The sanctuary designation
provides protection for numerous animals.
Scores of cormorants and tufted puffins make
their way in and out of their homes in the sea
cliffs. Below in the water, sea lions swim from
cove to cove on the prowl for a meal. From
mid-March through mid-April, Cape Flattery
is a prime location for spotting migrating gray
whales; binoculars are a must. Cape Flattery
may be a long way from the rest of Washington, but North America's most northwestern
point is awesome.

User Groups: Hikers and leashed dogs. No
horses or mountain bikes are allowed. No
wheelchair access.

Permits: This trail is accessible year-round.
A Makah Recreation Pass is required to park
here. An annual pass costs $10 and is available
at most businesses in Neah Bay.

Maps: For topographic maps, ask Green Trails
for No. 98S, Cape Flattery, or ask the USGS
for Cape Flattery.

Directions: From Port Angeles, drive 5 miles
west on U.S. 101 to Highway 112. Turn right
(north) onto Highway 112 and drive 63 miles

to Neah Bay. At the west end of town, turn
left on Cape Flattery Road and drive to Cape
Loop Road. Turn right and drive to the signed
trailhead at road's end.

Contact: Makah Tribe, P.O. Box 115, Neah
Bay, WA 98357, 360/645-2201.

2 SHI SHI BEACH

4.0-9.6 mi/2.0 hr-2 days

south of the Makah Indian Reservation in
Olympic National Park

Protected from development by wilderness
designations, more than 75 miles of Olympic
Coast remain in pristine condition, untamed
by humans. This rich habitat sustains a bio-
diversity that offers unparalleled opportunities for seeing wildlife. And its most beautiful
section lies here, from the wide, sandy shores
of Shi Shi Beach to the rugged sea stacks at
Point of the Arches.

The Makah Tribe recently began rebuild-
ing Shi Shi Beach Trail from its reservation,
providing new and easier access to this beach.
The trail travels 2 muddy miles through forest before breaking out onto Shi Shi Beach.
Two miles of beach stretching southward offer
great strolling, even when the weather fails
to cooperate (which is often). The beach is a
good point to turn around, for those looking
for a shorter hike.

Shi Shi Beach ends where Point of the Arches begins. Here, a large grouping of enormous
sea stacks spread out into the sea off a point.
Tidal pools abound here, offering excellent
chances for seeing starfish and urchins. Sea
otters often play in the water while bald eagles
soar overhead in perpetual wind.

The trip to Point of the Arches (4.8 miles)
can easily be done in one day, but camping
is a popular activity along Shi Shi. Permits,
however, must be obtained from the park service. Good sites are found regularly along the
shore. Water should be obtained at Petroleum
Creek (3.3 miles), which must be forded to

HIKING

© SCOTT LEONARD

The views along the Olympic Coast are first-rate.

access Point of the Arches. It is an easy crossing made easier by low tides. Traveling south of Point of the Arches brings hikers to Cape Alava and the Ozette Triangle, not a recommended approach.

User Groups: Hikers only. No dogs, horses, or mountain bikes are allowed. No wheelchair access.

Permits: This trail is accessible year-round. A Makah Recreation Pass is required to park here. An annual pass costs $10 and is available at most businesses in Neah Bay. Overnight stays within the national park require backcountry camping permits, which are available at the Wilderness Information Center in Port Angeles.

Maps: For a map of Olympic National Park, contact the Outdoor Recreation Information Center at the downtown Seattle REI. For topographic maps, ask Green Trails for No. 98S, Cape Flattery, or ask the USGS for Makah Bay and Ozette.

Directions: From Port Angeles, drive 5 miles west on U.S. 101 to Highway 112. Turn right (north) onto Highway 112 and drive 63 miles to Neah Bay. At the west end of town, turn

left on Cape Flattery Road and drive 3 miles to Hobuck Beach Road. Turn left, cross the Waatch River, and drive to Sooes River. Here, Hobuck Beach Road becomes Sooes Beach Road. Cross the Sooes River and drive to the clearly marked trailhead on the right. The parking area here is for day use only. Overnight visitors can pay local homeowners (who have signs advertising parking) to park on their private property (where their cars will be secure).

Contact: Makah Tribe, P.O. Box 115, Neah Bay, WA 98357, 360/645-2201; Olympic Wilderness Information Center, located in the Olympic National Park, Wilderness Information Center, 3002 Mount Angeles Rd., Port Angeles, WA 98362-6798, 360/565-3130.

🖪 OZETTE TRIANGLE
9.0 mi/1-2 days 🏃1 ⛰10

northwest of Forks in Olympic National Park

BEST (

No route in Washington claims a heritage quite like the Ozette Triangle. Three trails form this triangle, with the leg along the beach home to Wedding Rocks. Wedding Rocks bear petroglyphs carved by Native Americans hundreds of years ago. Their illustrations depict orcas, the sun and moon, and even a ship of explorers. Even without Wedding Rocks, this beach would be highly popular. Large sea stacks set among larger islands, countless tide pools brimming with sea life, bald eagles aplenty, and possible sightings of gray whales make this a pleasurable trip.

Cape Alava and Sand Point Trails lead to the beach from Lake Ozette. Each trail is 3 miles long, flat, and forested by big trees. Boardwalk covers most of each trail and can be slippery; watch out! Starting on the northern route (Cape Alava) will drop you off at a coastline full of sea stacks and wildlife. The numerous campsites near Cape Alava require reservations (from the Port Angeles Wilderness Information Center) because of large summer crowds.

Head south from Cape Alava among countless tidal pools, brimming with life. Wedding Rocks are 1 mile south from Cape Alava, scattered around a jutting point; they are above the high tide line. The site is legendary for attracting cultists and other New Age folk, but you're more likely to run across sea otters floating offshore in beds of kelp. The beach extends south 2 miles before intersecting Sand Point Trail. Here, a large headland juts into the sea and provides an excellent vantage point from atop it. The Ozette Triangle is rightfully one of the peninsula's most beautiful hikes.

User Groups: Hikers only. No dogs, horses, or mountain bikes are allowed. No wheelchair access.

Permits: This trail is accessible year-round. There is a $1 daily parking fee here, payable at the trailhead. Overnight stays within the national park require backcountry camping permits, which are available at the Wilderness Information Center in Port Angeles.

Maps: For a map of Olympic National Park, contact the Outdoor Recreation Information Center at the downtown Seattle REI. For topographic maps, ask Green Trails for No. 135S, Ozette, or ask the USGS for Ozette.

Directions: From Port Angeles, drive east 5 miles on U.S. 101 to Highway 112. Turn right (west) and drive 49 miles to Hoko/Ozette Lake

HIKING

© SCOTT LEONARD

tide pools at Cape Alava along the Ozette Triangle

Road. Turn left and drive 21 miles to the well-signed trailhead at Lake Ozette.

Contact: Olympic National Park, Wilderness Information Center, 3002 Mount Angeles Rd., Port Angeles, WA 98362, 360/565-3100.

4 NORTH WILDERNESS BEACH

19.7 mi one-way/2-3 days 🏃3 ⛰10

west of Forks in Olympic National Park

This stretch of the Olympic coastline is one of the wildest and most scenic beaches anywhere in the United States. North Wilderness Beach features countless tidal pools packed with creatures crawling, swimming, or simply affixed to the rocks. Unremitting waves roll in through the fog to break apart on the sea stacks jutting into the Pacific Ocean. Sea otters, eagles, herons, cormorants, and ducks are all likely sightings.

Access to North Wilderness Beach Route is via Sandpoint Trail, 3 miles of virgin coastal forest. The travelway heads south along sandy beaches, but at times may test ankles with stretches of cobbles and boulders. Several times the trail is driven on land because of impassibility around a point. Circular signs (painted like bull's-eyes and visible from the shore) indicate these points. Also, it is important to carry a tide table, as 12 sections of trail require passage at low or medium tides. Green Trails maps indicate points that require passages during low tides.

The route encounters the tall cliffs of Yellow Bank (4.5 miles). A pair of memorials stand along the route; Norwegian Memorial (9.9 miles), marked by an obelisk, and Chilean Memorial (16.5 miles). The travelway crosses Cedar Creek (11.3 miles), a necessary ford, and rounds Cape Johnson (15 miles). South of Cape Johnson is Hole in the Wall, a rock formation forming a natural arch, where hikers can capture a postcard moment. The route ends at the sea stacks of Rialto Beach.

Throughout the route, camping is plentiful, with numerous sites on the shore. Campfies are not permitted along the beach between Wedding Rocks (north of Sand Point) and Yellow Banks. Elsewhere, be sure to gather only driftwood from the beach.

User Groups: Hikers only. No dogs, horses, or mountain bikes are allowed. No wheelchair access.

Permits: This trail is accessible year-round. There is a $1 daily parking fee here, payable at the trailhead. Reservations are required for camping between Norwegian Memorial and Point of the Arches May 1 through September 30. Overnight stays within the national park require backcountry camping permits, which are available at the Wilderness Information Center in Port Angeles.

Maps: For a map of Olympic National Park, contact the Outdoor Recreation Information Center at the downtown Seattle REI. For topographic maps, ask Green Trails for No. 130S, Lake Ozette, or ask the USGS for Ozette, Allens Bay, and La Push.

Directions: From Port Angeles, drive east 5 miles on U.S. 101 to Highway 112. Turn right (west) and drive 49 miles to Hoko/Ozette Lake Road. Turn left and drive 21 miles to the well-signed trailhead at Lake Ozette.

Contact: Olympic National Park, Wilderness Information Center, 3002 Mount Angeles Rd., Port Angeles, WA 98362, 360/565-3100.

5 PYRAMID MOUNTAIN

7.0 mi/3.5 hr 🏃3 ⛰6

north of Lake Crescent in Olympic National Park

Pyramid Mountain Trail provides a good workout through old-growth forest culminating at a wonderful cabin lookout. From the top, peer out over the Strait of Juan de Fuca to Canada and over Lake Crescent to the Olympics. The lookout was built during World War II so the army could watch for incoming enemy aircraft. Fortunately, none arrived, but the lookout remained. The cabin on stilts perches atop the 3,100-foot peak, not high by Olympic standards, but good enough to work up a sweat on the way up.

Pyramid Mountain Trail starts off in a previously logged forest but soon enters old-growth forest. Mixed with the large conifers are numerous Pacific madrona, the Northwest's distinctive broad-leaved evergreen. Madrona is known for its uniquely papery bark that comes off in ragged shreds to reveal fine, smooth wood. These handsome trees produce small, bell-shaped flowers in the spring. Madrona trees deserve close inspection and always garner admiration.

The trail climbs through forest, crossing June Creek, which often runs below ground at this spot. It's a good idea to bring your own water on this hike, especially on warm days. The trail eventually reaches the ridgeline, where devastating clear-cuts have revealed views of the strait. After several false summits, the trail finally reaches the lookout. Be a bit careful up here; the north side of the mountain features a precipitous drop. The views extend in every direction. Lake Crescent is a beautiful green jewel to the south, while the strait is wide and large to the north.

User Groups: Hikers only. No dogs, horses, or mountain bikes are allowed. No wheelchair access.

Permits: This trail is accessible April–October. Parking and access are free. Overnight stays within the national park require backcountry camping permits, which are available at the Wilderness Information Center in Port Angeles.

Maps: For a map of Olympic National Park, contact the Outdoor Recreation Information Center at the downtown Seattle REI. For topographic maps, ask Green Trails for No. 101, Lake Crescent, or ask the USGS for Lake Crescent.

Directions: From Port Angeles, drive west 28 miles on U.S. 101 to North Shore Road. Turn right and drive about 3 miles to the well-signed trailhead on the left side of the road.

Contact: Olympic National Park, Wilderness Information Center, 3002 Mount Angeles Rd., Port Angeles, WA 98362, 360/565-3100.

6 SPRUCE RAILROAD
8.0 mi/4.0 hr   🏃₁ ⛰₉

north shore of Lake Crescent in Olympic National Park

Anyone who has ever navigated the twisty section of U.S. 101 as it passes Lake Crescent knows the beauty of the emerald lake. With lush green forests and high mountain ridges encircling the waters, Lake Crescent often stands out in the memories of passing motorists. That is to say nothing of the memories it leaves with hikers who walk the shores of Lake Crescent on the Spruce Railroad Trail.

Four miles of trail edge the lake along a former railroad built by the U.S. Army. This rail route once carried high-quality spruce timber to Seattle and eastward for production of World War I airplanes. Metal eventually replaced wood in aircraft production and the army sold the route, allowing the railway to be successfully converted into a level, easy-to-walk trail. The highlight is Devil's Punchbowl, 1.1 miles from the east trailhead. Here, a small cove from the lake is ringed by cliffs of pillow basalt. The depth of this popular swimming hole is reportedly more than 300 feet. Spruce Railroad Trail continues another 3 miles below towering cliffs where Pacific madrona cling to the walls. Lush forest covers parts of the trail, but Lake Crescent rarely leaves your sight. A trailhead exists at the west end, also. This hike is extremely well suited for families and for the off-season. It's a local winter favorite.

User Groups: Hikers, horses, and bicycles allowed. No dogs are allowed. No wheelchair access.

Permits: This trail is accessible year-round. Parking and access are free. Overnight stays within the national park require backcountry camping permits, which are available

HIKING

HIKING

at the Wilderness Information Center in Port Angeles.

Maps: For a map of Olympic National Park, contact the Outdoor Recreation Information Center at the downtown Seattle REI. For topographic maps, ask Green Trails for No. 101, Lake Crescent, or ask the USGS for Lake Crescent.

Directions: From Port Angeles, drive west 28 miles on U.S. 101 to North Shore Road. Turn right and drive 5 miles to the well-signed trailhead.

Contact: Olympic National Park, Wilderness Information Center, 3002 Mount Angeles Rd., Port Angeles, WA 98362, 360/565-3100.

🄷 MARYMERE FALLS
1.4 mi/1.0 hr

south of Lake Crescent in Olympic National Park

BEST (

Marymere Falls Trail offers hikers of all ages and abilities a great view of the Olympics' best waterfall. A short stroll through old forest and a climb up a large series of crib steps presents visitors with a vantage point well positioned for the showcase cascade. Falls Creek shoots over Marymere Falls and tumbles more than 100 feet. With adequate flow, the creek plummets so fiercely that surrounding trees and ferns sway. A delicate mist covers all who lean over the railing. Marymere is a beautiful spot and is popular in the summer with the many people passing by on U.S. 101. Ferns and mosses grow upon everything in the forest, a great example of what the Olympic forests are all about. The route starts at Storm King Ranger Station, follows the Barnes Creek Trail for 0.5 mile, then cuts off by crossing Barnes Creek and Falls Creek before ascending to the viewpoint.

User Groups: Hikers only. No dogs, horses, or mountain bikes are allowed. No wheelchair access.

Permits: This trail is accessible year-round. Permits are not required. Parking and access are free.

Maps: For a map of Olympic National Park, contact the Outdoor Recreation Information Center at the downtown Seattle REI. For topographic maps, ask Green Trails for No. 101, Lake Crescent, or ask the USGS for Lake Crescent.

Directions: From Port Angeles, drive west 20 miles on U.S. 101 to the well-signed Storm King Ranger Station. Turn right and drive 200 yards to Lake Crescent Road. Turn right for the trailhead at Storm King Ranger Station.

Contact: Olympic National Park, Wilderness Information Center, 3002 Mount Angeles Rd., Port Angeles, WA 98362, 360/565-3100.

🄸 HEATHER PARK/MOUNT ANGELES
10.0 mi one-way/5.5 hr

south of Port Angeles in Olympic National Park

A popular route for Port Angeles visitors, Heather Park Trail delivers grand views into the Olympics from along windswept ridges. Meadows are the name of the game along the upper sections. An outstanding parkland basin is found at Heather Park, while several accessible peaks offer views stretching over the heart of the Olympic Range. The route can also be completed from Hurricane Ridge Visitor Center, a less strenuous but busier choice.

Heather Park Trail leaves Heart o' the Hills in pleasant but unspectacular second-growth forest and climbs steadily to timberline and Heather Park (4.1 miles). The wide-open basin rests between the pinnacles of First Peak and Second Peak. Meadows of heather and lupine fill in the voids between scattered subalpine fir trees, and several campsites are to be had. This is a good turnaround point.

Heather Park Trail continues, climbing below the base of Mount Angeles (6 miles), whose summit is accessible by an easy social trail. Beyond, the trail drops to a junction with Sunrise Trail (6.3 miles), a highly used route that leads west to Hurricane Ridge Visitor Center. It's 3.5 miles of ridgeline hiking through open forest and meadows. Sunrise Trail gains less elevation and has its own social trail to the top of Mount Angeles. Campfires are not allowed at Heather Park.

User Groups: Hikers and horses. No dogs or mountain bikes are allowed. No wheelchair access.

Permits: This trail is accessible mid-June–October. Parking and access are free. Overnight stays within the national park require backcountry camping permits, which are available at the Wilderness Information Center in Port Angeles.

Maps: For a map of Olympic National Park, contact the Outdoor Recreation Information Center at the downtown Seattle REI. For topographic maps, ask Green Trails for No. 103, Port Angeles, and No. 135, Mount Angeles, or ask the USGS for Port Angeles and Mount Angeles.

Directions: From Port Angeles, drive north 2 miles on Race Street as it turns into Mount Angeles Road. Veer right at the well-signed fork and continue on Mount Angeles Road 5 miles to the trailhead immediately prior to the national park entrance booth. The trailhead is down a short access road.

Contact: Olympic National Park, Wilderness Information Center, 3002 Mount Angeles Rd., Port Angeles, WA 98362, 360/565-3100.

9 KLAHHANE RIDGE

13.0 mi/6.5 hr

south of Port Angeles in Olympic National Park

Klahhane Ridge Trail offers much more than just Klahhane Ridge. For starters, the trail passes Lake Angeles, one of the peninsula's larger subalpine lakes, set beneath cliffs. Talk about picturesque. Second, it makes an outstanding loop when combined with Mount Angeles Trail. This 12.9-mile round-trip samples all of the best of the North Olym-

pics. And the trail leads out along Klahhane Ridge, a place where open meadows and small trees give way to sweeping views of the interior Olympics. It may well be the best sampler of the Olympics around.

Klahhane Ridge Trail leaves Heart o' the Hills and climbs steadily through forest to Lake Angeles (3.7 miles). The lake is very popular with visitors to the North Peninsula, particularly on weekends. One would think the steep trip would weed folks out, but apparently not enough. A few camps are found around the lake. The trail continues up to Klahhane Ridge (5 miles), where distant vistas make their appearance, extending in every direction. The cities of Port Angeles and Victoria are visible to the north. Klahhane Ridge Trail ends at a junction with Mount Angeles Trail (6.5 miles), where turning north takes you through spectacular Heather Park and back to Heart o' the Hills.

User Groups: Hikers and horses. No dogs or mountain bikes are allowed. No wheelchair access.

Permits: This trail is accessible mid-June–October. Parking and access are free. Overnight stays within the national park require backcountry camping permits, which are available at the Wilderness Information Center in Port Angeles.

Maps: For a map of Olympic National Park, contact the Outdoor Recreation Information Center at the downtown Seattle REI. For topographic maps, ask Green Trails for No. 103, Port Angeles, and No. 135, Mount Angeles, or ask the USGS for Port Angeles and Mount Angeles.

Directions: From Port Angeles, drive north 2 miles on Race Street as it turns into Mount Angeles Road. Veer right at the well-signed fork and continue on Mount Angeles Road 5 miles to the trailhead immediately prior to the national park entrance booth. The trailhead is down a short road on the right.

Contact: Olympic National Park, Wilderness Information Center, 3002 Mount Angeles Rd., Port Angeles, WA 98362, 360/565-3100.

HIKING

10 DUNGENESS SPIT

10.0 mi/5.0 hr

north of Sequim on the northeast tip of the
Olympic Peninsula

BEST (

Set within Dungeness National Wildlife Refuge, Dungeness Spit is undoubtedly one of the state's premier sites for watching wildlife. The refuge hosts a rich and diverse ecosystem that is home to birds, critters of land and sea, and numerous fish and shellfish. The trail is more of a walk on a great beach than it is a traditional hike.

Dungeness Spit juts into the Strait of Juan de Fuca 5.5 miles, creating a quiet harbor and bay of tide flats. The spit is constantly growing, as nearby bluffs erode sandy sediments into the strait. At the end of the spit stands a historic lighthouse that was built in 1857 and is still open to the public.

The refuge sees more than 250 species of birds each year—mainly shorebirds and waterfowl, but some migratory and some permanent residents. It's definitely a bird-watcher's dream. More than 50 species of mammals of both land and sea live here, too. Harbor seals occasionally use the tip of the spit as a pup-raising site. In the bay, eelgrass beds provide a nursery for young salmon and steelhead adjusting to saltwater. This is a wonderful place to enjoy regional wildlife.

User Groups: Hikers only. No dogs or mountains bikes are allowed. The trail is wheelchair accessible (to several lookouts, not the spit).

Permits: Most of this area is accessible year-round (some parts are closed seasonally to protect wildlife feeding and nesting). The entrance fee is $3 per family daily. Admission is free with a federal duck stamp, a Golden Eagle Pass, a Golden Age Pass, or a Golden Access passport.

Maps: For a topographic map, ask the USGS for Dungeness.

Directions: From U.S. 101, go just west of Sequim and turn north on Kitchen-Dick Road. Continue for 3 miles to the Dungeness Recreation Area. Go through the recreation area to the refuge parking lot at the end of the road. The well-marked trailhead is located immediately prior to the parking area.

Contact: Dungeness National Wildlife Refuge, Washington Maritime NWR Complex, 33 South Barr Rd., Port Angeles, WA 98362, 360/457-8451.

11 SECOND BEACH

2.4 mi/2.0 hr

south of La Push on the central Olympic Coast

Second Beach is a place to do some thinking. Sit and stare at the many sea stacks out among the waves. Watch waves crash through the large archway to the north. Spy eagles and gulls tangling high overhead. During the months of March, April, and October you may glimpse migrating whales not far offshore. When you tire of resting, walk along the sandy beach. It is in pristine condition, save for a little garbage that floats in from the ocean. Well over a mile long, Second Beach provides lots to see: driftwood, crabs, eagles, sea otters, and who knows what else. The trail down to the beach (0.7 mile) is easy to negotiate; it's flat and wide the whole way save for the last few hundred yards. A wide pile of driftwood stands between the trail and beach, requiring a bit of scrambling, but it's nothing much. Second Beach is well worth a couple of extra hours for anyone on the way to La Push.

User Groups: Hikers and leashed dogs. No horses or mountain bikes are allowed. No wheelchair access.

Permits: This trail is accessible year-round. Permits are not required. Parking and access are free.

Maps: For a map of Olympic National Park, contact the Outdoor Recreation Information Center at the downtown Seattle REI. For topographic maps, ask Green Trails for No. 163S, La Push, or ask the USGS for Toleak Point.

Directions: From Port Angeles, drive west 54 miles on U.S. 101 to La Push Road (Highway 110; just before the town of Forks). Turn right and drive 8 miles to a Y, where the road splits. Stay left, on La Push Road, and drive 4.5 miles to the signed trailhead on the left.

Contact: Olympic National Park, Wilderness Information Center, 3002 Mount Angeles Rd., Port Angeles, WA 98362, 360/565-3100.

12 THIRD BEACH
2.6 mi/2.0-3.0 hr   🏃‍1 ⛰5

south of La Push on the central Olympic Coast

Snaking its way through a nice lowland forest, Third Beach Trail accesses a long strip of extravagant Olympic coast. The beach is wide and sandy for nearly its entire length, well over a mile, and bends inward slightly to make a crescent. The resulting bay was named Strawberry Bay for the ubiquitous strawberry plant in the coastal forests. Tall, rocky cliffs mark the north end of the crescent and are impassable, no matter your skill level. As you look to the south, beyond Taylor Point, a number of sea stacks are visible in the distance. It's easy for hikers of all abilities to enjoy all this, as the trail down to the beach loses very little elevation and is wide and well maintained. As you hike through the forest, the increasing roar of the ocean signals your progress, as does the increasing size of massive cedar trees. Although some may say that Second Beach is more scenic, Third Beach is a great trip as well.

User Groups: Hikers and leashed dogs. No horses or mountain bikes are allowed. No wheelchair access.

Permits: This trail is accessible year-round. Permits are not required. Parking and access are free.

Maps: For a map of Olympic National Park, contact the Outdoor Recreation Information Center at the downtown Seattle REI. For topographic maps, ask Green Trails for No.

163S, La Push, or ask the USGS for Toleak Point.

Directions: From Port Angeles, drive west 54 miles on U.S. 101 to La Push Road (Highway 110; just before the town of Forks). Turn right and drive 8 miles to a Y, where the road splits. Stay left, on La Push Road, and drive 3 miles to the signed trailhead on the left.

Contact: Olympic National Park, Wilderness Information Center, 3002 Mount Angeles Rd., Port Angeles, WA 98362, 360/565-3100.

13 CENTRAL WILDERNESS BEACH
16.7 mi one-way/2 days   🏃‍3 ⛰10

south of La Push on the central Olympic Coast

As beautiful as the other long beach routes, Third Beach to Oil City provides a bit more of a hiking challenge. This is the South Coast Beach Travelway, and it requires that several overland bypasses and three creeks be crossed. Not that any of these obstacles is too much to overcome. The South Travelway has some great scenery, including Giants Graveyard, Alexander Island, and an extraordinary abundance of birds and sea life. Bald eagles and blue herons regularly sweep the shores in search of dinner, while sea otters play it cool, reclining in the water and eating shellfish off their stomachs.

Access the route via Third Beach, hiking south above Taylor's Point, impassable along the water. Many times hikers must avoid impassable coastline by hiking trails on land; it's important to carry a map to properly identify these sections. Five miles of great beach present views of Giants Graveyard (4.2 miles), Strawberry Point (6.5 miles), and Toleak Point (7.2 miles), appropriate images of the rugged coastline.

The middle section of Southern Travelway requires fords of Falls Creek (8.5 miles), Goodman Creek (9 miles), and Mosquito Creek (11.5 miles). If it's been wet recently, expect them

HIKING

to be difficult. The lower section of Southern Travelway uses beach, with Alexander Island offshore, and a long 3.5-mile overland route bypassing Hoh Head. This leaves you just north of the trailhead at Oil City (16.7 miles), near the mouth of the Hoh River. Campsites are spread throughout the trip, usually tucked away on shore but visible from the beach.

User Groups: Hikers only. No dogs, horses, or mountain bikes are allowed. No wheelchair access.

Permits: This trail is accessible year-round. Permits are not required. Parking and access are free.

Maps: For a map of Olympic National Park, contact the Outdoor Recreation Information Center at the downtown Seattle REI. For topographic maps, ask Green Trails for No. 163, La Push, or ask the USGS for Toleak Point and Hoh Head.

Directions: From Port Angeles, drive west 54 miles on U.S. 101 to La Push Road (Highway 110; just before the town of Forks). Turn right and drive 8 miles to a Y, where the road splits. Stay left, on La Push Road, and drive 3 miles to the signed trailhead on the left.

Contact: Olympic National Park, Wilderness Information Center, 3002 Mount Angeles Rd., Port Angeles, WA 98362, 360/565-3100.

14 BOGACHIEL RIVER
41.6 mi/4 days 👫3 ⛺9

southeast of Forks in Olympic National Park

Let the masses drive the road up the Hoh River and visit the overpopulated Hoh River Valley. Follow the wiser hikers who access the Bogachiel River for the same gargantuan trees covered in moss, the same cascading streams filled with juvenile salmon, and the same forests teeming with wildlife—but with considerably more solitude.

While the Bogachiel River Trail is a fine day hike, the route increasingly gets wilder as it heads into the mountains, making it an outstanding overnight trip. Beginning along an old logging road, the trail soon enters the national park and virgin rainforest (2 miles). Massive trees fill the forests, awash in green from the heavy rains off the Pacific Ocean. The mostly flat trail moves in and out of the forest, regularly nearing the river and passing camps. Maintenance on the trail often fails to keep up with the regular washouts from heavy winter rains, so be ready for some route-finding along the way.

After Flapjack Camp (10 miles), Bogachiel River Trail leaves the main branch of the river and slowly climbs with North Fork Bogachiel River toward High Divide. This is the trail's best section, where at 15 Mile Shelter (14.5 miles) the river surges through a deep gorge. After Hyak Camp (17.6 miles) and 21 Mile Camp (20.8 miles), the trail overlooks the Bogachiel and vast meadows. Those who plan for it can connect this trail to Mink Lake or Deer Lake Trails (25.5 miles) for through-hikes via the Sol Duc Valley. This route is truly wild country, where elk and ancient trees far outnumber bipeds.

User Groups: Hikers and horses. No dogs or mountain bikes are allowed. No wheelchair access.

Permits: This trail is usually accessible year-round (up to about 15 Mile Camp, where the winter snowpack becomes quite deep). A federal Northwest Forest Pass is required to park here. Overnight stays within the national park require backcountry camping permits, which are available at the Wilderness Information Center in Port Angeles.

Maps: For a map of Olympic National Park, contact the Outdoor Recreation Information Center at the downtown Seattle REI. For topographic maps, ask Green Trails for No. 132, Spruce Mountain, No. 133, Mount Tom, and No. 134, Mount Olympus, or ask the USGS for Reade Hill, Indian Pass, Hunger Mountain, Slide Peak, and Bogachiel Peak.

Directions: From Forks, drive south 6 miles on U.S. 101 to Undie Road. Turn left (east) and drive 4 miles to the trailhead at road's end.

Contact: Olympic National Park, Wilderness Information Center, 3002 Mount Angeles Rd., Port Angeles, WA 98362, 360/565-3100.

15 SOL DUC FALLS/ LOVER'S LANE

5.6 mi/3.0 hr

south of Lake Crescent in Olympic National Park

This is not an exclusive trail for sweethearts. Sure, a couple in love are apt to find this the perfect stroll. But those even more likely to find this a great trail are those who love an easy hike along a great trail through the forest. That group includes couples and kids, seasoned hikers, singles, groups, and anyone between. Add to the pleasure of Lover's Lane the excitement of Sol Duc Falls, one of the Olympics' premier photo ops, and you have a widely agreed-upon fun hike.

The trail departs from the Sol Duc Hot Springs Resort, where folks can relax weary muscles in a number of springs, and starts off into an old-growth forest. The Sol Duc River is never far away and calls out with its incessant rushing. The trail crosses three streams on easy-to-negotiate footbridges, each a nice interruption in the scenery.

Before 3 miles are underfoot, the trail arrives at Sol Duc Falls. Here, the river makes an abrupt turn and cascades from three notches into a narrow gorge. The forest is incredibly green in these parts and moss seems omnipresent. Regardless of your romantic pursuits, Lover's Lane is a trail for all.

User Groups: Hikers only. No dogs, horses, or mountain bikes are allowed. No wheelchair access.

Permits: This trail is accessible year-round. A federal National Parks Pass is required to park here.

Maps: For a map of Olympic National Park, contact the Outdoor Recreation Information Center at the downtown Seattle REI. For topographic maps, ask Green Trails for

Sol Duc Falls is a popular and easy hike to access.

No. 133, Mount Tom, or ask the USGS for Bogachiel Peak.

Directions: From Port Angeles, drive west 30 miles on U.S. 101 to well-signed Sol Duc Hot Springs Road. Turn left (south) and drive 14 miles to the trailhead at road's end.

Contact: Olympic National Park, Wilderness Information Center, 3002 Mount Angeles Rd., Port Angeles, WA 98362, 360/565-3100.

16 SEVEN LAKES BASIN LOOP

20.1 mi/2 days

south of Lake Crescent in Olympic National Park

This is one of the peninsula's greatest hikes, a exceptional journey into one of the best lake basins in Washington. This is one of the peninsula's greatest hikes, an exceptional journey into the heart of the Olympic Mountains. The trip revels in the views of High Divide and

Seven Lakes Basin offers some of the Olympic Mountains' best lake fishing.

offers great camping and fishing in the Seven Lakes Basin. The divide is more than 5,000 feet in elevation, making this meadow territory. Views open wide to the south, revealing Mount Olympus at close range. Wildlife is plentiful in this part of the park, where regular sightings include black bear, ravens, Roosevelt elk, picas, and Olympic marmots. If you have a camera, you'd best bring it. During July, wildflowers are prolific and difficult not to trample underfoot.

The trail makes a loop by heading up the Sol Duc River to High Divide, then coming back via Deer Lake and Canyon Creek. The trail up the Sol Duc River is a trip through pristine old-growth forests along a river that makes constant cascades and falls. After the Appleton Pass Trail cuts off at 4.8 miles, the Sol Duc Trail climbs vigorously up Bridge Creek to High Divide. Camps are frequent,

but Sol Duc Park and Heart Lake are highly recommended.

From High Divide, Mount Olympus and the Bailey Range ring the Hoh Valley. Head north on the High Divide to the Seven Lakes Basin, a series of not seven but actually eight subalpine lakes. The lakes lie on a gentle slope facing the north, meaning snow can linger well into July. To curb overuse, campsites here must be reserved with the Wilderness Information Center. The trail leaves the basin and drops to Deer Lake. Here, one trail leads down to the trailhead via Canyon Creek, another long string of waterfalls.

User Groups: Hikers only. No dogs, horses, or mountain bikes are allowed. No wheelchair access.

Permits: This trail is accessible July–October. A National Parks Pass is required to park here. Overnight stays within the national park require backcountry camping permits, which are available at the Wilderness Information Center in Port Angeles.

Maps: For a map of Olympic National Park, contact the Outdoor Recreation Information Center at the downtown Seattle REI. For topographic maps, ask Green Trails for No. 133, Mount Tom, and No. 134, Mount Olympus, or ask the USGS for Bogachiel Peak and Mount Carrie.

Directions: From Port Angeles, drive west 30 miles on U.S. 101 to well-signed Sol Duc Hot Springs Road. Turn left (south) and drive 14 miles to the trailhead at road's end.

Contact: Olympic National Park, Wilderness Information Center, 3002 Mount Angeles Rd., Port Angeles, WA 98362, 360/565-3100.

17 APPLETON PASS
14.8 mi/8.0 hr

south of Lake Crescent in Olympic National Park

Appleton Pass Trail provides a crossing from the Sol Duc to the Elwha drainages. It's also an alternate route up to Boulder Lake and a great entry to acres of open meadows and parkland. The Sol Duc Valley is full of waterfalls, and this route passes by several of them.

From the trailhead, the route uses Sol Duc River Trail for the first 4.8 miles. Along the way is Sol Duc Falls, a popular day hike. This section of trail passes through cool forests of old-growth timber. Appleton Pass Trail climbs steeply via a tiring number of switchbacks to the pass. Just before the pass, it reaches the timberline, and spacious meadows break out in abundance.

The diminutive Oyster Lake is a short side trail from the pass and well recommended. Mount Appleton stands to the north, cloaked in wildflowers and heather during the early summer. For through-hikers, the trail continues beyond the pass down the South Fork of Boulder Creek. Just before the trail converges with North Fork Trail, Boulder Creek makes a tremendous leap into a deep pool, followed by several smaller cascades—a wonderful sight.

User Groups: Hikers and horses. No dogs or mountain bikes are allowed. No wheelchair access.

Permits: This trail is accessible July–October. A National Parks Pass is required to park here. Overnight stays within the national park require backcountry camping permits, which are available at the Wilderness Information Center in Port Angeles.

Maps: For a map of Olympic National Park, contact the Outdoor Recreation Information Center at the downtown Seattle REI. For topographic maps, ask Green Trails for No. 133, Mount Tom, and No. 134, Mount Olympus, or ask the USGS for Bogachiel Peak and Mount Carrie.

Directions: From Port Angeles, drive west 30 miles on U.S. 101 to well-signed Sol Duc Hot Springs Road. Turn left (south) and drive 14 miles to the trailhead at road's end.

Contact: Olympic National Park, Wilderness Information Center, 3002 Mount Angeles Rd., Port Angeles, WA 98362, 360/565-3100.

18 BOULDER LAKE
11.2 mi/6.0 hr 🏃2 ⛰8

southwest of Port Angeles in Olympic National Park

Although Boulder Lake is a great destination, it's often overlooked for the soothing waters of Olympic Hot Springs. The hot springs draw the majority of visitors (understandably), but those soakers miss out on a great hike. The hike is a relatively easy one, climbing gradually through virgin forests. At the base of Boulder Peak, the small Boulder Lake sits within open forests of subalpine fir and mountain hemlock. In spite of the lake's beauty, you're more likely to remember your soak in the Olympic Hot Springs if you take it on your way back down the trail.

The first 2.2 miles of the trail are old roadbed, terminating at Boulder Creek Camp. The hot springs are just across Boulder Creek. Consisting of several pools collecting hot mineral water, the springs feel primitive and natural. Save it for your muscles on the way down, when they'll be more thankful. The trail splits 0.5 mile beyond the camp; the left fork goes to Appleton Pass, the right fork travels another 2 miles to Boulder Lake. Campsites can be found around the lake within the open forest. View seekers can scramble Boulder Peak.

At the lake, the trail turns into Happy Lake Ridge Trail, an optional return of 10 miles to Hot Springs Road, 2 miles below the trailhead. Most of the hike is on the ridge, within open spreads of subalpine meadows. Happy Lake sits at the midpoint of the ridge, perfect for longer stays. It's nice, but most prefer the hot springs.

User Groups: Hikers and horses. No dogs or mountain bikes are allowed. No wheelchair access.

Permits: This trail is accessible June–October. A National Parks Pass is required to park here. Overnight stays within the national park require backcountry camping permits, which

HIKING

are available at the Wilderness Information Center in Port Angeles.

Maps: For a map of Olympic National Park, contact the Outdoor Recreation Information Center at the downtown Seattle REI. For topographic maps, ask Green Trails for No. 134, Mount Olympus, or ask the USGS for Mount Carrie.

Directions: From Port Angeles, drive west 8 miles on U.S. 101 to Elwha Hot Springs Road. Turn left (south) and drive 10 miles, into the national park, to the road's end at a barrier with a well-signed trailhead.

Contact: Olympic National Park, Wilderness Information Center, 3002 Mount Angeles Rd., Port Angeles, WA 98362, 360/565-3100.

19 ELWHA RIVER
54.2 mi/3-5 days

southwest of Port Angeles in Olympic National Park

The Elwha River serves as the main artery of the Olympic Mountains. For more than 25 miles, the trail closely follows a historic and well-traveled route deep into the heart of the range. The Elwha was used for ages by local tribes to delve into the mountains for hunting and ceremonial reasons. In the late 1800s, the Press Expedition (a contingent of newspapermen and explorers) followed it on their trek across the mountain range. It has been an often-visited trail by backpackers and hikers for decades and is thought of as the spirit of the Olympics. The glacially fed waters boom through magnificent forests, a setting for many a backcountry tale. Sounds like a great place, doesn't it?

Elwha Trail travels deep into the Olympics to Low Divide. There are many campsites and shelters, and they receive heavy use in the summer. Old-growth forest breaks to reveal the river in stands of alder and maple. The trail forks at Chicago Camp (25 miles). The north fork heads to Elwha Basin, while the south fork proceeds up

to Low Divide and the North Fork Quinault. It's an amazing trek for those who complete it, and especially great when done with a friend.

Day hikers will also find much to see and do within several miles of the trailhead. Side trails (1.2 miles in) lead down to Goblin's Gate (1.7 miles), where the Elwha passes through a narrow gorge. From here, a small network of trails finds the sites of old homesteads and large meadows. These are great places to see deer, elk, and even black bears.

User Groups: Hikers and horses. No dogs or mountain bikes are allowed. No wheelchair access.

Permits: The lower part of this trail is usually accessible year-round (upper part is accessible May–October). A National Parks Pass is required to park here. Overnight stays within the national park require backcountry camping permits, which are available at the Wilderness Information Center in Port Angeles.

Maps: For a map of Olympic National Park, contact the Outdoor Recreation Information Center at the downtown Seattle REI. For topographic maps, ask Green Trails for No. 134, Mount Olympus, No. 135, Mount Angeles, No. 166, Mount Christie, and No. 167, Mount Steel, or ask the USGS for Hurricane Hill, Mount Angeles, McCartney Peak, Chimney Peak, and Mount Christie.

Directions: From Port Angeles, drive west 8 miles on U.S. 101 to Elwha Hot Springs Road. Turn left (south) and drive 4 miles to the cutoff for Whiskey Bend Road. Turn left and drive 5 miles to the trailhead at road's end.

Contact: Olympic National Park, Wilderness Information Center, 3002 Mount Angeles Rd., Port Angeles, WA 98362, 360/565-3100.

20 HURRICANE HILL
3.2 mi/2.0 hr

south of Port Angeles in Olympic National Park

BEST (

Visitors to Hurricane Ridge should and very often do hike this trail. Why? Because no trail in the Olympics offers such easy access to such exceptional views. The trail is completely within the high country, where windswept ridges are covered in lush, green meadows. The open trail offers nonstop views to the north and south, and the summit of Hurricane Hill is one giant panoramic vista. The hike is relatively easy and can be made by hikers of all abilities at their own pace.

Hurricane Hill Trail starts off on a cleared roadbed and gently climbs for its entire length. Wildflowers are in full gear during late June, while the last vestiges of the winter's snowpack hang on. Eventually the roadbed ends, but the trail remains wide and easy to hike. At the top of Hurricane Hill are wide knolls, perfect for a picnic or extended rest before heading back to the car. It's likely you'll want to stick around for awhile, mostly for the views. Much of the Olympic interior is revealed, including the Bailey Range and most of the Elwha drainage. The views to the north include the Strait of Juan de Fuca, Vancouver Island, and to the east, the Cascades. If there is any one trail that will endear the Olympics to its visitors, this is surely it.

User Groups: Hikers only. No dogs, horses, or mountain bikes are allowed. No wheelchair access.

Permits: This trail is accessible June–October. A National Parks Pass is required to park here.

Maps: For a map of Olympic National Park, contact the Outdoor Recreation Information Center at the downtown Seattle REI. For topographic maps, ask Green Trails for No. 134, Mount Olympus, or ask the USGS for Hurricane Hill.

Directions: From Port Angeles, drive north 2 miles on Race Street as it turns into Mount Angeles Road. Veer right at the well-signed fork and continue on Mount Angeles Road 19 miles, past the lower and upper visitors centers, to the well-signed trailhead.

Contact: Olympic National Park, Wilderness Information Center, 3002 Mount Angeles Rd., Port Angeles, WA 98362, 360/565-3100.

21 GRAND RIDGE
8.0 mi/4.0 hr   🏃‍♂️1 ⛰️9

south of Port Angeles in Olympic National Park

The National Park Service was once crazy about cars. It hoped to build a road through the park connecting Obstruction Point to Deer Park. Fortunately, the park service realized it would be insane to destroy such a beautiful area and abandoned the idea after surveying the route. Survey markers from the Bureau of Public Roads still line the trail, the intended course. Barren, open, and windy, Grand Ridge offers views of the Gray Wolf River drainage and many northern Olympic peaks. It's a great trip for those visiting Obstruction Point and the Hurricane Ridge area.

The trail primarily follows the southern side of Grand Ridge. This area is extremely barren, where even krummholz (small, distorted trees that look more like bushes) struggle to establish a foothold. Thin soils and intense winds work together to keep this area devoid of trees and full of views. A couple of high points offer good scramble opportunities and panoramic views of Elk Mountain (1.5 miles) and Maiden Peak (4 miles). Be sure to bring water, as hot days are even hotter on this south-facing slope. And be aware that when the wind picks up, which is often, you can expect 50–60 mph gusts to knock you around. Usually the wind blows you into the mountain, a good thing, because the drop down the mountain is precipitous.

User Groups: Hikers only. No dogs, horses, or mountain bikes are allowed. No wheelchair access.

Permits: This trail is usually accessible May–October. A National Parks Pass is required to park at Hurricane Hill; parking at Deer Park is free. Camping is limited between May 1 and September 30. Obtain permits at the WIC in Port Angeles during business hours.

Maps: For a map of Olympic National Park, contact the Outdoor Recreation Information Center at the downtown Seattle REI. For top-

HIKING

HIKING

ographic maps, ask Green Trails for No. 135, Mount Angeles, or ask the USGS for Mount Angeles and Maiden Peak.

Directions: From Port Angeles, drive north 2 miles on Race Street as it turns into Mount Angeles Road. Veer right at the well-signed fork and continue on Mount Angeles Road 17 miles to Obstruction Point Road. Turn left and drive 7 miles to the road's end and Obstruction Point Trailhead.

Contact: Olympic National Park, Wilderness Information Center, 3002 Mount Angeles Rd., Port Angeles, WA 98362, 360/565-3100.

22 GRAND PASS
12.0 mi/1-2 days

south of Port Angeles in Olympic National Park

There's good reason that this is one of the Olympics' most popular destinations. Easily accessible and very beautiful, Grand and Moose Lakes are favorite campgrounds. Farther up Grand Valley are plentiful subalpine meadows and rough, rocky slopes leading to Grand Pass, where views reach for miles around. Throw in two routes to the valley from Obstruction Peak (each of which is terrific), and you have a popular and well-visited spot in the North Olympics.

Leaving Obstruction Point, you are faced with two possible routes. Grand Pass Trail traverses Lillian Ridge, well above 6,000 feet and awash in mountain views, before dropping to Grand Lake. Alternatively, Badger Valley Trail makes its way through meadows and Alaskan cedar groves before climbing to Grand Lake. The best option is to make this a small loop, along the ridge on the way in and up the valley on the way out.

Overnight guests to Grand and Moose Lakes are required to secure a permit and reservation from the Wilderness Information Center. While there are numerous sites, they often fill up in the summer. The lakes are bordered by beautiful forests and rocky val-

ley hillsides. Beyond, Grand Pass Trail passes small Gladys Lake and climbs steeply to Grand Pass. The rocky and barren territory is a testament to the snowpacks that linger well into summer along these north-facing inclines. From Grand Pass, the Olympics are at hand and breathtaking.

User Groups: Hikers only. No dogs, horses, or mountain bikes are allowed. No wheelchair access.

Permits: This trail is usually accessible June–October. A National Parks Pass is required to park here. Overnight stays at Grand or Moose Lake require reservations and backcountry camping permits, which are available at the Wilderness Information Center in Port Angeles.

Maps: For a map of Olympic National Park, contact the Outdoor Recreation Information Center at the downtown Seattle REI. For topographic maps, ask Green Trails for No. 135, Mount Angeles, or ask the USGS for Mount Angeles, Maiden Peak, and Wellesley Peak.

Directions: From Port Angeles, drive north 2 miles on Race Street as it turns into Mount Angeles Road. Veer right at the well-signed fork and continue on Mount Angeles Road 17 miles to Obstruction Point Road. Turn left and drive 7 miles to the road's end and Obstruction Point Trailhead.

Contact: Olympic National Park, Wilderness Information Center, 3002 Mount Angeles Rd., Port Angeles, WA 98362, 360/565-3100.

23 CAMERON CREEK
32.0 mi/4 days

south of Sequim in Olympic National Park

The best backcountry locations often require an extra bit of effort to reach. Perhaps it is that extra exertion that makes some places so special and memorable. Cameron Creek is one of those places. It requires more than a few miles of approach hiking before you even embark on the long trail itself. Don't fret, time-conscious hikers; the journey along the trail and the vast mountain meadows deep within Cameron Basin are reward enough.

Cameron Creek Trail begins at Three Forks, where the creek joins Grand Creek and Gray Wolf River. The best access is via Three Forks Trail, a steep drop from Deer Park. While it's possible to hike up from the Lower Gray Wolf, river crossings are necessary and difficult. Cameron Creek Trail heads up the valley 7 miles, passing through beautiful forests of Douglas fir. Lower Cameron Camp (4 miles from Three Forks) is the primary campground.

Cameron Trail becomes more rugged near its headwaters, sometimes blown out by the creek. The upper basin is pure parkland, where wildflowers and waterfalls cover the landscape. Although it's a tough climb, Cameron Pass rewards with deep wilderness views. Mount Claywood and Sentinel Peak beckon from across Lost River Basin, one of the wildest places on the peninsula. The trail eventually drops to Dosewallips River. Campsites for the second night are scattered along the trail and throughout Cameron Basin.

User Groups: Hikers only. No dogs, horses, or mountain bikes are allowed. No wheelchair access.

Permits: This trail is accessible June–early October. Parking and access are free. Overnight stays within the national park require backcountry camping permits, which are available at the Wilderness Information Center in Port Angeles.

Maps: For a map of Olympic National Park, contact the Outdoor Recreation Information Center at the downtown Seattle REI. For topographic maps, ask Green Trails for No. 135, Mount Angeles, and No. 136, Tyler Peak, or ask the USGS for Tyler Peak, Maiden Peak, and Wellesley Peak.

Directions: From Port Angeles, drive east 5 miles on U.S. 101 to Deer Park Road. Turn right (south) and drive 17 miles to the well-signed trailhead.

Contact: Olympic National Park, Wilderness

Information Center, 3002 Mount Angeles Rd., Port Angeles, WA 98362, 360/565-3100.

24 HOH RIVER
34.0 mi/1-4 days

southeast of Forks in Olympic National Park

The Hoh Valley is world famous for the enormous size of its forests. Known as a cathedral forest, the massive trees' canopy stands more than 200 feet above the trail, filtering sunlight onto numerous ferns and draping mosses. This trail is also popular because it is the route for those seeking the pinnacle of the Olympic Mountains, Mount Olympus. Never mind the herds of people (or elk)—trees with trunks that wouldn't fit in your living room focus your attention upward.

The entire trail is outstanding. The first 12 miles are flat and well laid out, avoiding many ups and downs. It's a constant biology lesson in growth limits, as behemoth trees compete to outgrow each other. Many places along the trail allow for full appreciation of a river's ecology. Eagles and ravens stand atop trees looking for salmon or steelhead within the river. American dippers patrol the waterline while herds of Roosevelt elk graze along the forest floor. There are several well-interspersed campgrounds throughout. At 9.5 miles is Hoh Lake Trail cutoff, a trip for another day.

After 12 miles, the trail begins to slowly climb. The river courses through a spectacular canyon more than 100 feet deep by the time a hiker reaches the 13-mile mark. Hoh Trail crosses the canyon on a well-built bridge and begins its true ascent. Through a series of switchbacks, the trail passes through the forest and into a deep ravine. Beyond lies Glacier Meadows, where Olympus stands tall above terminating glaciers, revealing fields of blooming wildflowers among piles of glacial moraine. There are numerous camps here; all sites must be reserved at the Wilderness Information Center and may fill up quickly with

HIKING

backpackers and mountain climbers. This is the climax of the Olympics, standing between mighty Olympus above and miles and miles of rainforest below. Enjoy your hike out.

User Groups: Hikers and horses. No dogs or mountain bikes are allowed. No wheelchair access.

Permits: This trail is usually accessible April–October. A National Parks Pass is required to park here. Overnight stays within the national park require backcountry camping permits, which are available at the Hoh Ranger Station (at the end of Hoh River Road, 360/374-6925). Permits are limited May 1 through September 30. Reservations are recommended once the lake is snow free. For reservations call 360/565-3100.

Maps: For a map of Olympic National Park, contact the Outdoor Recreation Information Center at the downtown Seattle REI. For topographic maps, ask Green Trails for No. 133, Mount Tom, and No. 134, Mount Olympus, or ask the USGS for Owl Mountain, Mount Tom, Bogachiel Peak, Mount Carrie, and Mount Olympus.

Directions: From Port Angeles, drive south 14 miles on U.S. 101 to Upper Hoh River Road. Turn left (east) and drive 18 miles to the Hoh Ranger Station and trailhead.

Contact: Olympic National Park, Wilderness Information Center, 3002 Mount Angeles Rd., Port Angeles, WA 98362, 360/565-3100.

25 QUEETS RIVER

30.8 mi/2-3 days

south of Forks in Olympic National Park

Queets River Trail is all about two things: forests chock-full of enormous trees and total seclusion. Trees here grow to tremendous sizes, with Sitka spruce, western hemlock, western red cedar, and Douglas fir creating a community of giants. In fact, the Queets is home to the world's largest living Douglas fir, a monster with a trunk 14.5 feet in diameter

and a broken top 221 feet above the ground. While as impressive as the Hoh, this valley receives just a fraction of the visitors. That's because of a necessary river ford just beyond the trailhead. The river can be forded only during times of low water (late summer or fall) and should be undertaken with care at any time; once you're past it, though, traveling is easy.

The trail travels roughly 15 miles along the river. The forest often gives way to glades of big leaf maple and the cutting river. Bears outnumber people here. The world's largest Douglas fir is 2 miles in, just off Kloochman Rock Trail heading north. There are three established camps along the trail, easily providing sufficient camping for the few backpackers on this trail. The first is Spruce Bottom (6 miles). Sticking on the trail will eventually take you to the Pelton Creek Shelter (15 miles), where the trail ends. It is certainly possible to carry on farther to Queets Basin, but it's a bushwhack. It's enough to sit down, enjoy the permeating quiet of the wilderness, and smile.

User Groups: Hikers and horses. No dogs or mountain bikes are allowed. No wheelchair access.

Permits: This trail is usually accessible May–October. Parking is free. Overnight stays within the national park require backcountry camping permits, which are available at the Wilderness Information Center in Port Angeles.

Maps: For a map of Olympic National Park, contact the Outdoor Recreation Information Center at the downtown Seattle REI. For topographic maps, ask Green Trails for No. 165, Kloochman Rock, or ask the USGS for Stequaleho Creek, Kloochman Rock, and Bob Creek.

Directions: From Forks, drive south on U.S. 101 to Forest Service Road 21. Turn left and drive about 10 miles north to Upper Queets Road. Turn right and drive about 2 miles to the trailhead at road's end.

Contact: Olympic National Park, Wilderness

Information Center, 3002 Mount Angeles Rd., Port Angeles, WA 98362, 360/565-3100.

26 SKYLINE RIDGE
45.0 mi/5-6 days

 4 ▲ 10

northeast of Quinault in Olympic National Park

Sure to test even the toughest hikers, Skyline Ridge rewards with one of the most beautiful hikes on the peninsula. The trail never leaves the high country as it follows the ridge separating the large Quinault and Queets Valleys. The views up here are unbelievable, with Mount Olympus standing just one ridge away. From this high perch, watch the sun set or the fog roll in from the Pacific Ocean, which is visible in the distance. And stay on your toes, as this is the perfect place to spot black bears as they drunkenly wolf down huckleberries. The Quinault is said to sport some of the highest black bear concentrations in the state, so be ready for some excitement. Mile after mile, Skyline Ridge consistently offers the best of the Olympics.

The route must be accessed by Three Lakes Trail (6.5 miles) or North Fork Quinault Trail (16 miles; see listing in this chapter). The best route is via North Fork Quinault, making a loop. Climbing out of Low Divide, Skyline Trail skirts several basins of meadows and rises to Beauty Pass (7.4 miles from Low Divide). A side trail heads to Lake Beauty and campsites with views of Olympus.

Beyond, the trail is difficult to follow and marked by rock cairns. Excellent map and route-finding skills are needed here. Skyline Trail heads for Three Prune Camp (18 miles), switching between the Quinault and Queets Valleys several times. Water can be difficult to find here until Three Prune. The trail begins its decent to Three Lakes, the last spot for camping, and Three Lakes Trail back to the trailhead. By the time you get back to the car, you'll already be planning next year's trip.

User Groups: Hikers only. No dogs, horses, or mountain bikes are allowed. No wheelchair access.

Permits: This trail is usually accessible August–September (depending on the previous winter's snowpack). Parking is free. Overnight stays within the national park require backcountry camping permits, which are available at Quinault Ranger Station.

Maps: For a map of Olympic National Park, contact the Outdoor Recreation Information Center at the downtown Seattle REI. For topographic maps, ask Green Trails for No. 166, Mount Christie, or ask the USGS for Bunch Lake, Kimta Peak, and Mount Christie.

Directions: From Forks, travel south on U.S. 101 to North Shore Road at Lake Quinault. Turn left (east) and drive 17 miles to North Fork Ranger Station at road's end.

Contact: Olympic National Park, Wilderness Information Center, 3002 Mount Angeles Rd., Port Angeles, WA 98362, 360/565-3100.

27 NORTH FORK QUINAULT
31.4 mi/3-4 days

🏃 2 ▲ 8

northeast of Quinault in Olympic National Park

With headwaters at Low Divide, North Fork Trail provided the way for many a party of explorers. From this popular junction, used by the Press Expedition, Army Lieutenant Joseph P. O'Neil, and others, the river flows more than 30 miles to the Pacific through beautiful high country and forests of enormous size in the lowlands. Its link to Low Divide makes it a well-used route for folks coming or going to the Elwha River. It also makes a great counterpart to Skyline Trail, which skirts the North Fork's upper ridge. There's no end to things to see as the trail crosses numerous beautiful creeks and even the river itself. It passes through superb forests of trees swollen to rainforest dimensions, and hikers often encounter wildlife.

The trail follows the river all the way to its source at Low Divide. Campsites and shel-

HIKING

ters occur regularly throughout this section of trail, including Wolf Bar (2.5 miles), Halfway House (5.2 miles), Elip Creek (6.5 miles), Trapper Shelter (8.5 miles), and 12 Mile (11.5 miles). Be prepared for several easy creek crossings. The ascent up the valley is modest, making these 12 miles pass quickly underfoot.

After a good day's hike, the trail crosses the North Fork at 16 Mile Camp (12.3 miles). This river crossing can be difficult if not impassable during times of high flow. If coming from the Elwha, beware. A U-turn here makes the return trip more than 40 miles. Beyond, the trail climbs to Low Divide, an open meadow surrounded by waterfalls. Low Divide Ranger Station lies just beyond the Skyline Trail junction.

User Groups: Hikers and horses. No dogs or mountain bikes are allowed. No wheelchair access.

Permits: This trail is accessible May–October. No fee is required to park here. Overnight stays within the national park require backcountry camping permits, which are available at the Wilderness Information Center in Port Angeles.

Maps: For a map of Olympic National Park, contact the Outdoor Recreation Information Center at the downtown Seattle REI. For topographic maps, ask Green Trails for No. 166, Mount Christie, or ask the USGS for Bunch Lake, Kitma Peak, and Mount Christie.

Directions: From Forks, travel south on U.S. 101 to North Shore Road at Lake Quinault. Turn left (east) and drive 17 miles to North Fork Ranger Station at road's end.

Contact: Olympic National Park, Wilderness Information Center, 3002 Mount Angeles Rd., Port Angeles, WA 98362, 360/565-3100.

28 ENCHANTED VALLEY
36.0 mi/4 days 🚶3 ⛰10

east of Quinault in Olympic National Park

Undoubtedly one of Washington's most beautiful places, Enchanted Valley leaves visitors reminiscing about their trip here for years to come. East Fork Quinault Trail travels through old-growth forests of giant trees to the steep cliffs and waterfalls of Enchanted Valley. The wide and wild valley offers miles of exploration and loads of views of the tall peaks enclosing the Quinault. The trail eventually finds the high-country playground of Anderson Pass, home to glaciers and acres of meadows.

East Fork Quinault Trail immediately crosses Graves Creek, then travels 13 level and easy miles among ancient trees growing in a lush and humid forest. Elk and deer roam the thick understory. The forest gives way to clearings as the trail nears Enchanted Valley. A ford of the river is required here, difficult at times of high water. Countless waterfalls cascade from the vertical cliffs on both sides of the valley. The valley is home to a ranger station and old chalet, now closed to visitors except in emergencies.

East Quinault Trail continues out of Enchanted Valley and finally begins climbing to reach Anderson Pass and several glaciers. This high country is home to huckleberries and their biggest fans: black bears. Good places to pitch a tent are found at O'Neil Creek Camp (6.7 miles), Enchanted Valley Camp (13.1 miles), and Anderson Pass Camp (18 miles).

User Groups: Hikers and horses. No dogs or mountain bikes are allowed. No wheelchair access.

Permits: This trail is accessible May–September. Parking is free. Overnight stays within the national park require backcountry camping permits, which are available at the Wilderness Information Center in Port Angeles.

Maps: For a map of Olympic National Park, contact the Outdoor Recreation Information Center at the downtown Seattle REI. For topographic maps, ask Green Trails for No. 166, Mount Christie, and No. 167, Mount Steel, or ask the USGS for Mount Hoquiam, Mount Olson, Mount Steel, and Chimney Peak.

Directions: From Forks, drive south on U.S. 101 to South Shore Road. Turn left (east) and drive 18.5 miles to Graves Creek Ranger Station and the signed trailhead.

Contact: Olympic National Park, Wilderness Information Center, 3002 Mount Angeles Rd., Port Angeles, WA 98362, 360/565-3100.

29 GRAVES CREEK
18.0 mi/2 days   ⛹3 △8

northeast of Quinault in Olympic National Park

Sometimes the itch to visit the Quinault area cannot be denied. The desire to see big trees, experience high-country meadows, and hear the boom of a roaring creek must be met. Fortunately, Graves Creek Trail scratches these itches without the considerable crowds of people found in the Enchanted Valley.

Graves Creek Trail begins soon after crossing Graves Creek on Quinault River Trail. It climbs gently above Graves Creek, which roars from within a box canyon for most of its descent. The trail makes a lot of ups and downs, but the overall trend is definitely up. At 3.2 miles the trail crosses Graves Creek, which can be difficult at times of high water (fall and spring). The forest breaks as meadows take over, a place where most hikers linger to fill up on huckleberries. The trail reaches Sundown Lake, set within a small glacial cirque complete with campsites. The trail eventually winds up at Six Ridge Pass and continues as Six Ridge Trail.

User Groups: Hikers only. No dogs, horses, or mountain bikes are allowed. No wheelchair access.

Permits: This trail is accessible July–October. No permits are needed for parking. Overnight stays within the national park require backcountry camping permits, which are available at the Wilderness Information Center in Port Angeles.

Maps: For a map of Olympic National Park, contact the Outdoor Recreation Information Center at the downtown Seattle REI. For topographic maps, ask Green Trails for No. 166, Mount Christie, or ask the USGS for Mount Hoquim.

Directions: From Forks, drive south on U.S. 101 to South Shore Road. Turn left (east) and drive 18.5 miles to Graves Creek Ranger Station and the signed trailhead.

Contact: Olympic National Park, Wilderness Information Center, 3002 Mount Angeles Rd., Port Angeles, WA 98362, 360/565-3100.

30 LAKE QUINAULT TRAILS
0.6-4.0 mi/0.5-2.0 hr   ⛹1 △9

on the shores of Lake Quinault in Olympic National Forest

Lake Quinault Loop is one of three trails on the south side of the lake. Built within exceptional old-growth forests, the three trails offer two loops and a creek hike. The shortest of the three is Rain Forest Trail, a loop that finds its way into a stand of 500-year-old Douglas firs. Signs are placed along the path to enlighten hikers on the forest's ecology. The trail also passes a great stretch of Willaby Creek running through a gorge.

Rain Forest Trail is a larger undertaking of 4 miles. It ventures farther into the forest, crossing a swamp on well-built puncheons and passing Cascade Falls on Falls Creek. It returns to the trailhead via Lake Quinault Shoreline Trail. The final hike is into Willaby Creek. A steady forest of immense proportions follows hikers to a granddaddy of cedars. The trail crosses the creek, which can be tricky, and eventually peters out. All three trails offer typically large Olympic forests full of moss and ferns. These are trails for the whole family to relish, regardless of age or hiking ability.

User Groups: Hikers and leashed dogs. No horses or mountain bikes are allowed. No wheelchair access.

Permits: This area is accessible year-round. No permit is needed to park. Parking is free.

Maps: For a map of Olympic National Forest, contact the Outdoor Recreation Information Center at the downtown Seattle REI. For topographic maps, ask Green Trails for No.

HIKING

197, Quinault Lake, or ask the USGS for Lake Quinault East.

Directions: From Forks, drive south on U.S. 101 to South Shore Road. Turn left (east) and drive 1.5 miles to the signed trailhead on the right side of the road.

Contact: Olympic National Forest, Quilcene Ranger Station, 295142 U.S. 101 South, Quilcene, WA 98376, 360/765-2200.

31 COLONEL BOB MOUNTAIN
14.4 mi/8.0 hr   🏃4 ⛰9

east of Quinault in the Colonel Bob Wilderness of Olympic National Forest

It's a hard climb from the bottoms of the Quinault Valley to the peaks of the southern ridge, the home of Colonel Bob Mountain. The overall elevation gain is greater than 4,000 feet, much of which is covered twice on this hike. The trail climbs out of the rainforests of the lower valley to subalpine meadows, where ridges and views seem to extend for days on end. While crowds of folks bump into each other down in the Enchanted Valley, far fewer people are to be found up here. Trips to Colonel Bob during June and July are absolutely wonderful, when the wildflowers are in full bloom and snowfields linger on distant mountains.

Colonel Bob Trail is a true scaling of the peak, starting directly from the Quinault River. The trail heads up through a forest of Douglas fir and western red cedar. Mosses, lichens, and ferns grow on anything that can support them. The trail eventually reaches the camps of Mulkey Shelter (4 miles) and Moonshine Flats (6 miles).

The trail now climbs steeply to a ridge and dishearteningly drops down the other side. Take courage in knowing that while you must give back some elevation, open meadows await you. The trail navigates between the surrounding peaks before ascending Colonel Bob. The views are grand from on top, revealing much of the southern Olympics.

User Groups: Hikers and leashed dogs. No horses or mountain bikes are allowed. No wheelchair access.

Permits: This trail is accessible mid-June–October. No permit is required to park. Parking is free.

Maps: For a map of Olympic National Forest, contact the Outdoor Recreation Information Center at the downtown Seattle REI. For topographic maps, ask Green Trails for No. 197, Quinault Lake, and No. 198, Griswold, or ask the USGS for Lake Quinault East and Colonel Bob.

Directions: From Forks, drive south on U.S. 101 to South Shore Road. Turn left (east) and drive 6 miles to the signed trailhead on the right side of the road.

Contact: Olympic National Forest, Quilcene Ranger Station, 295142 U.S. 101 South, Quilcene, WA 98376, 360/765-2200.

32 WYNOOCHEE PASS
7.2 mi/4.0 hr   🏃2 ⛰8

east of Quinault in Olympic National Park

This is not a long trail, and that's the beauty of it. Smart hikers know that Wynoochee Pass provides easy access to Sundown Lake and the incredible high country of the area. These spots add many additional miles and feet of elevation when accessed via two other converging trails. The few hikers who visit this trail each year find superb forests of mountain hemlock and silver fir along the route. It's nearly the perfect trail; not too long, incredibly scenic, and rarely used.

Wynoochee Pass Trail begins along an old logging road within the national forest before quickly entering the pristine confines of the national park. The trail is set high above the Wynoochee River, which at this location has neared the end of its journey. The trail makes a few switchbacks up to the small meadow at Wynoochee Pass; at just over 2 miles from the trailhead, the elevation is 3,600 feet. From here, hikers should follow a lightly used footpath for 1 mile to Sundown Lake and meadowy Sundown Pass. Since it's so far out of the way, it's understandable that so few people visit this part of the Olympics. But others' loss is your gain on Wynoochee Pass Trail. In the best sense of the term, it really is a getaway.

User Groups: Hikers only. No dogs, horses, or mountain bikes are allowed. No wheelchair access.

Permits: This trail is accessible May–November. Permits are not required. Parking and access are free.

Maps: For a map of Olympic National Park, contact the Outdoor Recreation Information Center at the downtown Seattle REI. For topographic maps, ask Green Trails for No. 166, Mount Christie, or ask the USGS for Mount Hoquim.

Directions: This road has experienced washouts in recent years. Call the WIC before choosing this hike to find out current road status, because alternative routes may be available. From Aberdeen, drive east 9 miles to Wynoochee Valley Road (just before Montesano). Turn left (north) and drive 33 miles

to Forest Service Road 2270 (at a four-way intersection). Go straight on Forest Service Road 2270 and drive 12 miles to Forest Service Road 2270-400. Turn right and drive 2 miles to the signed trailhead.

Contact: Olympic National Park, Wilderness Information Center, 3002 Mount Angeles Rd., Port Angeles, WA 98362, 360/565-3100.

33 GRAY WOLF RIVER
30.2 mi/3-4 days   4 9

south of Sequim in Olympic National Park

When the rain gives you pause about your planned trip to the west side of the peninsula, the little-visited Gray Wolf may be one of your better options. It's conveniently situated in the rain shadow of the Olympics, where much less rain falls than in other parts of the peninsula. So when it's raining on the west side, you're likely to luck out and stay dry in the rain shadow. This hike is quite long with the best parts, of course, far up the trail. The lower section of Gray Wolf is lowland river hiking.

enjoying the rumble of the Gray Wolf River

It's only above Three Forks, where Cameron and Grand Creeks join Gray Wolf, that the trail develops real personality.

Skip the lower half of the river and access Gray Wolf via Three Forks Trail (5.5 miles). From here, Gray Wolf Trail passes through beautiful forests of hemlock, cedar, and Douglas fir. A shelter is at Falls Camp (10.7 miles). From here, one can hike a way trail 3 miles up to Cedar Lake, a very large subalpine lake set within a large meadow. This little-visited spot alone is well worth a trip of several days.

Gray Wolf Trail continues by crossing the river several times and then beginning its real ascent. The basin at the head of the Gray Wolf is rather large and expansive. Several high tarns are set amid groves of mountain hemlocks and bare slides of shale. The basin is surrounded by high peaks, including the Needles as they extend from Mount Deception. The trail continues by steeply descending to Dosewallips River Trail.

User Groups: Hikers only. No dogs, horses, or mountain bikes are allowed. No wheelchair access.

Permits: This trail is usually accessible May–October. A federal Northwest Forest Pass is required to park here. Overnight stays require backcountry camping permits, which are available at the Quilcene Ranger Station.

Maps: For a map of Olympic National Park, contact the Outdoor Recreation Information Center at the downtown Seattle REI. For topographic maps, ask Green Trails for No. 135, Mount Angeles, and No. 136, Tyler Peak, or ask the USGS for Tyler Peak, Maiden Peak, and Wellesley Peak.

Directions: From Sequim, drive 3 miles east on U.S. 101 to Palo Alto Road. Turn right (south) and drive 7.5 miles to Forest Service Road 2880. Turn right and drive 1 mile to Forest Service Road 2870. Turn right and drive 0.5 mile to the signed trailhead.

Contact: Olympic National Forest, Quilcene Ranger Station, 295142 U.S. 101 South, Quilcene, WA 98376, 360/765-2200.

34 MOUNT ZION
3.6 mi/2.0 hr

west of Quilcene in Olympic National Forest

This is one of the Olympics' easier, more accessible peaks. It's not one of the tallest peaks, yet it offers its fair share of views from the northeast corner of the peninsula. A forested trail deposits hikers at a fairly flat, open summit. In comparison with the rest of the Olympics, it is in close proximity to Seattle, making it a great day hike for those with an itch for the Olympics.

The trail's best attraction is the plethora of rhododendrons that grace the forest blanketing the route. They are in full bloom during June and will make for one of the lasting memories of the hike. The trail gains just 1,300 feet on its ascent, pretty light fare for summit hikes. The forest eventually gives way near the summit to grand views of Olympic ranges and peaks. Mount Baker and the Cascades are visible beyond Puget Sound on clear days. On days that aren't so clear, fear not. Mount Zion is in the Olympic rain shadow, a corner of the mountain range that receives much less rain than the other parts of the peninsula. So when it's raining elsewhere, Mount Zion will be much drier. In sum, Mount Zion is a wonderful trail for easy hiking and basking in the sun.

User Groups: Hikers, leashed dogs, horses, mountain bikes, and motorcycles are permitted. No wheelchair access.

Permits: This trail is accessible mid-May–November (accessible nearly year-round with snowshoes). A federal Northwest Forest Pass is required to park here.

Maps: For a map of Olympic National Forest, contact the Outdoor Recreation Information Center at the downtown Seattle REI. For topographic maps, ask Green Trails for No. 136, Tyler Peak, or ask the USGS for Mount Zion.

Directions: From Quilcene, drive north 1.5 miles on U.S. 101 to Lords Lake Road. Follow

Lords Lake Road to the lake and turn left onto Forest Service Road 28. Drive to Bon Jon Pass and turn right onto Forest Service Road 2810. The trailhead is 2 miles ahead on the left.

Contact: Olympic National Forest, Hood Canal Ranger Station, 295142 U.S. 101 South, Quilcene, WA 98376 (2 miles from Highway 101 on South Shore Quinault Road), 360/765-2200.

35 TUBAL CAIN
17.4 mi/2 days

west of Quilcene in the Buckhorn Wilderness of Olympic National Forest

Tubal Cain Trail is more than a secluded forest or place of expansive mountain views. Unlike most wilderness settings, the route features a good deal of evidence of mankind. Along the route are a pair of easy-to-find old mines. Here, copper, manganese, and other minerals were extracted from the flanks of Iron and Buckhorn Mountains. But another unexpected find is made along a side trail, deep within a high basin. Tull Canyon is the final resting place for an old Air Force B-17. The plane crashed here more than 50 years ago and has been left intact.

The trail immediately crosses Silver Creek to climb the valley within thick growth of rhododendrons, in full bloom in June. At 3.2 miles is the junction with Tull Canyon Trail. Tubal Cain Mine (and campground) lies on the east side of the creek a short 0.5 mile later. The shaft of the mine ventures into the mountain for a distance of nearly 3,000 feet. Although the mine shaft is unsafe for exploration, there are many old relics left outside the mine. From Tubal Cain Mine, the trail becomes more scenic as it climbs to Buckhorn Lake (5.5 miles). This is a good turnaround point for day hikers. Buckhorn and Iron Mountains stand imposingly across the valley at this point, guarding their treasures. The trail ends at

Marmot Pass, where meadows are awash in wildflowers during July.

User Groups: Hikers, leashed dogs, and horses. No mountain bikes are allowed. No wheelchair access.

Permits: This trail is accessible June–October. Permits are not required, parking and access are free.

Maps: For a map of Olympic National Forest, contact the Outdoor Recreation Information Center at the downtown Seattle REI. For topographic maps, ask Green Trails for No. 136, Tyler Peak, or ask the USGS for Mount Townsend and Mount Deception.

Directions: From Sequim, drive 3 miles east on U.S. 101 to Palo Alto Road. Turn right (south) and drive 7.5 miles to Forest Service Road 28. Stay left and drive 1 mile to Forest Service Road 2860. Turn right and drive a long 14.5 miles to the signed trailhead.

Contact: Olympic National Forest, Quinault Wilderness Information Office, 295142 U.S. 101 South, Quilcene, WA 98376 (2 miles from Highway 101 on South Shore Quinault Road), 360/288-0232.

36 ROYAL BASIN
16.2 mi/2 days

south of Sequim in Olympic National Park

Unrivaled in beauty, Royal Basin Trail travels miles of old-growth forest before reaching acres of parkland meadows beneath towering peaks. This is one trail that guidebook authors prefer to keep mum about.

Royal Basin Trail begins along Dungeness River Trail 1 mile from the trailhead, where Royal Creek enters the river. Stay to the right on Royal Basin Trail. Easy to follow and well maintained, the trail serves hikers of all abilities as it courses through forest and avalanche tracks. Progress up the trail is easy to gauge as the forest changes from Douglas firs and western hemlocks to silver firs, yellow cedars, and finally subalpine firs. Campsites are found at the first meadow; these make a good alternative to the traditional campground a mile farther at Royal Lake.

The trail clambers over a terrace to reach Royal Lake. The large basin reveals Mount Deception, the Olympics' second-highest peak, and the always-impressive Needles, a long, jagged ridge. Explore to your heart's content, but stay on established trails, please. Parkland and meadows abound here, with wildflowers that burst with color in early summer. At the top of the basin is Royal Glacier, which you can walk on, while a trip to the shoulder below Mount Deception is also possible, revealing the Elwha River drainage. Royal Basin is sure to capture your heart. So hike Royal Basin and then lie about where you've been to anyone who asks.

User Groups: Hikers only. No dogs, horses, or mountain bikes are allowed. No wheelchair access.

Permits: This trail is usually accessible mid-June–October. A federal Northwest Forest Pass is required to park here. Overnight stays require backcountry camping permits, which are available at the Port Angeles Wilderness Information Center. Camping is limited between May 1 and September 30. Reservations are required.

Maps: For a map of Olympic National Park, contact the Outdoor Recreation Information Center at the downtown Seattle REI. For topographic maps, ask Green Trails for No. 136, Tyler Peak, or ask the USGS for Mount Deception.

Directions: From Sequim, drive 3 miles east on U.S. 101 to Palo Alto Road. Turn right (south) and drive 7.5 miles to Forest Service Road 28. Stay left and drive 1 mile to Forest Service Road 2860. Turn right and drive 11 miles to the signed Dungeness Trailhead.

Contact: Olympic National Park, Wilderness Information Center, 3002 Mount Angeles Rd., Port Angeles, WA 98362, 360/565-3100; Olympic National Forest, Quinault Wilderness Information Office, 295142 U.S. 101 South, Quilcene, WA 98376 (2 miles from Highway 101 on South Shore Quinault Road), 360/288-0232.

37 UPPER DUNGENESS
12.4 mi/6.0 hr   👥3 ⛰9

west of Quilcene in the Buckhorn Wilderness of Olympic National Forest

BEST (

The Upper Dungeness River is one of the most picturesque of the Olympics' many rivers, and this trail captures much of its scenic beauty. The trail follows the Dungeness as it passes through outstanding forests and eventually reaches a major junction, high within a mountain basin. Along the way is Heather Creek Trail, a nonmaintained route heading directly into the Olympics' wild interior. Add the fact that the Dungeness receives less rain than most of the peninsula, and you have a popular off-season hike.

The trail makes its way along the valley bottom for the first mile to a junction with Royal Basin Trail. Cross Royal Creek to stay on Dungeness Trail. The forest here is superb, with large Douglas firs, red cedars, and western hemlocks towering over an open understory. The trail eventually crosses the Dungeness to the east side and comes to Camp Handy, at 3.2 miles. Great camps are found within this slightly wooded meadow.

From Camp Handy, Heather Creek Trail continues up the valley alongside the Dungeness for another 4 miles. This stretch is not maintained and is fairly undisturbed wilderness. Dungeness Trail leaves Camp Handy to begin climbing out of the valley and into parkland meadows. The trail ends at Boulder Camp, the junction with Constance Pass Trail and Big Quilcene Trail.

User Groups: Hikers, leashed dogs, and horses. No mountain bikes are allowed. No wheelchair access.

Permits: This trail is accessible June–October. A federal Northwest Forest Pass is required to park here. Overnight stays require backcountry camping permits, which are available at the Port Angeles Wilderness Information Center.

Maps: For a map of Olympic National Forest, contact the Outdoor Recreation Information Center at the downtown Seattle REI. For topographic maps, ask Green Trails for No. 136, Tyler Peak, or ask the USGS for Mount Deception, Tyler Peak, and Mount Zion.

Directions: From Sequim, drive 3 miles east on U.S. 101 to Palo Alto Road. Turn right (south) and drive 7.5 miles to Forest Service Road 28. Stay left and drive 1 mile to Forest Service Road 2860. Turn right and drive 11 miles to the signed Dungeness Trailhead.

Contact: Olympic National Forest, Hood Canal Ranger Station, 295142 U.S. 101 South, Quilcene, WA 98376, 360/765-2200.

38 MOUNT TOWNSEND
7.8 mi/4.5 hr

west of Quilcene in Buckhorn Wilderness of Olympic National Forest

Upon reaching the top of Mount Townsend, hikers may be hard-pressed to decide if they're in the midst of mountains or perched above long stretches of Puget waterways. This lofty summit strategically puts you smack-dab in the middle of the two settings. The grand, competing vistas are likely to vie for your attention during the length of your stay here. Be thankful. High mountain meadows scrubbed by forceful winds, complete with requisite berries, complement the experience. It's no wonder that Mount Townsend is one of the peninsula's more popular day hikes.

Mount Townsend Trail climbs steadily throughout its length. The first couple of miles pass through forest punctuated by rhododendrons (catch them blooming in June). At 2.5 miles lies Camp Windy (not nearly as windy as Townsend's summit), and the trail soon reaches a junction with Silver Lakes Trail. Mount Townsend Trail harshly climbs

through opening meadows, full of late summer's huckleberries. Snow and wind limit the growth of the subalpine trees, leaving vistas for hikers. The summit is long and flat with superb views. Nearly the full range of the Cascades lines the east, while Mount Deception and The Needles are highlights of the Olympic Range. The trail continues for another 1.4 miles down to Little Quilcene River Trail.

User Groups: Hikers, leashed dogs, and horses are permitted. No mountain bikes are allowed. No wheelchair access.

Permits: This trail is accessible June–October. A federal Northwest Forest Pass is required to park here.

Maps: For a map of Olympic National Forest, contact the Outdoor Recreation Information Center at the downtown Seattle REI. For topographic maps, ask Green Trails for No. 136, Tyler Peak, or ask the USGS for Mount Townsend.

Directions: From Quilcene, drive 1 mile south on U.S. 101 to Penny Creek Road. Turn right (west) and drive 1.5 miles to Big Quilcene Road. Stay to the left at this Y and drive 3 miles to the Forest Service boundary and paved Forest Service Road 27. Drive 9 miles to Forest Service Road 2760. Drive 1 mile to the trailhead at road's end.

Contact: Olympic National Forest, Quinault Wilderness Information Office, 295142 U.S. 101 South, Quilcene, WA 98376 (2 miles from Highway 101 on South Shore Quinault Road), 360/288-0232.

39 SILVER LAKES
10.8 mi/6.0 hr

west of Quilcene in the Buckhorn Wilderness of Olympic National Forest

BEST (

It takes a harsh rainstorm to ruin a trip to Silver Lakes. And that's a less-than-likely proposition since this trail is snugly tucked away in the peninsula's rain shadow. Silver Lakes nestle within a large basin rimmed with jagged peaks. Subalpine firs are amply spread around the lakes, mingling with meadows of heather. Alpine flowers add strokes of color and are likely to provide great memories and photo ops. Throw in some good scrambles at the end to an extremely pleasant hike and you have yourself a thoroughly agreeable trip.

Silver Lakes Trail begins on Mount Townsend Trail, 2.9 miles from the trailhead (see listing in this chapter). The trail immediately drops into the forested valley, crosses Silver Creek, and makes a quick ascent to the larger Silver Lake. The smaller and less visited lake is just before the larger one, to the west off a visible side trail.

Parkland surrounds the lake, with large meadows of wildflowers mingling with small stands of subalpine fir. There are several campsites for overnight guests. The lake is favored by swimmers and anglers alike. Be sure to scramble the slope rising to the south, between rocky peaks, for more wildflowers and the prime views.

User Groups: Hikers, leashed dogs, and horses. No mountain bikes are allowed. No wheelchair access.

Permits: This trail is accessible July–October. Permits are not required, parking and access are free.

Maps: For a map of Olympic National Forest, contact the Outdoor Recreation Information Center at the downtown Seattle REI. For topographic maps, ask Green Trails for No. 136, Tyler Peak, or ask the USGS for Mount Townsend.

Directions: From Quilcene, drive 1 mile south on U.S. 101 to Penny Creek Road. Turn right (west) and drive 1.5 miles to Big Quilcene Road. Stay to the left at this Y and drive 3 miles to the Forest Service boundary and paved Forest Service Road 27. Drive 9 miles to Forest Service Road 2760. Drive 1 mile to the trailhead at road's end.

Contact: Olympic National Forest, Quinault Wilderness Information Office, 295142 U.S. 101 South, Quilcene, WA 98376 (2 miles from Highway 101 on South Shore Quinault Road), 360/288-0232.

40 UPPER BIG QUILCENE
10.6 mi/5.5 hr   👣3 ⛰9

west of Quilcene in the Buckhorn Wilderness of Olympic National Forest

Rarely can hikers get to such an outstanding viewpoint, with so much wild country spread before them, than with Upper Big Quilcene Trail. Passing through virgin timber and open, pristine meadows, the trail delivers hikers to Marmot Pass. This is an opportunity to view many of the Olympics' most impressive peaks, including Mount Mystery and Mount Deception. The trail is one of the best on the peninsula's east side and perfect for an outing with the dog.

The trail follows the river for several miles, where the forest consists of old-growth Douglas fir, western hemlock, and western red cedar. In June, rhododendrons light up the understory with fragrant blossoms. The trail then climbs gently but steadily out of the valley. Good camps are at Shelter Rock (2.6 mi) and Camp Mystery (4.6 mi), each next to water. The trail eventually broaches the confines of forest and finds itself at Marmot Pass, where one can finally see all that is to the north of the ridge. Grand views of near and far mountains are plentiful. The trail junctions here with Tubal Cain Trail before dropping to Boulder Camp. Constance Pass and Upper Dungeness Trails meet at Boulder Camp.

User Groups: Hikers and leashed dogs. No horses or mountain bikes are allowed. No wheelchair access.

Permits: This trail is accessible July–October. A federal Northwest Forest Pass is required to park here.

Maps: For a map of Olympic National Forest, contact the Outdoor Recreation Information Center at the downtown Seattle REI. For topographic maps, ask Green Trails for No. 136, Tyler Peak, or ask the USGS for Mount Townsend and Mount Deception.

Directions: From Quilcene, drive 1 mile south on U.S. 101 to Penny Creek Road. Turn right (west) and drive 1.5 miles to Big Quilcene Road. Stay left at this Y and drive 3 miles to the Forest Service boundary and paved Forest Service Road 27. Drive 6 miles to Forest Service Road 2750. Stay to the left and drive 4.5 miles to the signed trailhead.

Contact: Olympic National Forest, Hood Canal Ranger Station, 295142 U.S. 101 South, Quilcene, WA 98376 (2 miles from Highway 101 on South Shore Quinault Road), 360/765-2200.

41 TUNNEL CREEK
8.2 mi/4.5 hr

west of Quilcene in the Buckhorn Wilderness of Olympic National Forest

The trail up Tunnel Creek leads to a pair of subalpine lakes and a pass with far-reaching views. It's a popular day hike, whisking hikers from old-growth forests along the valley floor to open meadows and views up high. Never mind the steep final ascent to the lakes and 50-50 Pass, as you'll have plenty of time to rest while surveying the mountainous horizon.

The trail ventures easily through great forests of Douglas fir and western red cedar accompanied by numerous rhododendrons (blooming in June) for 2.7 miles. Here, the trail encounters Tunnel Creek Shelter, where a few campsites can be found. Beyond this point, the route steeply climbs to the Twin Lakes (3.7 miles). The lakes are situated in a tiny basin and bounded by mountain hemlocks, an appealing setting. The trail climbs a bit more to 50-50 Pass, at elevation 5,050 feet. This is mostly just a rocky promontory, but the views are grand during clear weather. Nowhere is Mount Constance better seen, with

pockets of snow often finding refuge among the many crags and faces. Views toward Puget Sound stand out as well. This is the ideal place to turn around; otherwise, a sharp descent awaits, into a valley other than the one where your car is parked.

User Groups: Hikers, leashed dogs, and horses are permitted. No mountain bikes are allowed. No wheelchair access.

Permits: This trail is accessible mid-June–October. Permits are not required. Parking and access are free.

Maps: For a map of Olympic National Forest, contact the Outdoor Recreation Information Center at the downtown Seattle REI. For topographic maps, ask Green Trails for No. 136, Tyler Peak, and No. 168, The Brothers, or ask the USGS for Mount Townsend.

Directions: From Quilcene, drive 1 mile south on U.S. 101 to Penny Creek Road. Turn right (west) and drive 1.5 miles to Big Quilcene Road. Stay left at this Y and drive 3 miles to the Forest Service boundary and Forest Service Road 2740. Stay to the left at this Y and drive 6.5 miles to the signed trailhead.

Contact: Olympic National Forest, Quinault Wilderness Information Office, 295142 U.S. 101 South, Quilcene, WA 98376 (2 miles from Highway 101 on South Shore Quinault Road), 360/288-0232.

42 WEST FORK DOSEWALLIPS
31.0 mi/3-4 days

south of Quilcene in Olympic National Park

West Fork Dosewallips Trail is half of one of the premier routes for trekking across the Olympic Range. Making its way along the west fork of its namesake, the trail reaches Anderson Pass and connects to the legendary Enchanted Valley. This route has had its troubles in recent years. A suspension bridge has been repeatedly washed out and then rebuilt, only to be washed out again. Currently, a bridge is in place, but be sure to call the Wilderness Information Center for current access status.

West Fork Dosewallips Trail begins 1.4 miles up Dosewallips River Trail (actually 6.5 miles because the road is permanently out 5 miles below the trailhead) at a signed junction. After a short distance lies the troubled bridge crossing over a beautiful canyon. Beyond, the trail weaves through grand old-growth forest. Big Timber Camp is at 4.2 miles (from the Dosewallips Ranger Station) and Diamond Meadows is at 6.6 miles.

The trail climbs to Honeymoon Meadows, wide open meadows of grass and flowers, and eventually to Anderson Pass (access to the Enchanted Valley). This low pass is a real playground, with a trail leading to Anderson Glacier and its craggy home, the highlight of the trip. A final camp is just below the pass.

User Groups: Hikers and horses. No dogs or mountain bikes are allowed. No wheelchair access.

Permits: This trail is accessible June–October. Low elevations are usually accessible April through October, sometimes year-round. No permit is required to park here. Parking is free. Overnight stays within the national park require backcountry camping permits, which are available at the Wilderness Information Center in Port Angeles.

Maps: For a map of Olympic National Park, contact the Outdoor Recreation Information Center at the downtown Seattle REI. For topographic maps, ask Green Trails for No. 168, The Brothers, and No. 167, Mount Steel, or ask the USGS for The Brothers and Mount Steel.

Directions: From Quilcene, drive south 11.5 miles on U.S. 101 to Dosewallips River Road. Turn right (west) and drive about 10 miles to the road's end at a washout. The trail is on the right side of the road and climbs above the washout before returning to the road, 5 miles from Dosewallips Ranger Station.

Contact: Olympic National Park, Wilderness Information Center, 3002 Mount Angeles Rd., Port Angeles, WA 98362, 360/565-3100.

43 MAIN FORK DOSEWALLIPS RIVER
40.0 mi/4 days

south of Quilcene in Olympic National Park

This exceptionally beautiful river valley has suddenly become much more remote. A few years back, the river wiped out the road to the trailhead, adding roughly 5 miles to the hike. This has weeded out a considerable number of visitors, and now the hike is a wilderness lover's dream come true. But don't worry about hiking an extra 5 miles, all of it on the old road. The trek is easily worth it.

After 5 miles along the old road, the abandoned car camp of Muscott Flats appears. The trail begins here at the ranger station. Dosewallips River Trail follows the river before splitting at 1.5 miles. Stay on the right fork to continue along the main Dosewallips Trail. Dosewallips Trail makes a long journey through typically grand forests of Douglas fir, hemlock, and cedar and passes three established camps on its way to Dose Meadows Camp, 12.5 miles from the end of the road.

The final 2.5 miles is the best part as it breaks out into spacious meadows. The trail begins a more steady ascent from here to Hayden Pass. Along the way is 1,000 Acre Meadow, a wildflower mecca off trail to the southeast for adventurous types. Those who make it to the pass will be rewarded. Countless peaks outline several valleys streaking away from this point. And, of course, Mount Olympus shines from the west.

User Groups: Hikers and horses are permitted. No dogs or mountain bikes are allowed. No wheelchair access.

Permits: This trail is usually accessible mid-May–October. No permit is required to park here. Parking is free. Overnight stays within the national park require backcountry camping permits, which are available at the Wilderness Information Center in Port Angeles.

Maps: For a map of Olympic National Park, contact the Outdoor Recreation Information

Center at the downtown Seattle REI. For topographic maps, ask Green Trails for No. 135, Mount Angeles, No. 136, Tyler Peak, and No. 168, The Brothers, or ask the USGS for The Brothers, Mount Deception, and Wellesley Peak.

Directions: From Quilcene, drive south 11.5 miles on U.S. 101 to Dosewallips River Road. Turn right (west) and drive about 10 miles to the road's end at a washout. The trail is on the right side of the road and climbs above the washout before returning to the road, 5 miles from Dosewallips Ranger Station.

Contact: Olympic National Park, Wilderness Information Center, 3002 Mount Angeles Rd., Port Angeles, WA 98362, 360/565-3100.

44 LAKE CONSTANCE
10.0 mi/6.0 hr 🏃5 ⛰9

south of Quilcene in Olympic National Park

You're likely to hear two things about Lake Constance. First, folks always mention the incredible beauty of the lake. Craggy Mount Constance towers above mountain hemlocks and subalpine firs that border the deep blue lake. But there's a catch, which you're also likely to hear about Lake Constance. The trail is unbelievably steep—3,300 feet in just 2 miles. That's steep enough to be the toughest climb in the Olympics and steep enough that you can forget about switchbacks. The trail heads straight up the ridge. Your arms will get as much of a workout as your legs as you grab onto roots and branches, pulling yourself up what barely qualifies as a trail. It's a very difficult climb and should not be undertaken by those unprepared for a strenuous ascent.

Camping is available at the lake, but because of heavy use, a permit and reservation are required for overnight stays. There are lots of opportunities to explore around the lake, but staying on established trails is important to prevent further ecosystem damage. Also, don't forget that the road up the Dosewallips is out

and requires about 3 miles of hiking on the old road to get to the trail. For those in shape enough to make it up to Lake Constance, it is well worth the effort.

User Groups: Hikers only. No dogs, horses, or mountain bikes are allowed. No wheelchair access.

Permits: This trail is usually accessible June–October. No permit is required to park here. Parking is free. Overnight stays at Lake Constance require reservations and backcountry camping permits.

Maps: For a map of Olympic National Park, contact the Outdoor Recreation Information Center at the downtown Seattle REI. For topographic maps, ask Green Trails for No. 168, The Brothers, or ask the USGS for The Brothers.

Directions: From Quilcene, drive south 11.5 miles on U.S. 101 to Dosewallips River Road. Turn right (west) and drive about 10 miles to the road's end at a washout. The trail is on the right side of the road and climbs above the washout before returning to the road, 3 miles from Lake Constance Trail.

Contact: Olympic National Park, Wilderness Information Center, 3002 Mount Angeles Rd., Port Angeles, WA 98362, 360/565-3100.

45 DUCKABUSH RIVER
43.6 mi/3-4 days 🏃3 ⛰9

south of Quilcene in the Brothers Wilderness of Olympic National Forest and Olympic National Park

The Duckabush ranks as one of the longest river valley trails on the peninsula. It starts just 6 miles from Hood Canal and makes a long trek up to the river's headwaters. Much of the forest is big old-growth, and wildlife is regularly seen throughout the valley. Yet Duckabush Trail receives only moderate use, tapering off significantly farther up the lengthy valley. As wilderness lovers would say, "Other people's loss our gain."

The main reasons few people venture far into the Duckabush are Little Hump and Big Hump. Elevation gains of 500 feet and 1,100 feet weed out many a noncommitted day hiker. Thank Big Hump, however, for preventing timber-cutting in the upper river valley. This obstacle kept much of the valley forested in old-growth, the main theme of the trail.

Good spots to throw down for the night are found at 5 Mile and 10 Mile Camps. The trail finally reaches the steep walls of Duckabush Basin after 20 miles. The trail makes a steep ascent to La Crosse Basin, a beautiful collection of high-country lakes, and O'Neil Pass. O'Neil Pass features scenery so spectacular that it's pretty much beyond compare to anything else in the Olympics. Magnificent mountains, valleys, and rivers sum it up best. It may be a lot of hard work to get very far on Duckabush Trail, but it will be well remembered.

User Groups: Hikers and horses. No dogs or mountain bikes are allowed. No wheelchair access.

Permits: The lower part of this trail is accessible year-round (the upper part is accessible July–October). A federal Northwest Forest Pass is required to park here. Overnight stays require backcountry camping permits, which are available at the Wilderness Information Center in Port Angeles.

Maps: For a map of Olympic National Park, contact the Outdoor Recreation Information Center at the downtown Seattle REI. For topographic maps, ask Green Trails for No. 167, Mount Steel, and No. 168, The Brothers, or ask the USGS for Mount Steel, The Brothers, and Mount Jupiter.

Directions: From Quilcene, drive 16 miles south on U.S. 101 to the Duckabush River Road (Forest Service Road 2510). Turn right (west) and drive 5.5 miles to Forest Service Road 2510-060. Turn right and drive 0.1 mile to a large parking lot and the signed trailhead.

Contact: Olympic National Park, Wilderness Information Center, 3002 Mount Angeles Rd., Port Angeles, WA 98362, 360/565-

3100; Olympic National Forest, Hoodsport Ranger District, 150 N. Lake Cushman Rd., Hoodsport, WA 98548, 360/877-5254.

46 LENA LAKES
6.0-12.0 mi/3.5 hr-2 days 🥾5 ⛰10

south of Quilcene in Olympic National Park

BEST (

Upper Lena Lake may possibly render hikers speechless with its beauty and open views. Meanwhile, the trail up to Lena Lake will certainly leave hikers breathless with its intense steep ascent and sections that require something more akin to scrambling than hiking. Lower Lena Lake is a much less strenuous excursion. Both lakes are great day hikes but also feature many campsites for overnight visits.

Lena Lake Trail climbs gently but steadily through 3 miles of shady forest to Lower Lena Lake. Dogs and mountain bikes are allowed up to this point, where numerous camps encircle the large lake. Upper Lena Lake Trail continues from the northeast corner of the lake and climbs strenuously for another 3 miles. This section features switchback after switchback as it ascends the steep valley. Be prepared for a rocky, narrow, and brushy trip.

The upper lake sits among some of the Olympics' best parkland meadows. Mount Bretherton stands to the south while Mount Lena fills the northern horizon. The National Park Service maintains numerous campsites around the eastern and southern shores of the lake. Footpaths create weblike patterns into the lakeside meadows. Be careful of treading into revegetation plots, where the park is aiding regrowth of the very sensitive meadow ecosystem. Although Upper Lena Lake receives many visitors during the summer, it is worthy of all the attention it receives.

User Groups: Hikers only. No dogs, horses, or mountain bikes are allowed. No wheelchair access.

Permits: This trail is accessible July–October.

A federal Northwest Forest Pass is required to park here. Overnight stays require backcountry camping permits, which are available at the park boundary.

Maps: For a map of Olympic National Park, contact the Outdoor Recreation Information Center at the downtown Seattle REI. For topographic maps, ask Green Trails for No. 168, The Brothers, or ask the USGS for Mount Washington and The Brothers.

Directions: From Quilcene, drive south 24 miles on U.S. 101 to Forest Service Road 25. Turn right and drive 8 miles to the Lena Lakes Trailhead.

Contact: Olympic National Park, Wilderness Information Center, 3002 Mount Angeles Rd., Port Angeles, WA 98362, 360/565-3100.

47 THE BROTHERS
3.0 mi/2.0 hr

south of Quilcene in the Brothers Wilderness of Olympic National Forest

While The Brothers are the most easily recognized Olympic peaks from Seattle, visitors to the peninsula rarely hike this trail. That's because The Brothers Trail is primarily used by climbers to reach the base camp for a shot at the mountain's summit. The trail to the base camp is hikable for almost anyone, but since you won't see much, it's hardly worth it. To really appreciate The Brothers, you would have to go beyond the trail and ascend the mountain, which is not a job for amateurs. So unless you're ready for some real mountaineering, The Brothers Trail is best left as a through-way for climbers.

The trail begins near the northwest corner of Lena Lake, where Lena Creek empties into the lake. It is rocky and overcome with roots in places. It even requires some careful maneuvering over boulder fields. The trail enters the Valley of Silent Men, named for the climbers from Lena Lake passing through before the sun rises or the conversation heats

up. The trail passes back and forth over East Lena Creek several times and after 3 miles crosses one last time, skirts a small pond, and ends at The Brothers base camp. Most hikers should turn around here.

Beyond the base camp, climbing The Brothers is recommended only with the proper gear and training. It's a pretty serious ascent, not a scramble for novices. Hikers intending to go up to the summit should consult climbing guides that cover this peak or contact the ranger station in Quilcene.

User Groups: Hikers, leashed dogs, and horses. No mountain bikes are allowed. No wheelchair access.

Permits: This trail is accessible June–October. A Federal Northwest Forest Pass is required to park here.

Maps: For a map of Olympic National Forest, contact the Outdoor Recreation Information Center at the downtown Seattle REI. For topographic maps, ask Green Trails for No. 168, The Brothers, or ask the USGS for Mount Washington and The Brothers.

Directions: From Quilcene, drive south 24 miles on U.S. 101 to Forest Service Road 25. Turn right and drive 8 miles to the Lena Lakes Trailhead.

Contact: Olympic National Forest, Hoodsport Ranger Station, 150 N. Lake Cushman Rd., Hoodsport, WA 98548, 360/877-5254.

48 PUTVIN
8.0 mi/4.0 hr

south of Quilcene in Mount Skokomish Wilderness of Olympic National Forest and in Olympic National Park

Putvin Trail includes much of what is great about the Olympics. There are forests full of trees big enough to test the limits of how far you can crane your neck, and there are prime subalpine meadows, full of heather and huckleberries, enough to make your mouth water. And, of course, there are outstanding views,

HIKING

enough to make you rub your eyes. It's a steep trail, gaining 3,400 feet in just 4 miles. But as the pilgrims once said, there's redemption in suffering.

Putvin Trail starts off in the river bottom of the Hamma Hamma, climbing through an old logging tract. The trail eventually enters the Mount Skokomish Wilderness (1.5 miles) and a land of big trees. After briefly leveling out, Putvin resumes climbing, arriving at several small tarns. Keep going, as this is not Lake of the Angels. It is farther yet, set within a small glacier cirque called the Valley of Heaven. Heaven indeed. The lake is absolutely beautiful, surrounded by meadows and craggy peaks. Mount Skokomish and Mount Stone flank the valley's two ends. For outstanding views, hike the small footpath up to the long ridge separating the two peaks. From here, Putvin Trail's anonymity is hard to understand.

User Groups: Hikers and leashed dogs. No horses or mountain bikes are allowed. No wheelchair access.

Permits: This trail is accessible mid-June–November. Parking permit not required. Overnight stays require backcountry camping permits, which are available at Hoodsport Ranger Station.

Maps: For a map of Olympic National Park and Olympic National Forest, contact the Outdoor Recreation Information Center at the downtown Seattle REI. For topographic maps, ask Green Trails for No. 167, Mount Steel, and No. 168, The Brothers, or ask the USGS for Mount Skokomish.

Directions: From Hoodsport, drive 14 miles north on U.S. 101 to Forest Service Road 25 (Hamma Hamma Recreation Area). Turn left (west) and drive 12 miles to the Putvin Historical Marker. The trail is on the right side of the road. High clearance vehicles are recommended to access this trailhead.

Contact: Olympic National Forest, Hoodsport Ranger Station, 150 N. Lake Cushman Rd., Hoodsport, WA 98548, 360/877-5254; Olympic National Park, Wilderness Information Center, 3002 Mount Angeles Rd., Port Angeles, WA 98362, 360/565-3100.

49 MILDRED LAKES
9.8 mi/6.0 hr

northwest of Hoodsport in Mount Skokomish Wilderness of Olympic National Forest

Although Mildred Lakes is gaining in popularity, you're likely to experience fewer fellow hikers here than elsewhere in the Olympics. The Forest Service provides little maintenance on the trail to help keep this sensitive area in good condition, as an easy trail would likely lead to overuse. Nonetheless, Mildred Lakes are still out there and very much worth visiting.

The trail climbs through an old logging tract before entering virgin forest. The trail is relatively easy to follow through the pleasant forest of hemlock and fir. Before long, however, the trail becomes increasingly infested with rocks and roots. At about 3 miles, you must cross a ravine more than 20 feet deep. Now the trail becomes really rough. Head straight up the steep mountainside, pulling yourself up by rocks and roots. At 4.9 miles, crest the ridge to find the Mildred Lakes Basin.

The basin holds three lakes bordered by subalpine firs and meadows of heather. The Sawtooth Range runs along the north and western part of the basin, with Mount Cruiser and Mount Lincoln acting as bookends to the jagged ridge. There are a fair number of campsites up here, but Leave-No-Trace principles are to be emphasized, as heavy use has been detrimental to the area in the past.

User Groups: Hikers and leashed dogs. No horses or mountain bikes are allowed. No wheelchair access.

Permits: This trail is accessible July–October. A federal Northwest Forest Pass is required to park here.

Maps: For a map of Olympic National Forest, contact the Outdoor Recreation Information Center at the downtown Seattle REI. For topographic maps, ask Green Trails for No. 167, Mount Steel, or ask the USGS for Mount Skokomish.

Directions: From Hoodsport, drive north 14 miles on U.S. 101 to Forest Service Road 25 (Hamma Hamma Recreation Area). Turn left (west) and drive 14 miles to Mildred Lakes Trailhead at road's end.

Contact: Olympic National Forest, Hoodsport Ranger Station, 150 N. Lake Cushman Rd., Hoodsport, WA 98548, 360/877-5254.

50 STAIRCASE RAPIDS
2.0 mi/1.0 hr   🏃1 ⛰9

northwest of Hoodsport in Olympic National Park

BEST (

Walks through the forest rarely get better than this. Set along the North Fork Skokomish River within an old-growth forest, Staircase Rapids Trail is perfect for families and older hikers. The flat, level trail encounters several sites where the river pours over bedrock or rumbles over rapids. And it all occurs within one of the eastern Olympics' most beautiful old-growth forests. The trail has a bit of history, as well, as it was part of the original route taken by the O'Neil Expedition in 1890. This is either an excellent destination or just a great side trip to a bigger excursion.

The trail starts at Staircase Ranger Station on the west side of the river. The exceptional old-growth forest is highlighted by Big Cedar (accessible by a side trail signed "Big Cedar"). Definitely check it out. Along the way to the rapids are Red Reef, an outcropping of red limestone that does its best to hold back the rushing river, and Dolly Varden Pool, where rocky cliffs loom over the river as it rumbles between large boulders. The climax of the walk is Staircase Rapids, a series of regularly spaced terraces over which the river spills. This is easily one of the Olympics' most scenic stretches of river and well worth a visit.

User Groups: Hikers only. No dogs, horses, or mountain bikes are allowed. No wheelchair access.

Permits: This trail is accessible year-round. A National Parks Pass is required to park here.

Maps: For a map of Olympic National Park, contact the Outdoor Recreation Information Center at the downtown Seattle REI. For topographic maps, ask Green Trails for No. 167, Mount Steel, or ask the USGS for Mount Skokomish.

Directions: From Hoodsport, drive west 9 miles on Lake Cushman Road (Highway 119) to Forest Service Road 24 (a T intersection). Turn left and drive 6.5 miles to Staircase Ranger Station for the trailhead and trailhead parking.

Contact: Olympic National Park, Wilderness Information Center, 3002 Mount Angeles Rd., Port Angeles, WA 98362, 360/565-3100.

51 NORTH FORK SKOKOMISH
25.2 mi/2-3 days   🏃1 ⛰8

northwest of Hoodsport in Olympic National Park

The western rivers of the Olympic Mountains rightfully share reputations for forests of enormous proportions. While the North Fork Skokomish remains out of this limelight, it's no less impressive. The trail follows the North Fork Skokomish for 10 miles at relative ease, passing through a virgin forest full of massive trees. This route is historical, as well, having been blazed by Army Lieutenant Joseph P. O'Neil on the first east—west expedition of the Olympics in the winter of 1890.

The trail leaves Staircase Ranger Station along an old roadbed. It quickly encounters the Beaver Fire of 1985, where new firs are growing up among towering burned snags. At 5 miles, the trail crosses the Skokomish via a bridge where the slate-gray water passes through a beautiful box canyon bordered by colossal Douglas firs. The trail crosses several large streams, two of which lack a bridge and may be tricky in times of heavy runoff.

Camp Pleasant (6.4 miles) and Nine Stream Camp (9.3 miles) make for great places to spend the night and build a fire. After Nine Stream, the trail begins its ascent to First Divide through large mountain hemlocks and Douglas firs. After 3.5 miles of climbing, the trail reaches First Divide and several small tarns. Views into the upper Duckabush reward the long trek. Just beyond the pass, Home Sweet Home (13.5 miles) offers another great site for camping in a meadow setting.

User Groups: Hikers and horses. No dogs or mountain bikes are allowed. No wheelchair access.

Permits: The lower part of this trail is accessible year-round. The upper part is accessible June–October. A National Parks Pass is required to park here. Overnight stays in the national park require backcountry camping permits, which are available at the Wilderness Information Center in Port Angeles or at the Hoodsport Ranger Station.

Maps: For a map of Olympic National Park, contact the Outdoor Recreation Information Center at the downtown Seattle REI. For topographic maps, ask Green Trails for No. 167, Mount Steel, or ask the USGS for Mount Skokomish, Mount Olson, and Mount Steel.

Directions: From Hoodsport, drive west 9 miles on Lake Cushman Road (Highway 119) to Forest Service Road 24 (a T intersection). Turn left and drive 6.5 miles to Staircase Ranger Station for the trailhead and trailhead parking.

Contact: Olympic National Park, Wilderness Information Center, 3002 Mount Angeles Rd., Port Angeles, WA 98362, 360/565-3100; Olympic National Forest, Hoodsport Ranger Station, 150 N. Lake Cushman Rd., Hoodsport, WA 98548, 360/877-5254.

52 WAGONWHEEL LAKE
5.8 mi/3.5 hr   🥾5 ⛰6

northwest of Hoodsport in Olympic National Park

When people mention Wagonwheel Lake, they mostly condemn it to being nothing more than a conditioning hike. Consider that neither an insult nor compliment; it's mostly just the truth. After all, the trail makes a brutal ascent of 3,200 feet in less than 3 miles. For most hikers, a pace of 1,000 feet per mile is considered "difficult." Throw in the fact that there are few views to be had along the way or at the lake and you get only the diehards or the foolhardy on the trail.

Nearly the entire length of the trail is a steep climb through the forest. The lower part of the trail climbs via switchback through second-growth forest tamed by fire before eventually reaching some old-growth hemlock. After nearly 3 miles of huffing and puffing, hikers are delivered to Wagonwheel Lake, set within a small basin on the north side of Copper Mountain and bounded by a dense forest offering relatively no views. With all the hard work, why come here? Because a day in the woods is always a good day.

User Groups: Hikers only. No dogs, horses, or mountain bikes are allowed. No wheelchair access.

Permits: This trail is accessible July–November. A National Parks Pass is required to park here. Overnight stays in the national park require backcountry camping permits, which are available at Hoodsport Ranger Station.

Maps: For a map of Olympic National Park, contact the Outdoor Recreation Information Center at the downtown Seattle REI. For topographic maps, ask Green Trails for No. 167, Mount Steel, or ask the USGS for Mount Skokomish.

Directions: From Hoodsport, drive west 9 miles on Lake Cushman Road (Highway 119) to Forest Service Road 24 (a T intersection). Turn left and drive 6.5 miles to Staircase

Ranger Station for the trailhead and trailhead parking.

Contact: Olympic National Park, Wilderness Information Center, 3002 Mount Angeles Rd., Port Angeles, WA 98362, 360/565-3100; Olympic National Forest, Hoodsport Ranger Station, 150 N. Lake Cushman Rd., Hoodsport, WA 98548, 360/877-5254.

53 FLAPJACK LAKES
16.0 mi/2 days   🏃2 ⛰7

northwest of Hoodsport in Olympic National Park

BEST (

Flapjack Lakes is one of the most scenic and popular destinations in Olympic National Park. So popular, in fact, that the Park Service instituted a permit system limiting the number of overnight campers here. Don't let that deter you, however, as it's a must-hike on any to-do list of Olympic trails. Plus, Flapjack Lakes are easily accessible, especially for families on a weekend excursion.

The route follows North Fork Skokomish Trail for 3.5 miles, where Flapjack Lake Trail takes off to the east. The trail steadily ascends through a forest of impressively large trees while following Donahue Creek. At 7 miles, the trail splits, with the left fork heading to Black and White Lakes. Stay to the right and find old mountain hemlocks, subalpine firs, and yellow cedars surrounding the two lakes. Mount Cruiser and the jagged ridge leading to Mount Lincoln enclose the eastern view; a way trail leading up to the Gladys Divide is a great side trip.

If the thought of crowds at Flapjacks is unappealing, an attractive alternative is Black and White Lakes. From the fork in the trail (7 miles), a mile of walking brings hikers to an open ridge below Mount Gladys. The lakes are small and have fewer campsites, but they are much more open and offer outstanding views of the entire North Fork Skokomish drainage. With several options for exploration, the

Flapjack Lakes area is definitely a destination for Olympic enthusiasts to undertake.

User Groups: Hikers only. No dogs, horses, or mountain bikes are allowed. No wheelchair access.

Permits: This trail is accessible mid-May–October. A National Parks Pass is required to park at North Fork Skokomish Trailhead. Overnight stays in the national park require backcountry camping permits, which are available at Staircase Ranger Station. Camping permits are limited between May 1 and September 30th. Call 360/565-3100 for reservations.

Maps: For a map of Olympic National Park, contact the Outdoor Recreation Information Center at the downtown Seattle REI. For topographic maps, ask Green Trails for No. 167, Mount Steel, or ask the USGS for Mount Skokomish and Mount Olson.

Directions: From Hoodsport, drive west 9 miles on Lake Cushman Road (Highway 119) to Forest Service Road 24 (a T intersection). Turn left and drive 6.5 miles to Staircase Ranger Station for the trailhead and trailhead parking.

Contact: Olympic National Park, Wilderness Information Center, 3002 Mount Angeles Rd., Port Angeles, WA 98362, 360/565-3100.

54 SIX RIDGE
32.8 mi/3-4 days   🏃4 ⛰8

northwest of Hoodsport in Olympic National Park

BEST (

If you are considering hiking Six Ridge, you are to be commended. You have a thirst for adventure and are undeterred by difficult ascents. You appreciate grand mountain views, love mountain meadows full of blooming wildflowers, and enjoy wilderness best when it's solitary. Six Ridge Trail is all that and more.

To access Six Ridge, one must first travel North Fork Skokomish Trail 5.6 miles, a flat and easy walk. Skokomish Trail crosses the river

HIKING

here and Six Ridge turns south. After crossing Seven Stream, the trail climbs gradually through forest to achieve the eastern end of Six Ridge. From here are 8 miles of ridge walking. The trail passes through exceptional subalpine meadows for much of the route, although fields of scree, talus, and even snow are common. There are several camps on the ridge, most notably McGravey Lakes at 8.5 miles up the ridge. The trail technically ends at Six Ridge Pass, where it becomes Graves Creek Trail but continues to Lake Sundown in 1.2 miles.

User Groups: Hikers only. No dogs, horses, or mountain bikes are allowed. No wheelchair access.

Permits: This trail is accessible mid-July–October. A National Parks Pass is required to park here. Overnight stays in the national park require backcountry camping permits, which are available at the Staircase Ranger Station.

Maps: For a map of Olympic National Park, contact the Outdoor Recreation Information Center at the downtown Seattle REI. For topographic maps, ask Green Trails for No. 166, Mount Christie, and No. 167, Mount Steel, or ask the USGS for Mount Skokomish, Mount Olson, and Mount Hoquim.

Directions: From Hoodsport, drive west 9 miles on Lake Cushman Road (Highway 119) to Forest Service Road 24 (a T intersection). Turn left and drive 6.5 miles to Staircase Ranger Station for the trailhead and trailhead parking.

Contact: Olympic National Park, Wilderness Information Center, 3002 Mount Angeles Rd., Port Angeles, WA 98362, 360/565-3100.

55 MOUNT ELLINOR
6.2 mi/3.0 hr

northwest of Hoodsport in Mount Skokomish Wilderness of Olympic National Forest

Tucked away in the southeastern corner of the Olympic Peninsula, Mount Ellinor is rarely high on peoples' radar when they are looking for a hike. It gets less attention than other nearby spots, such as Mount Rose or Flapjack Lakes. But the trip is no less beautiful and actually features some the area's best views.

The trail has two trailheads, the lower one adding about 1.5 miles and 800 feet elevation gain to the trip. Since it's not much farther, the lower trailhead is the better choice, as it follows a well-forested ridge that should not be missed. The trail is a steady climb, rarely leveling out for more than a few yards. The forest breaks into avalanche chutes and meadows about 0.5 mile from the summit. At the top, views of Hood Canal, Lake Cushman, and neighboring Olympic peaks can be found. Neither well known nor frequently visited, Mount Ellinor makes for a perfect one-day getaway.

User Groups: Hikers and leashed dogs. No horses or mountain bikes are allowed. No wheelchair access.

Permits: This trail is accessible mid-June–November (accessible year-round with ice ax). A federal Northwest Forest Pass is required to park here.

Maps: For a map of Olympic National Forest, contact the Outdoor Recreation Information Center at the downtown Seattle REI. For topographic maps, ask Green Trails for No. 167, Mount Steel, and No. 168, The Brothers, or ask the USGS for Mount Washington and Mount Skokomish.

Directions: From Hoodsport, drive east 9 miles on Hoodsport Road (County Road 44) to Forest Service Road 24. Turn right and drive 1.5 miles to Forest Service Road 2419 (Big Creek Road). Turn left and drive 6 miles to Forest Service Road 2419-014. Turn left and drive 1 mile to the signed trailhead at road's end.

Contact: Olympic National Forest, Hoodsport Ranger Station, 150 N. Lake Cushman Rd., Hoodsport, WA 98548, 360/877-5254.

HIKING

56 MOUNT ROSE
6.4 mi/3.5 hr

northwest of Hoodsport in Mount Skokomish Wilderness of Olympic National Forest

Mount Rose is one of the more popular summits in the southeastern Olympic Mountains. Which means it must be awfully scenic, as it is certainly not an easy route. The trail is unique for a summit route in that it is a loop. Laid out like a lasso, the trail ascends straight to the summit and then makes a circle along the ridge to the trail again. Overall elevation gain is 3,500 feet in just about 3 miles.

The trail navigates a mile of second-growth timber before entering the wilderness. The rise to the junction (1.8 miles) is rather steep despite the many switchbacks. Head to the right for the more gradual route along the ridge. The trail has peek-a-boo views of neighboring peaks and drainages. The summit is forested save for a small chuck of basalt that reaches up roughly 30 feet. From the top are grand, panoramic views of Hood Canal and numerous Olympic peaks. Good luck, and enjoy the workout.

User Groups: Hikers and leashed dogs. No horses or mountain bikes are allowed. No wheelchair access.

Permits: This trail is accessible July–October. Permits are not required. Parking and access are free.

Maps: For a map of Olympic National Forest, contact the Outdoor Recreation Information Center at the downtown Seattle REI. For topographic maps, ask Green Trails for No. 167, Mount Steel, or ask the USGS for Lightning Peak and Mount Skokomish.

Directions: From Hoodsport, drive west 9 miles on Lake Cushman Road (Highway 119) to Forest Service Road 24 (a T intersection). Turn left and drive 3 miles to the signed trailhead on the right side of the road.

Contact: Olympic National Forest, Hoodsport Ranger Station, 150 N. Lake Cushman Rd., Hoodsport, WA 98548, 360/877-5254.

57 UPPER SOUTH FORK SKOKOMISH
15.0 mi/1-2 days

west of Hoodsport in the Wonder Mountain Wilderness and Olympic National Park

Upper South Fork Skokomish Trail is a great route through a typically great Olympic river valley. Unfortunately, an extension of the access road has made this hike much shorter than it was once. This trail has just what one could want out of Olympic river hike: a forest composed of large trees, a river carving occasional canyons, and meadows at the river's headwaters along a high mountain ridge. And throw in an absence of people on the trail, which is all right with the folks who know of this place.

The trail leaves the road and sets off into a forest of large cedars, firs, and hemlocks, all old-growth and of good size. Streams and creeks regularly cross the trail, but few give any trouble. The trail crosses the river twice via bridges and makes a detour into the Startup Creek valley. Soon after the route enters the national park, it becomes little more than a beaten footpath. It's not exceptionally difficult to follow as long as snow isn't lingering on the ground (after mid-June). The trail climbs gradually through the headwaters of the South Fork of the Skokomish, eventually reaching Sundown Pass and Lake Sundown, a remote place of meadows and open subalpine forests. Backpackers will find overnight spots at Camp Riley (5.4 miles) and Sundown Pass.

User Groups: Hikers and horses. No dogs or mountain bikes are allowed. No wheelchair access.

Permits: This trail is accessible mid-June–October. Permits are not required. Parking and access are free.

Maps: For a map of Olympic National Park and Olympic National Forest, contact the Outdoor Recreation Information Center at the downtown Seattle REI. For topographic maps, ask Green Trails for No. 166, Mount

Christie, No. 167, Mount Steel, and No. 199, Mount Tebo, or ask the USGS for Lightning Peak, Mount Tebo, Mount Olson, and Mount Hoquim.

Directions: From Hoodsport, drive south 7 miles to Skokomish Valley Road. Turn right (west) and drive 5.5 miles to Forest Service Road 23. Turn right and drive 13 miles to Forest Service Road 2361. Turn right and drive 5.5 miles to the signed trailhead at road's end.

Contact: Olympic National Forest, Hoodsport Ranger Station, 150 N. Lake Cushman Rd., Hoodsport, WA 98548, 360/877-5254.

58 RAINBOW CANYON
1.0 mi/0.5 hr   🏃1 ⛰8

south of Quilcene in the Buckhorn Wilderness
of Olympic National Forest

This is a great leg-stretcher for those making a long trek along U.S. 101. Just outside Rainbow Campground (which is right off the highway), a short 0.5-mile hike accesses a nice waterfall on the way to Rainbow Canyon on the Big Quilcene River. The trail's drop is not much to speak of, making it easily accessible to hikers of all abilities.

Forests of Douglas fir tower over an understory that includes vine maple, a tangle of brilliant colors in September. An overlook peers into Elbo Creek, where the waterfall cascades into a small pool. The trail continues down to the Big Quilcene River, where it makes a gentle turn within the canyon walls. Moss and ferns line the sides. When the kids are getting antsy in the back seat, Rainbow Canyon is just the thing to burn off a little energy. Total distance for the round-trip excursion is just 1 mile.

User Groups: Hikers and leashed dogs. No horses or mountain bikes are allowed. No wheelchair access.

Permits: This trail is accessible year-round. Permits are not required. Parking and access are free.

Maps: For a map of Olympic National Forest, contact the Outdoor Recreation Information Center at the downtown Seattle REI. For topographic maps, ask the USGS for Mount Walker.

Directions: From Quilcene, drive 5 miles south on U.S. 101 to Rainbow Campground. While the trail begins from within the campground, it is a group site and the gate will be locked. Park across Highway 101 and walk into the site. The trailhead is at the back of the campground.

Contact: Olympic National Forest, Hood Canal Ranger Station, 295142 U.S. 101 South, Quilcene, WA 98376 (2 miles from Highway 101 on South Shore Quinault Road), 360/765-2200.

59 LEADBETTER POINT
2.6-8.3 mi/1.5-4.5 hr   🏃1 ⛰9

northern tip of Long Beach in southwestern
Washington

It may not appear as though there is much going on at Leadbetter Point, but in fact the tip of Long Beach is extremely rich in wildlife. Comprising sand dunes and miles of grasses waving in the strong breeze, the area can look barren and a bit forbidding. On closer inspection, however, you'll see that hundreds of thousands of seabirds and shorebirds make this place home for a part of each year. Leadbetter Point is a bird-watcher's dream, home to snowy plovers, grouse, bald eagles, great herons, and woodpeckers. Although it's a good visit anytime of the year, winter is the peak of bird season. Just be ready for soggy trail in places.

A small network of trails courses around the ever-changing peninsula. Taken altogether, they make an 8.3-mile loop that includes sand dunes, coastal forest, Willapa Bay, and a stretch along the beach. Shorter hikes include Blue Trail, a 2.6-mile round-trip out to the Pacific Ocean. All of the trails are fairly level, climbing only over sand dunes and grassy knolls. The park is managed by State Parks but is also a National Wildlife Refuge because of its importance as a migratory stop for birds. Dogs are not allowed on any trails.

User Groups: Hikers only. No dogs, horses, or mountain bikes are allowed. No wheelchair access.

Permits: This trail is accessible year-round. No permits are required. Parking and access are free.

Maps: For topographic maps, ask the USGS for Oysterville and North Cove.

Directions: From Long Beach, drive north 18 miles on Highway 103 (Pacific Way) to Leadbetter Point State Park. The route passes through Oysterville and is well signed. The trailhead is at the end of the road within the Leadbetter Point State Park.

Contact: Willapa National Wildlife Refuge, 3888 U.S. 101, Ilwaco, WA 98624-9707, 360/484-3482.

60 LONG ISLAND
1.0-5.0 mi/2.0-5.0 hr

in Willapa Bay in Southwestern Washington

Talk about secluded. As the name implies, this is an island, and it's one with no bridges. One reaches Long Island by boat or kayak, with no other options. If that's not a problem (it actually makes the trip all the more special), then Long Island is a real gem.

Roughly 5 miles of trail and even more old road crisscross the island, 2 miles wide by 7 miles long. Hiking along the shore is a real wildlife getaway, with a plethora of seabirds and shorebirds stopping by on their yearly migrations. Bald eagles, grouse, great herons, and snowy plovers are just a few of the many winged inhabitants. Inland, deer, bear, and elk are some of the bigger mammals to be found.

The highlight of the island is the ancient cedar grove in the center of the island. After crossing the bay to the island by boat (the crossing is about 200 feet and can be done only at high tide), hike north on the old logging road about 2.5 miles to the signed "Trail of the Ancient Cedars." Turn left and in 0.5 mile you will be among a large grove of massive cedars. Spared from logging because of its hard-to-reach locale, the stand is certain to instill a sense of awe for a forest that once covered the entire island. There are a number of primitive campgrounds around the lake, although there is no water during the summer.

User Groups: Hikers only. No dogs, horses, or mountain bikes are allowed. No wheelchair access.

Permits: This trail is accessible year-round. Permits are not required. Parking and access are free.

Maps: For topographic maps, ask the USGS for Long Island.

Directions: From Long Beach, drive north 13 miles on U.S. 101 to the signed Refuge Headquarters and trailhead.

Contact: Willapa National Wildlife Refuge, 3888 U.S. 101, Ilwaco, WA 98624-9707, 360/484-3482.

61 CAPE DISAPPOINTMENT STATE PARK
0.5-9.0 mi /0.5-4.5 hr

southwest of Ilwaco in southwest Washington

A network of trails through Cape Disappointment State Park makes for a great combination of forest and coastal hiking. All of the trails are extremely easy and highly scenic, providing parents a prime locale to take the kids on the weekend. Formerly known as Fort Canby, the state park covers the grounds where Lewis and Clark spent a wet winter. On Cape Disappointment, Washington's most southwestern point, the park overlooks both the Columbia River and Pacific Ocean.

The main route through the park is Washington Coast Trail, a long trek that gets its southern start here. Patched together from several trails, this 4.5-mile segment bisects the park through old-growth forest to link a pair of old lighthouses. Folks spending a full day here will want to hike the length of it, the best way to see the park.

Families looking for a shorter trip should hike to Beard's Hollow. The trail travels just 0.5 mile through coastal forest and sand dunes before finding the secluded cove, a gateway to more than 20 miles of beach to the north. Another beauty is Cape Disappointment Lighthouse Trail, 1.4 miles to the West Coast's oldest working lighthouse. Be sure to check out the Lewis and Clark Interpretive Center, atop a pair of enormous gun emplacements from World Wars I and II. The center features a cornucopia of artifacts from the Corps of Discovery's journey 200 years ago.

User Groups: Hikers, leashed dogs, and mountain bikes. No horses are allowed. Parts of the trails are wheelchair accessible.

Permits: This area is accessible year-round. No permits are required. Parking and access are free.

Maps: For topographic maps, ask the USGS for Cape Disappointment.

Directions: From Long Beach, drive south 3.5 miles on Pacific Way to Ilwaco. Turn right on North Head Road and drive 2.5 miles to North Head Lighthouse Road. Turn right and drive 0.5 miles to the well-signed park entrance. The main trailhead is located at the Lewis and Clark Interpretive Center, inside the park entrance.

Contact: Cape Disappointment State Park, P.O. Box 488, Ilwaco WA, 98624, 360/642-3078.

Index

www.moon.com

MOON.COM is ready to help plan your next trip! Filled with fresh trip ideas and strategies, author interviews, informative travel blogs, a detailed map library, and descriptions of all the Moon guidebooks, Moon.com is all you need to get out and explore the world—or even places in your own backyard. While at Moon.com, sign up for our monthly e-newsletter for updates on new releases, travel tips, and expert advice from our on-the-go Moon authors. As always, when you travel with Moon, expect an experience that is uncommon and truly unique.

MOON IS ON FACEBOOK—BECOME A FAN!
JOIN THE MOON PHOTO GROUP ON FLICKR

 OUTDOORS

"Well written, thoroughly researched, and packed full of useful information and advice, these guides really do get you into the outdoors."

—GORP.COM

ALSO AVAILABLE AS FOGHORN OUTDOORS ACTIVITY GUIDES:

250 Great Hikes in
  California's National Parks
California Golf
California Waterfalls
California Wildlife
Camper's Companion
Easy Biking in Northern
  California
Easy Hiking in Northern
  California

Easy Hiking in Southern
  California
Georgia & Alabama Camping
Maine Hiking
Massachusetts Hiking
New England Cabins
  & Cottages
New England Camping

New Hampshire Hiking
Southern California
  Cabins & Cottages
Tom Stienstra's Bay Area
  Recreation
Vermont Hiking
Washington Boating
  & Water Sports

MOON OLYMPIC PENINSULA CAMPING & HIKING

Avalon Travel
a member of the Perseus Books Group
1700 Fourth Street
Berkeley, CA 94710, USA
www.moon.com

Editors: Elizabeth Hollis Hansen, Sabrina Young
Series Manager: Sabrina Young
Copy Editors: Valerie Sellers Blanton, Maura
    Brown, Ellie Winters
Graphics and Production Coordinator:
    Domini Dragoone
Cover Designer: Kathryn Osgood
Interior Designer: Darren Alessi
Map Editors: Albert Angulo, Mike Morgenfeld
Cartographers: Mike Morgenfeld, Kat Bennett,
    Brice Ticen

ISBN-13: 978-1-59880-570-3

Text © 2010 by Tom Stienstra and
    Scott Leonard.
Maps © 2010 by Avalon Travel.
All rights reserved.

ABOUT THE AUTHORS

© JOHN BEATH

Tom Stienstra

For 30 years, Tom Stienstra's full-time job has been to capture and communicate the outdoor experience. Tom writes a weekly outdoors column that is distributed across America. He has won more than 100 national and regional writing awards, and has twice been named National Outdoors Writer of the Year. His television show, *The Great Outdoors*, is broadcast weekly on CBS/CW. His first edition of *Pacific Northwest Camping* was acclaimed by the *Portland Oregonian*.

Tom takes part in all facets of the outdoors, and as a pilot and airplane owner, can cover great distances quickly in the pursuit of adventure. He lives with his wife Stephani at their ranch in the "State of Jefferson," near the Oregon border.

You can contact Tom directly via his website at www.tom stienstra.com. His guidebooks include:

Moon Oregon Camping
Moon Washington Camping
Moon Pacific Northwest Camping
Moon West Coast RV Camping
Moon California Camping
Moon California Hiking (with Ann Marie Brown)
Moon California Fishing
Moon California Recreational Lakes & Rivers
California Wildlife
Moon Northern California Cabins & Cottages
Tom Stienstra's Bay Area Recreation

© ERIC MELTZER

Scott Leonard

Scott Leonard spent his childhood fishing, skiing, and hunting in the Oregon outdoors. He began hiking and backpacking when he started college at the University of Puget Sound in Tacoma. He fell in love with the wilderness areas of Washington – and has never grown tired of pounding out miles of trail.

After college, Scott spent several years building and maintaining trails, and teaching others to do the same. He spent a year researching and hiking for *Moon Washington Hiking* and *Moon Pacific Northwest Hiking*, and yet another summer on *Moon Take a Hike Seattle* – never has a job been so easy to get up for each morning.

In addition to writing, Scott works as an attorney in Portland, Oregon, where he has a successful criminal defense practice.